Vectorworks for Entertainment Design

Vectorworks for Entertainment Design:

Using Vectorworks to Design and Document Scenery, Lighting, and Sound

by Kevin Lee Allen

Focal Press
Taylor & Francis Group

NEW YORK AND LONDON

First published 2015
by Focal Press
70 Blanchard Rd Suite 402
Burlington, MA 01803

Simultaneously published in the UK
by Focal Press
2 Park Square, Milton Park, Abingdon, Oxon OX14 4RN

Focal Press is an imprint of the Taylor & Francis Group, an informa business

Notices
Knowledge and best practice in this field are constantly changing. As new research and experience broaden our understanding, changes in research methods, professional practices, or medical treatment may become necessary.

Practitioners and researchers must always rely on their own experience and knowledge in evaluating and using any information, methods, compounds, or experiments described herein. In using such information or methods they should be mindful of their own safety and the safety of others, including parties for whom they have a professional responsibility.

Product or corporate names may be trademarks or registered trademarks, and are used only for identification and explanation without intent to infringe.

Library of Congress Cataloging in Publication Data
CIP data has been applied for
ISBN: 978-0-415-72613-9 (pbk)
ISBN: 978-1-315-85612-4 (ebk)

Typeset in Gill Sans
By Kevin Lee Allen

Table of Contents

Introduction: About the Book

Design is Storytelling. Drawing, drafting, and documentation tell the story of the design. Vectorworks is the entertainment industry's preferred tool for design, drafting, and documentation.

I hope this book is also useful for interior designers, exhibit designers, industrial designers and others, as well as entertainment designers and technicians. There is a brief explanation of some theatrical terminology elsewhere in the introduction.

As a professional scenic and lighting designer in the entertainment industries, I have been using Vectorworks for many years. Vectorworks has streamlined my work, and increased my precision.

I have taught and lectured on Vectorworks techniques, and I've tried to present as much as possible in this book. A program as complex as Vectorworks allows different users to find their own best way to work, or their own workflow. Sometimes, tools can be manipulated from their original purpose to the individual user's advantage. We'll look at some of those techniques.

Vectorworks is a design tool, as well as a documentation tool. The book will stress developing ideas, visualizing the ideas, and evolving them for presentation.

In general, even with shortcuts and optional ways of getting to a desired end result, everything herein is a best practice for the use of the software. The text is as linear as possible, given the complexity of the application.

This book was written using the Vectorworks Designer package of software, which includes the Spotlight, Architect, Landmark (Landscape Architecture), and Renderworks modules, with special focus on the Spotlight module. Renderworks using the Cinema 4D rendering engine can create amazing visuals, but if you do not have the full Designer package, renderings can be accomplished in the OpenGL mode. Nemetschek Vectorworks makes evaluation and student packages available from their website. References will be made to the additional Vectorworks modules, third-party plug-ins for the application, and related applications that designers will usually add to their arsenals.

We begin with some basic modeling and an overview of the working process. On that foundation we will go through the steps to design and document the scenery, lighting, and sound for a Broadway-scale production. To get there, we will explore a process of design development and collaboration with other designers and technical staff.

This book doubles as a handy desktop reference.

Well-made drawings inspire well-done work.

Save Early and Save Often

There are illustrations throughout the text. Each chapter is punctuated with a spread showing professional work created using Vectorworks. I hope the readers find that work inspirational and aspirational. There are illustrations that explain the text included; these are appropriately captioned. There are many illustrations in the text that relate directly to the text above; these capture Vectorworks performing the functions explained and are not captioned.

The Website associated with this book at **focalpress.com/cw/Allen** contains the work files required, and additional information about the projects shown throughout the text.

The Vectorworks Environment

I'm a US based, Mac user. All of the screen shots show the Mac OS interface, but the PC interface looks very much the same. Keyboard shortcuts are given using Command/Control, or Alt/Option, as that is generally how the keys translate from the Mac OS to the Windows OS.
- A right-click in Windows is the same as Control+click or a two-finger tap on the track pad in the Mac OS is used to open contextual or context menus which *pop-up* in the working window. These available commands vary based on the context or situation from which they have been chosen.
- Measurements given are imperial US-based measurements, with converted metric equivalents in millimeters. If your document is set up for metric but you enter imperial data, appropriately notated, Vectorworks will translate the numbers.

General Rules for a good Workflow

This manual covers a lot of ground quickly, so that you can get up to speed with Vectorworks. Keep these points in mind as you work through the guide:
- Don't put your coffee cup on your drawing board, or your computer.
- Read the entire section before beginning the work described, then go back to the beginning and follow the directions. As you progress through, fewer specific steps are dictated in the instructions.
- Alternate methods are shown for activating/ using many tools, commands, and modes. Use what works best for you. Experiment with different tools and techniques. Find your own workflow.
- Watch for the **SmartCursor**: cues that appear as you hover your cursor over **significant geometry.**
- The text assumes you are familiar with basic computer terms and basic theatrical concepts. For review, or if theatre isn't your

Create a redundant back up plan and use it.

course of study: House left and right are your left and right as you face the stage. Stage left and right are your left and right as you stand on stage and face the audience. Up stage is away from the audience. Downstage is near the audience. At one time, stages were raked, that is to say they were like ramps with the lower end near the audience.

- Save early, and save often. Save after every operation.
- Establish a back-up ritual. Macintosh users should take advantage of the Time Machine feature within the OS.
- Use the Vectorworks auto back up in addition to your own back-up plan.
- Use **Save As** frequently, so you can always access earlier ideas and solutions.
- Use symbols, and get to know and understand them early on.
- Most tools have options that are available for selection in the Tool Bar; always look for them, until they are second nature.
- When mentioned to explore or experiment, it is incumbent on the reader to do so; consider that digital doodling.
- The text assumes a basic working knowledge of geometry; points, planes, and axis are not defined.
- A **Palette** is a floating window that contains tools or resources for working. The Vectorworks interface is similar to many other drawing and graphics applications.

Find your own workflow. Make the work your own.

There is a companion website to the text at **focalpress.com/cw/Allen.** Text about an application is incomplete without application files and other resources. The Website contains a zip file called *WorkFiles.zip* that includes the files and references needed for the work in this book, additional files and images from the projects shown here, and up to the minute descriptions of new features in Vectorworks. Download and expand the zip file now.

Separating each chapter will be a two page spread showing work done professionally using Vectorworks. Additionally there is professional work used to llustrate soem key points of the text not addressed in the *Lysistrata* project.

This might not all make sense, but it will. Read on.

About the Author

Kevin Lee Allen is a multiple-award-winning scenic and lighting designer who works in theatre, film, television, museums, and corporate environments, including architainment, exhibits, fashion, and special events. Notable projects include work for the United States Government, CNN and CNN International, a virtual interview with Benjamin Franklin, productions of *Romeo & Juliet* (both the ballet and play), *All I ask of You,* and *The Tempest*, and the Chase Bank Flagship Signage in Times Square. His design sketches are held in private collections and in the permanent collection of the Library of Congress.

Mr. Allen is a longtime Vectorworks user and has taught, lectured, and demonstrated the application on the university level and at the Broadway Lighting Master Classes.

Kevin Lee Allen's work can be seen at http://klad.com. Kevin Lee Allen and Kathleen McDonough blog at http://klad.com/blog. Sometimes he blogs about Vectorworks.

If you have comments or questions, e-mail Kevin at klad@klad.com.

Acknowledgments

No one works alone, especially in show business, and writing. Despite the rumors.

My Vectorworks posse has offered guidance, advice, and support: lighting designer and author Steven Shelley (creator of the Field Templates and Soft Symbols, author of *A Practical Guide to Stage Lighting*); scenic and lighting designer Cris Dopher; lighting designer Shawn Kaufman; designers and developers John McKernon, C. Andrew Dunning, and Joshua Benghiat. You are all thankful for Dopher's technical edit on the first draft. You just don't know that.

Jeremy Powell of Nemetschek Vectorworks, and AJ from ESP Vision sent me down the writing path. Jeremy along with Frank Brault, Sue Collins, Dave Donley, Theresa Downs, Tara Grant, Lisa Lance, Kevin Linzey, and Kristine Sherwood at Nemetschek Vectorworks have been continuously supportive and helpful on many levels.

Everything I've written has been based on my classroom experience. Dean Geoffrey Newman, Professor Michael Allen, and Professor John Wiese of Montclair State University made that happen, and to them I am grateful. I am equally grateful to the students whom I taught. I hope they learned as much from me as I did from them.

I am thankful for the people who taught and mentored me, among them: Reagan Cook, John Figola, Keith Gonzales, Phillip Graneto, Mark Kruger, W. Scott MacConnell, Lester Polikov, Peter Politanoff, Phillip Louis Rodzen, Tom Schwinn, David Steigerwalt, and Peter Wexler. From these talents, I learned the importance of precision and the crucial need for clarity of communication in order for the vision to be properly executed.

Many talented, professional Vectorworks users have contributed their work to this publication. You will find illustrations of that work between each chapter. It is all worth study. Those names are sprinkled throughout, and I thank them.

In addition to the many talented designers whose work is presented here, friends and colleagues like Lighting Designer Steven Rust, Broadway Producers Tim Laczynski and Roy Miller, Kevin Hersh, Gerald Lee Ratliff, Michael Eddy, and playwright Robert Patrick have all helped to advance this book, each in their own way.

This book could not have happened without Stacey D. Walker and Meagan White of Focal Press.

Of course, this book, and much of my life would not have been possible without the love and support of my wife and partner Kathleen McDonough.

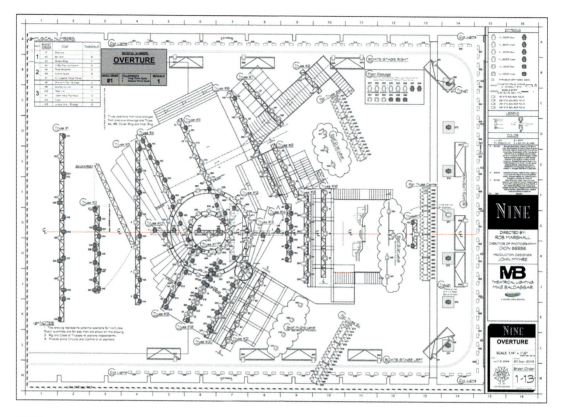

NINE

Light Plot for the Overture sequence.

NINE: the film

NINE
Photo by: David James, © The Weinstein Company, 2009.

NINE: the film

Directed by: Rob Marshall
Director of Photography: Dion Beebe
Production Designer: John Myhre
Theatrical Lighting Designer: Mike Baldassari
    Theatrical Lighting Design Draftsperson: Kristina Kloss

1. Basic Drafting Principles and Standards

Before we begin to draw, let's take a look at what we are drawing, and why.

This book will teach you how to create, draft, and document project designs. For the most part, CAD is the way professionals work. Vectorworks is the CAD tool generally chosen by designers. There are occasions when the lessons learned here will need to be transported to a hand-drawn world.

Although there is really only a minimal place for hand-drawn or drafted work in the modern professional world, those skills remain necessary. There are times when a scenic designer might be in a shop and explaining a detail to a carpenter. That would likely be done with a pencil on scrap paper, or scrap wood, and possibly a nail, or a

screw rather than a pencil. That takes skill.

A Lighting Designer might find him or herself in a field with a half dozen or so sky-trackers. The light plot then might be scraped into the ground with the heel of the designer's shoe. It might not sound that way, but that is drafting and design on the fly.

Meetings often rely on quick scribbles on pads or iPads. Everyone draws. It is expected that the designers can communicate clearly and concisely with a pencil or pen.

The brain to hand connection at every stage of the design process, especially the beginning of the design process, is critical.

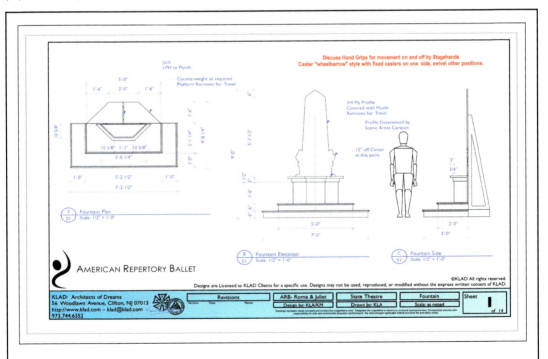

This plate of drawings provides basic information for a simple scenic element for a ballet..

Design is storytelling.

Drafting is Design, and Design requires clear drafting. We will start at the beginning. You do not need to know how to hand draft at this point, but you can apply the principles here to learn to hand draft. Develop your hand skills as you develop your computer skills.

The first rule is there are no rules.

Architects have rules. Engineers have lots of rules. Theatrical drawing, drafting, and documentation is often like an untamed frontier defined by the designer or draftsperson's own style, technique, and taste. The only rule is you must get the show built and installed. The producer has sold tickets for a certain day and time, and before that, the company needs to rehearse. You must have clearly communicated the needs of the design, and the look, well before.

OK, so there's a rule.

While a hand-drawn object may be converted to a computer-drawn document to be sent to a computer-controlled (CnC) router, or a 3D printer, the CnC router can do nothing with hand drafting. The technology of construction and rigging is state-of-the-art and technology driven. Make no mistake, 3D printers can be used to create scenic models today, and they will be used to make scenery in the immediate future.

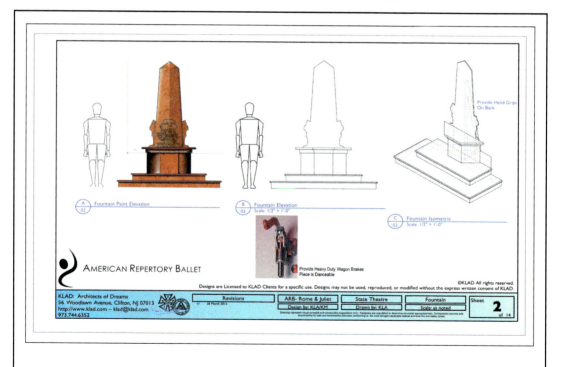

This plate of drawings details a simple scenic element for a ballet..

There are two basic types of drawing that we're discussing: engineering drawing, and artistic drawing, and both may simply be called drawing when the context is clear. Engineering drawing, and artistic drawing both create pictures, both help tell a story. Typically, any story requires both kinds of drawing. The purpose of artistic drawing is to express emotion, or render a moment, an object, an instance in a subjective manner. Engineering drawings convey objective information.

Accuracy and precision are everything. Tell the stagehand to put a light or a speaker in the wrong place and you've cost the producer money. You'll also have cost the production time. There is never enough of either of these commodities.

So, there's a second rule; you must be accurate in your drawing.

Here's a third rule; for the most part when creating a set of drawings, when telling the story of the design, the drawings would be complete enough that if the designer were to be hit by a bus when the documentation is completed, others should be able to execute the design without the designer. This is less true of lighting and sound than scenery, but the rule holds.

Line Weight

When theatrical drawing (like architectural or engineering drawing) was done by hand, the draftsperson sought to master three different line weights:
- A Thin Line for leaders, invisible objects, and dimensions.
- A Thick Line mostly reserved to delineate the cutaway of a section view.
- A Medium Line Weight for pretty much everything else. Although a lot of scenic drafting was very pictorial, the basic outline of shapes, including individual lighting instruments drawn from a template, all maintained this line quality.

These were plenty of line weights to be consistently drawn by hand. Even though we have many more options available using Vectorworks, it is generally still true. As you grow as an artist, you may see this rule change. You may opt to have a few more line weights.

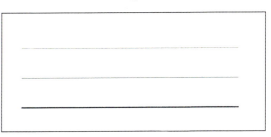

Drawing/CAD is the art of telling the story of the design.

On a Light Plot, or a Sound Plot, the darkest lines are reserved for the lighting instruments and audio gear. That is definitely not to say that these are places to use your heavy/thick line. However, the venue architecture, scenery, masking, and audience must not draw the crew's attention from clearly seeing the proper placement of the lighting equipment.

Line Types

The same is also true of Line Types:
- A solid line to indicate the outlines of objects, in a medium line weight, and possibly a light line weight to indicate some lesser details.
- A short dashed line in a light line weight to indicate details below or inside an object.
- A medium dashed line for annotations or exploded views.
- A long dashed line in a light line weight to indicate objects above.
- A dashed line in a light line weight with a long dash, a short, and then another long (repeating) to indicate the centerline of an object or a stage.
- A dashed line in a heavy line weight with a long dash, two short dashes, and then another long (repeating) to indicate the cut line, and the outline of a section view.

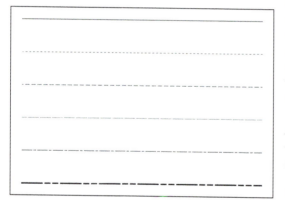

So, what's a section view? That is sometimes, and for many, a challenging concept. Fortunately, Vectorworks makes a Section View easy to draw, and easy to understand, just not first thing.

Line weights, and line types clarify objects.

This book addresses, or will speak to, many different types of drawings. Let's begin with some definitions, and a look at the basic types of views required to illustrate and execute a design.

Preliminary sketch for a television project. By the author.

The first doodle is likely a hand-drawn perspective view and/or plan (aerial) view by the designer. We'll spend a considerable amount of time on perspective and rendering, but for the moment let's just define perspective as the drawing of objects in two-dimensions, giving the correct impressions of height, width, depth, and position in relation to each other when viewed from a specific spot. Perspective creates the illusion of depth where there is none.

A good draftsperson can visually reverse engineer a properly drawn (or even badly drawn) perspective view to create all other views.

Perspective views give life to a design; they can express the emotion of the design, but they are not detailed enough to execute a design. Perspective views can be drawn from a point of having scale, but they are, by their nature, not to scale.

Figures should always be included in perspective views, elevations, and sections to help indicate scale, even when dimensions (indications of size) are present.

Scale

What is scale?

Scale is relative size, or a ratio between actual size and reduced size.

If you have a sheet of paper, say letter size or A4, it is possible to draw a 2" or 4cm cube in actual size. If you need to draw a 200' (6,0960mm) cube, you either need a really big piece of paper, or you need to draw it to scale such that it fits on your paper.

In the US, theatrical drawings are typically in 1/2" or 1/4" scales. Detail views are shown at larger scales like 1 1/2"=1'-0" or 3"=1'-0" and often even 1:1 or 1:2 to provide very specific information. 1:1 is obviously full scale, also known as *to scale* or *actual*. 1:2 then becomes *half scale*.

Architectural Scales, like 1/2"=1'-0" (commonly referred to as 1/2" scale) divide one-half inch of the ruler into 12 equal increments to represent inches. So, an object that is 2' (609.6mm) long, drawn in 1/2" scale is shown at 1" (254mm) long.

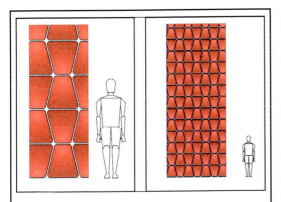

Two similar objects, the one on the left is clearly smaller than the one on the right as the scale of the pattern shows. The human figure adjacent to the images reinforces the sense of scale.

Orthographic Projections *must* be properly aligned.

Of course, the rest of the civilized world uses the Metric system, and the more logical 1:25 and 1:50 proportional scales. To translate 1/4" and 1/2" scales closer to metric, you would have to use 1:24 and 1:48 scales.

Orthographic Projection

Perhaps the most basic to-scale view is then a plan (or plan projection) view of an object. That is simply an overhead view of an object; *a bird's eye view without perspective.* There is no depth to a typical plan view. A Light Plot, a Sound Plot, and a theatrical Groundplan are all plan views.

A graphic projection is a convention where an image of one side view of a three-dimensional object is *projected* flat-onto a planar surface without the aid of mathematical calculation. In a traditional hand-drawn perspective view, the plane is called the picture plane; this is the one place where the objects are to scale. The picture plane is an invisible vertical plane perpendicular to the sightline of the subject. For a Plan view, the Plane of the view is a horizontal plane, above the floor or the bottom of an object.

A Plan view is a type of Orthographic Projection; a means of projecting different views of a three-dimensional object as measurable two-dimensional views arranged on a sheet, and providing enough information for a craftsperson to build the object. Typically, at least three views are required: a plan view, a front elevation, and a side elevation. For more complicated objects, additional views are needed. A section view is often one of those additional views.

When Orthographic views are presented on a sheet, they are all of the same scale, and they are consistently dimensioned. The positions of all measurements, are lined up, such that any dimension can be readily transferred between views by drawing vertical, horizontal, or diagonal lines. Details can be added, and often those details are in a larger scale than the basic Orthographic views.

Typically in the US, a full arrangement of orthographic views of an object has the front view centered, with a top, or plane view above, and a bottom view below, if needed. The right side view would be to the right of the Front view, and the left side view to the left. A rear view, if required, would be located to the left of the left side view.

A typical scenic elevation of a flat is the Front View in an Orthographic Projection.

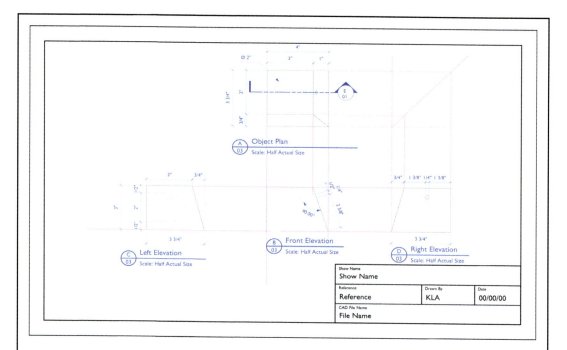

Each view in a basic Orthographic Projection is aligned with the other views such that with some dimensional information, each view can be constructed, or projected from the others. This drawing shows a simple object with straight sides, tapered sides, and a sphere removed from the middle. There is a hole drilled from one tapered side into the sphere.

Isometric Views

Sometimes a set of flat orthographic elevations is not enough to describe an object. Sometimes a pictorial view is needed, a to-scale pictorial view without perspective. An Isometric View is a to-scale pictorial view, without perspective.

An Isometric View is an Axonometric Projection; a type of parallel projection used to create a pictorial drawing of an object, where the object is rotated along one or more of its axes relative to the plane of projection. Axonometric means to measure along axis, therefore it is a pictorial view that is also to scale.

This is also to say that Isometric views don't truly appear correct.

Isometric means *Equal Measure,* and an isometric view shows equal amounts of three sides. Isometrics have the three major axis lines at equal angles (120 degrees) to the plane of projection.

A Right Isometric
02 Scale: Actual Size

An Isometric View of the same object.

An Isometric View is mechanically correct, and pictorial, but it does not appear correct—there is no perspective.

You can choose to orient any isometric view to be the most informative for your specific needs.

When looking at an isometric view of an object, notice that:
- The major isometric axis lines may be placed in any position.
- Each of the three angles between the axis lines must be 120 degrees.
- Vertical lines remain vertical, and parallel lines remain parallel.

Only axiometric lines are measurable. Those are the vertical lines and lines drawn on the defined axis. Curved lines and lines projected off-axis are not measurable.

An isometric view of a circle is an ellipse. The isometric of a square containing the circle will be a parallelogram with each side equal to the diameter of the circle.

Section Views

So all right already, what is a Section View?

Even with dotted lines indicating object interior details, there are often things left unclear. A Section View is a cutaway elevation, in effect slicing through an object, as if hinging the object, and opening at the hinge to look inside.

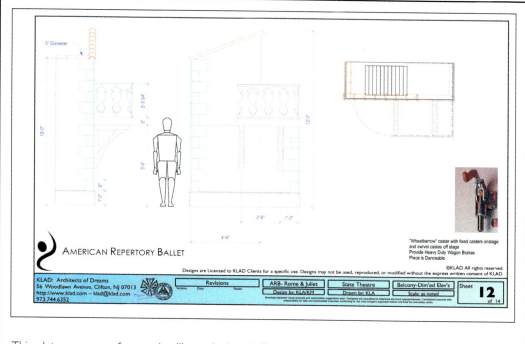

This plate was one of many detailing a single unit. The sheets were laid out for publication using a tabloid page size on an office printer, requiring additional sheets.

Typically, the cut line or cutting plane of the section is placed on center, but that cut line, or hinge-point, could be anywhere needed to best tell the story of the object. The cutting plane is identified by the placement of a Section Line, and reference markers.

Objects cut by the cutting plane are typically outlined with the thickest line, and filled with a cross hatch, or descriptive fill pattern.

A Plan View is a section view, with the cut line placed, usually, 4-5 feet (about 1,500mm) above the ground. The cutting plane of that section dictates where you use solid lines, and different types of dashed lines.

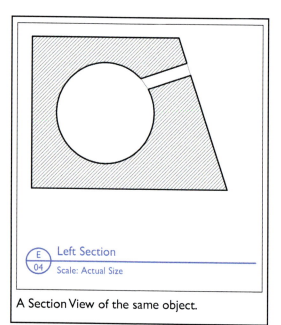

A Section View of the same object.

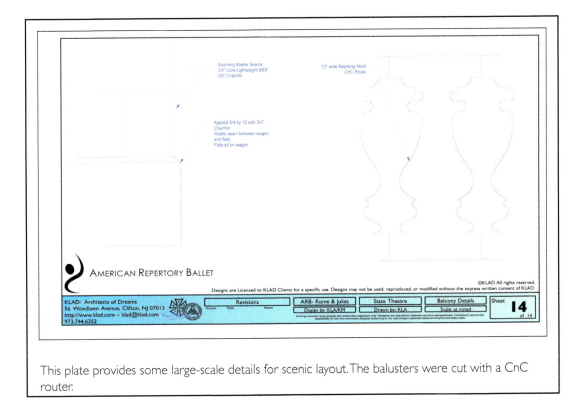

AMERICAN REPERTORY BALLET

KLAD: Architects of Dreams 56 Woodlawn Avenue, Clifton, NJ 07013 http://www.klad.com – klad@klad.com 973.744.6352	Revisions		ARB- Rome & Juliet	State Theatre	Balcony Details	Sheet
	Version	Date	Notes	Design by: KLA/KM	State Theatre	Balcony Details	**14** of 14

This plate provides some large-scale details for scenic layout. The balusters were cut with a CnC router.

Title Blocks

Every drawing of every type requires a title block. Period. End of Statement. Another rule.

The Title Block is your signature: it will contain copyright and contact information, as well as identify the specific drawing within a set of drawings.

Specific Annotations

There is a graphic convention in which drawings and sections are noted from one sheet within a set to another. Some **Reference Markers** appear in the illustrations and will be covered in the course of the text.

Building Information Model (BIM)

In the architectural world a working process for collaboration has been created called the Building Information Model, or BIM. Simply put, BIM is the creation of a 3D Model of a building that can be shared and modified by a team of architects, engineers, and designers.

This process is completely applicable to theatrical and entertainment designers. This book addresses design collaboration through a BIM process for the entertainment world. Instead of architects and engineers, although those types might be involved in larger projects, the collaboration here would be between scenic, lighting, and sound designers.

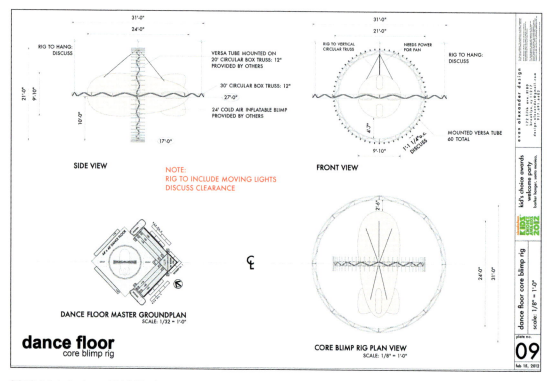

SIDE VIEW

RIG TO HANG:
DISCUSS

31'-0"
24'-0"

21'-0"
9'-10"

10'-0"

17'-0"

VERSA TUBE MOUNTED ON
20' CIRCULAR BOX TRUSS: 12"
PROVIDED BY OTHERS

30' CIRCULAR BOX TRUSS: 12"

27'-0"

24' COLD AIR INFLATABLE BLIMP
PROVIDED BY OTHERS

NOTE:
RIG TO INCLUDE MOVING LIGHTS
DISCUSS CLEARANCE

FRONT VIEW

RIG TO VERTICAL
CIRCULAR TRUSS

NEEDS POWER
FOR FAN

RIG TO HANG:
DISCUSS

31'-0"
21'-0"

4'7"

9'-10"

1'.1 1/4"o.c.
DISCUSS

MOUNTED VERSA TUBE
60 TOTAL

DANCE FLOOR MASTER GROUNDPLAN
SCALE: 1/32 = 1'0"

44 x 48 DANCE FLOOR

CORE BLIMP RIG PLAN VIEW
SCALE: 1/8" = 1'0"

2'-6"

24'-0"
31'-0"

dance floor
core blimp rig

kid's choice awards
welcome party
barker hanger, santa monica.

evan alexander design

dance floor core blimp rig

scale: 1/8" = 1'-0"

plate no.
09

feb 15, 2012

2012 Nickelodeon Kids' Choice Awards Welcome Party
Designs for the Kids Choice Awards courtesy of Nickelodeon. Copyright 2012, Viacom International Inc.

Nickelodeon Kids' Choice Awards Welcome Party

2012 Nickelodeon Kids' Choice Awards Welcome Party
Designs for the Kids Choice Awards courtesy of Nickelodeon. Copyright 2012, Viacom International Inc.

2012 Nickelodeon Kids' Choice Awards Welcome Party
Barker Hangar, Santa Monica, CA

Production Designer: Evan Alexander
    Design Associates: Sarah Tester & Rebecca Lord-Surratt
    Graphics Assistant: Benjamin Wheelock
Executive Producer: Jane Volpe
Production Manager: Joe Lewis
Lighting Designer: Matt Levesque

This design was explored and built out in Vectorworks in 3D. From there, the models were exported into Cinema 4D for material adjustments, lighting, and camera work. Those renders then went through Photoshop for color balance, overlays, and additional lighting effects.

2. The Vectorworks Screen

If you've ever hand-drawn, hand drafted, or worked with most any art application, the visual metaphor of the Vectorworks screen will look and feel familiar. To begin we must take a quick look around at the readily available tools.

The Spotlight Workspace

Open Vectorworks, and go to **Tools>Workspaces>Spotlight** to select the Spotlight Workspace. Your palettes and menus may then rearrange. A Vectorworks Workspace is a collection of tools and menus assembled to create a working environment in order to accomplish a focused set of tasks. Vectorworks comes with Workspaces created to accomplish different tasks. In our case, those

tasks are designing scenery, lighting, and sound, and the Spotlight Workspace is focused on those tasks.

Your screen should now look something like the illustration below. For clarity of illustration, some of the *palettes* have been carefully arranged. By default, Vectorworks will create a blank document when the application is opened. If you do not have a blank document window open, go to **File>New** and select *Create blank document.*

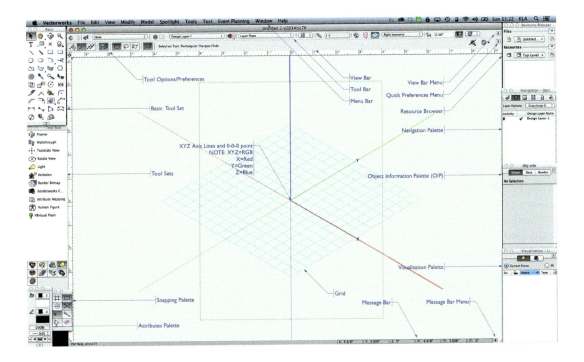

Organize Vectorworks to suit you.

○ ○		Navigation
○ ○	○	Resource Browser
○ ○		**Obj Info**
○ ○		Visualization – Lights

This allows fast clicking between palettes, while showing as much information as possible, and lets you easily window-shade (Mac OS) to show and reveal the palettes needed, as needed.

On the left side of your screen you should see the Basic Tool Palette and the Tool Sets Palette, which allow you to access additional tools for particular jobs. The Attributes Palette and the Snapping Palette are also to the left. On the right you should see the OIP, Navigation Palette, Visualization Palette, and Resource Browser.

At the top of the active window, you will see the View Bar where there are selections to be made affecting the screen display.

Below the **View Bar** is the **Tool Bar**. Virtually every Tool in Vectorworks has Modes that can be chosen from the Tool Bar. The Tool Bar is divided into sections grouped by mode function. To move easily through the mode sections from the keyboard, press the **U, I, O, P, [,** and **]** keys. Each key corresponds to a consecutive Tool Bar section.

The Message/Data Bar is located at the bottom of the window.

| X: -2.391" | Y: -.641" | L: 2.475" | A: -165.00" | ▶ |

Palettes

The palettes that surround the drawing window in Vectorworks allow ready access to the tools you'll use to create drawings, and the means to modify what you've drawn.

On a PC, the palettes should line up on either side of the screen. On a Macintosh, palettes have to be aligned manually. The right-hand side of the Object Information Palette (OIP), the Resource Browser, the Navigation Palette, and the Visualization Palette will dock to the right side of the screen when you click right side of the title bar and drag the palette. These palettes can be resized by selecting the lower-right-hand corner and clicking and dragging. When re-sizing, you will be constrained to the screen.

If you have multiple monitors, palettes can be kept separately from the main drawing window.

On a Macintosh, the windows can be collapsed (or *window shaded*) by double-clicking the title bar. While the arrangement shown above is clean, most users will find the need to reshape and reorganize the palettes as part of their workflow. When the palettes are docked to the right side of the screen, a click on the green button in the top left of the document window should resize that window to fit between the palettes. Resizing is an option in the **Vectorworks Preferences Session Tab**.

As you work, you may find a different workflow. To begin, stack the Resource Browser, Navigation Palette, OIP, and Visualization Palette in that order, as full-height as possible, and aligned to the right, wide enough for two or three objects to show as thumbnails in the Resource Browser.

Basic Tool Set

The Basic Tool set provides ready access to a collection of 2D drawing tools, 2D and 3D drawing modifiers, and basic dimensioning tools.

On the top left of the Basic Tool Set you will find the Selection Tool. Hover your cursor over the arrow-shaped icon and see the hint indicating the functionality of the tool and the keyboard shortcut for accessing the tool. You can choose the Selection tool by clicking on the icon or by pressing the **x** key (unless you are editing text).

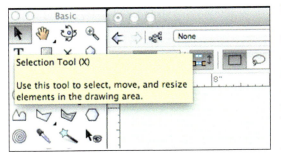

Now, hover over the other Tools to begin to familiarize yourself with what's available in this palette. Select some of the Tools and note how the options change in the Tool Bar.

The Selection Tool will be used frequently to choose objects for modification, move, or duplicate by pressing the Alt (Windows) or the Option (Macintosh) key and dragging any object.

The Selection Tool can be readily accessed by pressing the **X** key, or the **Esc** key.

Next to the Selection Tool is the Pan Tool, which is very useful for navigating around a drawing when you have zoomed in on a detail area. The Pan tool can be activated in *Boomerang* mode at any time (unless you are editing text) by pressing and holding the spacebar. Boomerang mode means simply that you can switch to the

Pan tool while the spacebar is pressed and you will return to the previously selected tool when the spacebar is released.

Notice the **Access Arrow** at the bottom of the Palette; click here to see and choose viewing options for the Tools in the Palette.

Tool Sets

Tool Sets are collections of tools grouped for specific tasks. Note, for example, that there is a Dims/Notes tool set that provides other dimensioning and labeling tools beyond those in the Dimensioning Tools provided in the Basic Tool Set of the Spotlight Workspace.

The Tool Sets can be viewed in a number of different ways. Note that, you can click in the access arrow at the bottom of the Tool sets palette to choose different ways of viewing the tools and the tool sets. I personally choose to view the tools as icons and text and the Tool Sets as icons.

The Attributes Palette

The Attributes palette sets various graphic attributes of 2D and 3D objects. When an object is selected, the line, fill, and opacity of an object may be changed. Arrows can be added to lines, line thickness can be changed, and opacity can be modified. Notice the access arrow at the bottom of the palette and the choices available. **Make All Attributes By Class** can often save many clicks.

The Snapping/Constraints Palette

The Snapping Palette sets options for drawing with precise alignment. Constraints can be temporarily turned off by pressing and holding the single quote ' key. This works in the same way as the Boomerang Mode with the Pan Tool.

Users may set Preferences for the constraints and the displayed grid by double-clicking on any of the constraint icons. Constraints help with precise drawing and provide cues to the SmartCursor.

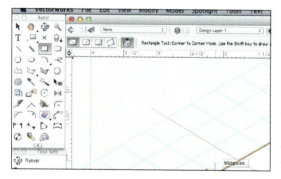

If you do not see the grid and the XYZ guidelines, double-click on a tool in the Snapping Palette, or press Command/Control+8 to access the Snapping Preferences, select **Grid**, and check the boxes to show the grid and the XYZ axis.

Hover over the options to see what they do for you. The Snap to Grid option should be turned off. This option can be useful or not depending on the drawing and grid specification.

SmartCursor

The SmartCursor provides a series of visual cues displayed as text at the cursor's current location. It can create snaps to specific points relative to other objects. These cues will be obvious as soon as we begin to draw.

Smart Points

Smart Points allow the use of existing geometry as drawing guides. When Smart Points snapping is on, a Smart Point can be defined by pausing the cursor over an object point and pressing the "T" key. Drawing can then be aligned with that point. The alignment is visually shown with a dotted red line.

Working Planes

The Working Planes palette is not opened by default and is not shown in the main illustration. To familiarize yourself with this palette, go to **Window>Palettes>Working Plane** to open the palette. When needed, locate the palette so it is accessible but not in the way of drawing.

Working planes allow you to change the base geometric plane on which you are drawing. Typically, the base plane is a flat horizontal plane located at zero elevation. This palette will allow you to access multiple saved planes. Vectorworks automatically finds the Working Plane when you hover over objects. For example, if you are working with a raked deck, or multiple level, you will want to save those surfaces as working planes.

Those same saved planes are also accessible via the Planes drop-down menu in the View Bar.

Object Information Palette (OIP)

The Object Information Palette (OIP) is a critical design control point; any object selected in Vectorworks can be manipulated via the OIP. This is wheresizes of objects can be changed, where Spotlight Lighting Devices can be modified, and one place where the visual appearance of objects can be altered.

The OIP has three tabs: Shape, Data, and Render. Shape affects size, location, and specific parameters associated with different types of objects. Data references information associated with the object for use in worksheets, and Render affects the look of 3D objects in presentations.

Depending on the type of object selected, the OIP offers different options. In the illustration at left, a Spotlight Lighting Device has been inserted into a document and is selected. The OIP then shows a myriad of default options. In the specific case of a Spotlight Lighting Device, data entered in the OIP can be shared with Lightwright 5 in a dynamic exchange that allows Vectorworks, via the OIP, to modify Lightwright data, and Lightwright to modify data and instrument placement in Vectorworks.

Resource Browser

The Resource Browser accesses and organizes symbols, textures, Line Styles, Text Styles, Data, and other resources stored in your file, as well as other files that may or may not be open. Select the disclosure arrow at the top right of the Resource Browser and note the **Add New Favorite Files** option. This allows you to navigate to other files, select the file(s), and always have access to frequently used Resources.

There is a wealth of Default Content available from within Vectorworks. For example, Default Textures can be accessed from the OIP, and when editing class definitions. When Default Content is added to a file, that content can then be accessed and edited from within the Resource Browser.

Navigation

The Navigation Palette allows you to quickly access Classes, Design Layers, Sheet Layers, Viewports, Saved Views, and References. Each of these terms will be defined and explained. From the Navigation palette you can activate, navigate, and control visibilities. This palette allows quick access to settings also located via the **Tools>Organization** command.

Visualization

The Visualization Palette allows control of Vectorworks Light Objects, Spotlight Lighting Devices, and Camera Objects.

The Visualization Palette is useful for setting lighting cues when pre-visualizing scenes.

Learn the Palettes.
Work the Palettes.

The Document Window

The Document Window in the main working area, or window.

View Bar

The View Bar is at the top of the document window and allows immediate access to many important functions. View Bar functions can be hidden and displayed from the drop-down list accessed via the **Disclosure Triangle** on the right end of the View Bar. From the left you will see forward and backward arrows; clicking on these will take you back and forth between recent document views. Skip to the center right, and you will see two magnifying glass icons. The first **Fits the View to the Page Area**. The second can take you to a view of either a selected item, or to a view of all items in the visible drawing (when nothing is selected). Command/Control+6 have the same functionality.

In the View Bar a drop-down menu allows you to select the working plane of your drawing. There are up to three basic options available here (excluding any saved planes): *Layer, Screen,* and *Automatic.*

Drawing in the Screen Plane with a 2D drawing tool from the Basic tool set gives you a 2D object that is locked to the screen or the front of the drawing space. As you change orthographic or isometric views, the object remains as a flat 2D elevation. In the Layer Plane mode, drawing 2D or 3D objects places the objects on the working plane. This is immediately evident when drawing an object in an isometric view; the object can be immediately seen in 3D space. Switching views shows the object move with the view. Working in the Layer Plane allows you to design entirely in 3D space.

The Automatic Layer Plane option is active and

can be selected when you have a 3D object and are drawing other 2D or 3D objects adjacent to the original. Hovering the 2D or 3D Primitive tool over the surface of the original 3D object causes the face plane of the original object to be highlighted. With the Push/Pull tool option selected, objects can be extruded (expanded into the third dimension) into the active working plane.

When working on different planes, the red, blue, and green axes will shift to the active working plane, if that option has been selected in the **Snapping Palette Preferences**.

There is a drop-down menu for your view of the drawing. This view defaults to Top/Plan (Command/Control+5), which is the 2D overhead view. In the illustration of the working area, that view has been set to Right Isometric.

Top is a 3D overhead view, and the others should all make logical sense, based on the definitions of orthographic and isometric projection. You may also access each of these views from a numeric keypad, with 5 being Plan, 2 being Front, 4 being the left view, 6 being the right view, 8 being the back, 0 being the Top/Plan, and the isometric views are the four corner numbers.

On the right of the View Bar you can select the disclosure arrow and choose the options to be visible. These are choices made based on your individual workflow. For our purposes, please select the options illustrated. Over time, you will likely adapt this list to your own workflow.

Tool Bar

The Tool Bar is just below the View Bar and displays different options available for each tool selected from the Basic tool set or one of the task-specific tool sets.

From within the Tool Bar, each tool has a variety of settings or Modes available on the left. For example, rectangles can be drawn diagonally, from the center out, from two sides, and rotated. The option to activate the Push/Pull capability allows you to immediately draw an extrude into 3D. You can shift between drawing modes by pressing the **U** key. When there are multiple types of Modes, tey are divided into sections, and then the **I, O, P, [** and **]** toggle between Modes in subsequent sections

Select available options via the **Disclosure Arrow** on the right of the Tool Bar.

Quick Preferences

Preferences are settings and options within the application, or documents. Vectorworks Application Preferences are accessed by going to **Vectorworks>Preferences** on a Mac, or by going to **Tools>Options>Vectorworks Preferences** on either a Mac or a PC. There are also document specific preferences that can be chosen at **File>Document Settings.** These settings will be detailed at length.

On the right of the Tool Bar are the **Quick Preferences**, which are frequently used settings available from within the **Vectorworks Preferences**. These options allow the user to make rapid interface changes, as and when desired. Select options via the Gear Icon near the right of the Tool Bar, and add toggles using the **Disclosure Triangle** on the far right.

Experiment with some of the options. You may find you prefer working on drawings against a black background, or with a full-screen cursor.

Message Bar

The Message Bar at the bottom right of the drawing window displays precise information about the location of the cursor in the drawing space. Preferences accessed via the Disclosure Arrow in the far right-hand corner of the screen can affect this display. Additionally, the Message Bar displays important alerts, back up information, and rendering progress.

Moving the View

It bears repeating here; that to pan across the drawing at any time (even if a tool or command is active), hold down the Space bar and drag the cursor. The Boomerang mode will return you to

the active tool as soon as the space bar is released. Boomerang mode does not work when editing text. Pressing and holding the space bar when adding text will obviously add spaces to the text.

You may also directly select the Pan tool from the Basic tool set. Scroll bars can be activated or deactivated from the Vectorworks Preferences.

Pressing the **H** key will also activate the Pan Tool.

Zooming

By default, the application's preferences set the scroll wheel of the mouse to zoom in and out. Similarly, two-fingers on a multi-touch track pad will zoom in and out of a drawing.

From the View Bar, click **Fit to Objects** (Command/Control+6). The view is adjusted to fit the selected object to the screen. When nothing is selected, the same action will fit all objects to the screen.

Command/Control+1 will zoom in, Command/Control+2 will zoom out, Command/Control+3 returns to the last view, and Command/Control+4 shows the full-page view

There are many keyboard shortcuts in Vectorworks. Making use of these shortcuts will speed your work. Vectorworks is incredibly customizable, and we will discuss how shortcuts can be changed or modified to suit your workflow.

Provide the right amount of information on every drawing.

There will be redundancy within a set of drawings.

Don't force the craftspeople hunt for information.

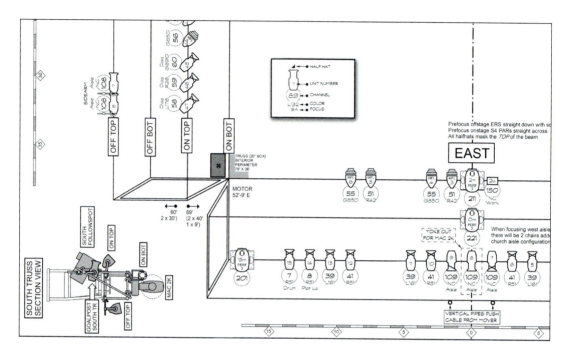

2013 Paul Winter Solstice Concert

Detail of Steven Louis Shelley's Plot for the 2013 Paul Winter Solstice Concert, with the key to the Label Legend overlaid by the author. Note the detailed section explaining the hanging of instruments on the truss rig.

2013 Paul Winter Solstice Concert

2013 Paul Winter Solstice Concert

2013 Paul Winter Solstice Concert
The Cathedral Church of St. John the Divine, New York City

Lighting Designer: Steven Louis Shelley

Designer Steven Louis Shelley is also the creator of the Soft Symbols collection of Spotlight Lighting Device symbols. Obviously he uses those symbols, and you can see a few of them on the detail of the Light Plot, at left.

3. Document Organization and Stationery

When creating a new document (**File>New**), Vectorworks will ask if you want to create a blank document or use a stationery file. Vectorworks comes with a selection of stationery files, most geared for architecture and engineering. There is a Spotlight template file that is worth reviewing. It is a useful time-saver to create your own template files.

Unless you have created a Default.sta file, saved in a specific location, when you create a new blank document, all custom settings are lost to the application defaults. When you save your personal settings in a stationery document, you set them and forget them. Stationery documents usually evolve as they are used over time.

Stationery, also known as **Template files,** can be used in many ways. If you frequently work in one venue, a template file can be created with the base architecture and standard views. Frequently used gear can be kept in a template file. It certainly makes sense to keep your graphic and organizational standards set in a stationery file.

Create a new Blank document in either A4 or Letter Size. Page size can be changed to standard or custom sizes in the **File>Page Setup** Dialog. This dialog accesses attached printers, standard size papers, and large-format output sizes in a number of standards when *Choose size unavailable in printer setup* is checked.

Save this file as you adjust these settings.

Go to the **Vectorworks Preferences**. On a Macintosh, Vectorworks preferences can be accessed at **Vectorworks>Preferences.** On either a Mac or a PC preferences can be accessed at **Tools>Options>Vectorworks Preferences**.

Application Preferences are saved when the application is quit.

Vectorworks Preferences

When the Preferences dialog opens, there will be seven tabs:
- Edit
- Display
- Session
- 3D
- Autosave
- Interactive
- User Folders

Let's take a look at each, and make some choices.

Edit

Under Edit, be sure that **2D conversion res** is set to high and that **Allow option-click-in-place duplication** is turned off. **Mouse wheel zooms** also allows two-finger zooming with a track pad.

It is best to be warned before scaling a symbol. Symbols are bits of a drawing that can be reused and that can be scaled in the OIP, and it is useful to know if they are scaled accidentally.

Display

The Display tab allows users to customize the look of the drawing window. Note the choices here to **Display light objects** and **Display 3D loci** only in the wireframe rendering. This helps to keep the rendered images clean.

It is important to remember these settings are there for times when you may want to toggle these back on to make specific adjustments. **Create text without fill** creates text without a block of white behind the characters.

Check **Use VectorCaching for faster drawing**.

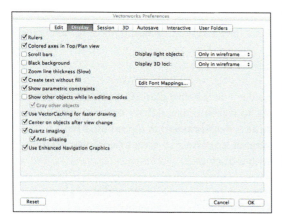

Session

If you're billing by the hour or want to track the time it takes you to perform certain tasks, you can log your time in Vectorworks here. This is also where you set the number of undos; the lower the number, the more memory you will have free. Most objects can be edited by double-clicking or right-clicking on the object so that fewer undos are actually required. Note that if you have added a 3D Chamfer or a 3D Fillet to an object, you must UnGroup the object to edit past that point. The Fillet or Chamfer will have to be recreated.

Some users like the Vectorworks sounds to help them know things, like when the SmartCursor has found a point, just as some users like to always have a fresh document when they enter Vectorworks.

It is important here to allow for palette margins on both sides of the screen, if you have only one monitor.

Mac OS users can opt in or out of the restore windows functionality here.

3D

Since we will be working in 3D, set the **3D Conversion** to **Very High**. That setting may impact performance with large files or complex models. If need be, reduce the conversion quality.

Interactive

The settings in the Interactive tab allow users to customize the look and feel of the user interface to suit their tastes and needs. Users should experiment with these settings and the choices.

Clicking the *Interactive Appearance Settings* button allows you to choose the colors for the SmartCursor highlighting and all of the different background colors, planes, and views.

Autosave

Save early, save often, and back up. Create a redundant back up system.

Vectorworks will back up your work for you and create files you can use to restore your work should you need to. By default, Vectorworks will create back ups in the same folder or directory as the original file. I prefer to keep all of the back ups in one place. I do have to remember to go clean out that folder from time to time, but it keeps my project folders cleaner. Since I have an hourly system back up, I only keep three Vectorworks back ups.

User Folders

A **User Folder** is a folder and file directory similar to the application directory. It makes your own data easier to find than if they were to be saved in the application directory. Create a folder on your system in a place that you can readily access, such as the documents folder in the home directory. Create a folder, and select the **Choose** button in the **User Folder Tab** of the **Application Preferences**. You will be taken to a standard file directory. Navigate to the folder you have created, and click **OK.**

Workgroup Folders allow a team or a firm to share resources.

In a project situation, the Project or Workgroup Folder could be on a server so that several designers, associates, and assistants could work on the project at the same time. The workgroup folder could be on a Local Area Network (LAN) for users working in the same office, or on a Wide Area Network (WAN), meaning that the network allows access from most anywhere. Services like **Drop Box** allow small offices or sole practitioners to create a (WAN) for projects. The **Vectorworks Nomad application** interfaces with **Drop Box**.

You will need to quit and restart Vectorworks for the application to find these folders.

Quick Preferences

Frequently Used Settings can be toggled from the Tool Bar Quick Preferences. Perhaps that section makes more sense now.

Document Setup

Go to **File>Page Setup** and **Show page boundary**, uncheck **Show page breaks** (which would add gray lines showing how your large sheet might print on letter size pages), and check **Show watermarks** (which will help to keep your information clear of watermarks if using an Educational version of the software).

It is always best practice to *draw* on a page the same size as you expect to use when printing. It is also best practice to export to PDF, and print from the PDF file.

Document Preferences and Settings

Go to **File>Document Settings> Document Preferences**; you will see five tabs:
* Display
* Dimensions
* Resolution
* Plane Mode
* Plan Shadows

In the **Display** tab, check **Save Viewport Cache**, which will speed rendering of Sheet Layers.

Select the **Dimensions** tab. Make sure the three check boxes are checked and that the drop-down menu is set to **Arch**.

Auto Associate "ties" dimensions to objects. When the object is edited or changed, the associated dimension will update.

The **Resolution** Preference Pane selects the print resolution. For our purposes, we will accept the defaults. Ultimately, print resolution depends on the printer of the plotter you will be using.

These preferences can be over-ridden in Layer Setting and PDF Export settings.

Select the **Plane Mode** tab, and be sure the preference is set to both **Screen Plane** and **Working Plane** mode.

Plan Shadows are applied to Plant objects and Massing Models. They are primarily used in Landscape Architecture presentation documents. As such, Entertainment Designers might find these settings useful in the design of film exteriors and themed entertainment installations.

Plant Objects, like Spotlight Lighting Devices, are symbols with specific data attached to the symbol. This data defines the objects beyond the basic geometry.

So, when a plant from the file **Library>Objects-Landscape & Site> Plant Objects 02.vwx** is inserted into a document, it looks like the illustration below.

The Plan Shadows can be defined in the Preference Pane to modify the look of the symbol.

For the Plan Shadow settings to be active, the Render Definition of the Plant Symbol must be modified.

The final result changes the look dramatically. A simple bit of 2D geometry now has the illusion of depth.

The same type of data record can be added to other 2D or hybrid symbols to create plan views that are more dramatic, and possibly more visually clear to some viewers.

Click **OK** to exit the dialog.

Go to **File>Document Settings>Units**, and set your document to feet and inches, or metric units, as appropriate for your use.

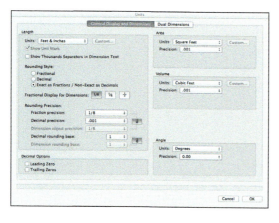

If you design a project in one system, you can go back later and convert the document from imperial to metric, or vice versa. Click **OK.**

In this dialog, you can also establish the criteria for Dual Dimensioning, which will display two sets of values, such as inches and millimeters, within a single dimension. These values have independent unit settings and attributes. Dual dimensions can be displayed side by side or stacked.

Dual Dimensions are activated in the Dimensions tab of the Document Preferences by selecting the ASME Dual SideBySide or ASME Dual Stacked Dimension Standard from the drop-down menu.

File>Document Settings>Patterns allows you to edit default pattern fill content. Pattern, Hatch, Tile, Gradient, and Picture fills are available for 2D forms in the Attributes palette. These same fills can be used when defining classes.

Save the file you're working in as you go here: the settings you are choosing will be used again.

Spotlight Preferences

File>Document Settings>Spotlight Preferences allows you to establish specific settings for configuring the light plot and communicating with Lightwright 5.

In the **Lighting Device Tab** you can configure the automatic positioning of lighting devices and set certain attributes for Spotlight Lighting Devices.

Vectorworks Classes allow designers to assign graphic attributes to objects, to organize, and to choose visibility options. Classes can be defined in the **Tools>Organization Palette,** via the Class drop-down menu on the View Bar, the OIP, via the Navigation palette, and throughout the application.

Check **Enable lighting device auto positioning,** and set **Pick Radius** to 18" or 500mm. Check **Automatically assigns the classes of all lighting devices**. Since no Class has been created, go to the drop-down menu and select **New**. This will open the **New Class** dialog. Create a new class called

Lighting-Spotlight Lighting Device. Check the box that says **Edit properties after creation.** Click **OK**, and the **Edit Class(es)** dialog opens. Check **Use at Creation** in the Graphic Attributes of the new class.

You may also Class lighting devices by the value of associated data filed, like the color, or the unit position. Consider if you Class by color: some units may appear difficult to read if they have a pale color assigned.

In this same section, you can class lighting devices using data fields assigned to the Lighting Device Object. For instance, lighting devices can be classed by the Lighting Positions to which they are assigned: the beam angle (if you want to differentiate between 19° and 36° Degree Source 4 units, for example) or focus, to name only a few options. Examine the drop-down menu.

In the next section, check **Modify lighting device color** and then **Lighting device**. This allows the selection of units to be colored manually using the Attributes Palette.

Checking **Color field** allows you to color the device outline or fill with the color assigned to the unit. This might be useful in some circumstances, or for some users. As an example, this option allows you to color, and then differentiate, rental units, or specials on a plot. Be aware of the color values to be used and how they will print.

Label Legends provide detail about each unit on the plot. Label Legends are configurable and will be discussed at length, but this is where you put information like color, circuit, or channel around instruments. Select **Use lighting device attributes** from the drop-down menu.

Lighting Devices, assigned to a Focus Point Object can illustrate the throw of the instrument from the Lighting Position to the Focus Point. Beam class allows the user to assign a class to the beams. Accept the default: you might want to change this option later.

Additional Default Records allows the the option to add an unlimited amount of data fields to a Spotlight Lighting Device. These fields can be displayed and modified in the OIP when a device is selected.

The **Lighting Device Parameters** button allows designers to configure and customize the data fields associated with the Lighting device symbols. The data fields are displayed in the OIP. As you can see, the list is very long. To reduce the amount of scrolling when creating a Light Plot, turn off:
- Circuit Name and Number
- User Fields
- Beam and Field Angles
- Frame Size
- Falloff Distance
- Lamp Rotation
- Shutter Fields

Once these visibilities have been changed, click on the Save button near the upper-right and create the **Plot Set.** You can create additional sets of visibilities as needed.

The Universe tab allows you to manually assign Dimmers and Universe or to automatically assign the Universe. We will assign manually.

When you configure Vectorworks to communicate with Lightwright using **Automatic Data Exchange,** Vectorworks creates an XML file that Lightwright 5 and Vectorworks can both modify. Once the link is established in Lightwright, changes made in either program are updated in the other. Right now, we want to be aware of this, set up the defaults, but not establish a connection. That connection would continually create new XML files when they may not be needed.

It is best practice (another rule) to create the XML file in the same folder as the Lightwright file and the Vectorworks file with the Light Plot. It is also best then to run Vectorworks and Lightwright at the same time.

Check **Use Automatic Lightwright Data Exchange.** Then select **Focus** and **Num Channels** from the **Available Fields** column and **Move** those into the **Export Fields** column. **Move** the **User Fields** from the **Export Fields** column back into the **Available Fields** column. Uncheck **Use Automatic Lightwright Data Exchange,** and be sure that **Save as default** is checked and click **OK.**

Lightwright will occasionally ask you to **Perform a complete export on exit.** Checking that box refreshes the XML file when the preferences dialog is closed and the box becomes unchecked.

Default Scale

Go to the View Bar. There should be a data field that says "1:1," and next to that, on the right, there should be a ruler icon. If not, select **Layer Scale** from the View Bar menu. Click on the ruler and note that you can change the Layer scale quickly with this tool from the document window.

Click on the Ruler Icon and change the scale to 1/2"=1'-0" if using Imperial measurements and check 1:25 if using the Metric System.

Layer Scale can also be changed by editing a Design Layer from either the Navigation palette or the Organization Dialog.

Line Weight

Go to **Tools>Options>Line Thickness** and review the default settings. Using mm as the Unit, change the defaults to .05, .15, .2, .25, .5, .75. 1, 1.5, and 2.

Even with **Zoom Line Thickness** turned on in either Vectorworks Preferences, or Quick Preferences, it can be difficult to see the slight variation in the thinner line weights without zooming in to look closely.

From the **Basic Tool Set**, select the **Line Tool,** and choose the **Constrained Mode**, and the **Vertex Mode** from the **Tool Bar.** Draw a line across the page. Select the line with the **Selection Too**l and go to **Edit>Duplicate Array.** Make nine duplicates .-12" (Vectorworks will convert 12" to 1'-0") or -100mm. Select one line at a time, and with the line selected go to the **Attributes Palette** and use the **Line Thickness** drop-down menu to assign a line weight.

It is advisable to test these line weights with your printer or plotter. As you work with Vectorworks, you will likely edit these defaults to suit your personal design style. This is a place to start.

Default Font Settings

Fonts are system resources. The fonts you have and use might not be available on a colleague's system. Bear that in mind if you are working in a collaborative. If you are using Vectorworks Nomad, consider the fonts available with Nomad. It is possible to add your preferred fonts to Nomad, simply by copying them to the Vectorworks Cloud Services folder on your desktop.

As with many defaults, to set a default font, deselect all and go to **Text>Font** and choose your preferred font to establish that font as your default. Your default font should be something generally readable, and if you will be sharing files, it should be one that is available across-platforms, and is installed on your colleagues' systems. With nothing selected, you can also select the default font size, style, and alignment.

This book is set in Gill Sans and will be using Gill Sans at 12 points for most of the annotations in the Vectorworks files.

Font settings can be adjusted again using the Text Menu or via the OIP when text is selected.

Text Styles

If you use a word processing program you might be familiar with Text Styles, or the concept. In Vectorworks, Text Styles are a Resource. Go to the Resource Browser and right-click in the empty window. Scroll to **New Resource** and then to **Text Style** in the fly-off of the contextual menu.

Your choices do not have to match the illustration, but create a basic look for Notes to be added to drawings. Using a Text Style, when you change the Style Definition, all instances that have the Stye applied will change.

Snapping Preferences

Snapping allows the user to align objects visually and with precision. Snapping and the SmartCursor are key to good drafting and design.

Snapping can be temporarily disabled by pressing the ` (back quote) key. This works in the same way as the Boomerang mode works; once the key is released, the snaps will appear again.

Single-click on the individual icons to set your Snapping Palette choices. Notice the hint as the cursor snaps to the Center Left position on the rectangle. As always, experiment with different options beyond those described.

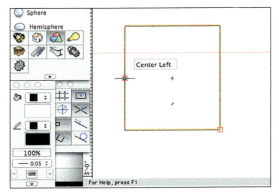

Notice that the Snap to Grid option is turned off: the Snap to Grid option, along with the Grid Preferences, can be very useful for placing lighting instruments on specific centers, and for working with other precise geometric arrangements. Sometimes, the grid just gets in the way.

When you double-click on a tool in the Snapping palette (to open the SmartCursor Settings) you will see a dialog that reminds you that Snapping can be suspended by pressing the ` key. If you like, you can check the box that says **Don't show this dialog again**.

Open the SmartCursor Settings.

In the General Settings Pane, you can select snaps, and access the Interactive Appearance Settings of Vectorworks Preferences. As you hover over the options, a description of the choice becomes visible in the dark gray panel at the bottom of the dialog.

The Grid pane allows you to make choices about the visibility of the drawing grid, the sizes of the visible grid, the size of the snapping grid, and the XYZ Axis lines. Note that the XYZ Axis lines are colored RGB, and they correspond in that order.

Red = X Axis/Length

Green = Y Axis/Width

Blue = Z Axis/Depth

The Object Pane affects how 2D and 3D objects snap to one another. These snaps and alignment options properly position elements in precise relation to other objects

The Angle pane specifies snapping angles. Note that 15.00° has been added to the default options. Angles can be adjusted and added/or deleted as needed for the needs of specific projects.

Smart Points allow the user to snap to specific points on an object, and align other, new objects.

The dialog refers to the use of the **T** key in snapping. Experiment with that now. Select the **Rectangle Tool** from the **Basic Tool Set**, and click and drag to create a rectangle. Use the SmartCursor to snap to a **Smart Edge** of the rectangle (a corner, or a midpoint), and then press the **T** key: the cursor will lock to that point and stay aligned with that point. That *locking* is indicated by a dashed red line.

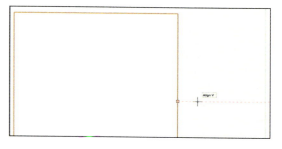

Snapping to Objects allows drawing by snapping to edges of objects, not just specific points.

Distance settings allow the designer to set the placement of specific points for snapping. The settings shown are a general setting, but these can be changed on an as needed basis for precision in design. This setting allows for **Snap Points** on an object at the 25% mark. There are times when that might better be set at 10% or 33.33%. Distance can also be specified as a specific in distance. Check **Multiple Divisions** to repeat snap points along a line at specified percentages or distances.

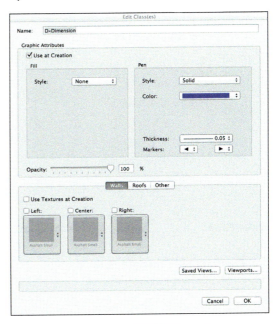

Drawing/Document Organization

Select **Tools>Organization,** or press **Command/Control+Shift+O** to open the **Organization Dialog**. Note the differences and similarities between this dialog and the Navigation Palette. This dialog can also be accessed from the Edit Classes and Edit Layers buttons in the View Bar, adjacent to their respective drop-down menus.

Vectorworks organizes documents by:
- Classes
- Design Layers
- Sheet Layers
- Viewports
- Saved Views
- Referenced Files

Classes

Classes assign graphic attributes, and control visibility. Vectorworks provides two classes by default: **Dimension** and **None**. We have added the class Lighting-Spotlight Lighting Device. The dash in the name is important; Vectorworks creates an alphabetical hierarchy of classes based on the prefix. In the Organization Dialog, Class lists can be collapsed by clicking the reveal triangle next to the prefix. Shift-Option or Alt will collapse/expand all classes. Prefixes shorten the Class lists in the drop-down menus.

You will likely have many Classes. Organize early.

As best practice, no object should be created without having a class assigned. Switch between classes for drawing by selecting from the class drop-down in the View Bar. Selected objects, can have a class assigned from the drop-down menu in the OIP.

Select the Classes Tab from the Organization Dialog, click on the Dimension Class and select **Edit** from the bottom of the window. In the ensuing dialog, change the name to D-Dimension, check **Use at creation,** and review the other options.

From this window, you can access many Vectorworks resources and Attributes.

The default Fill Style is Solid and the default Color is white. Click on the drop-down menu that shows the white fill: there are options at the bottom for Active Document and Standard Vectorworks Colors. In the upper-right there are buttons to the Standard Color Picker, Pick Color, and the Color Palette Manager. The Standard Color Picker is a system standard that shows a color wheel or sliders to specify colors. Pick Color allows access to the many color libraries that ship with Vectorworks. These include Pantone colors, commercial lines of paint, and libraries of gel colors. The Color Palette Manager allows users to check off those libraries they would want included in the list at the bottom of the main list. Lighting Designers might want to check off their preferred gel libraries now.

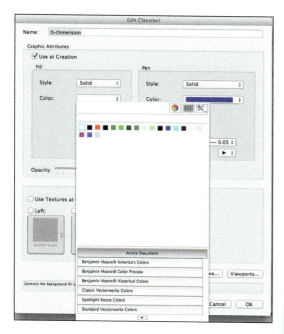

The **Disclosure Triangle** at the bottom reveals choices for viewing Palettes.

Click on the **Fill Style** drop-down. Review the available choices:
- Solid
- Pattern
- Hatch
- Tile
- Gradient
- Image

Select each and see how that changes what's available in the **Color** drop-down menu. This dialog and the Attributes palette access files in the directory **Vectorworks>Libraries>Defaults** and the same location also in your User Folder. Examine and explore this content: it can be added to or modified to suit your needs.

Select **None**.

The **Pen Style** should be set to Solid, but you can also assign a Pattern, or a Line Type. Make the color a dark blue, or you might change that to suit your own style. It often helps to see different types of objects in different colors. The line weight should be .05mm, and dimension markers are determined in the Document Preferences.

Although not applicable here, the lower portion of the dialog assigns textures to 3D or hybrid (2D+3D) objects. Click on a texture button to see that you have access to a variety of textures from the default content. Set Designers will want to create their own set of default textures. Lighting and Sound designers may also want specific finishes Who doesn't like a chrome-plated unit?

Who doesn't like, want, need, or have to have a chrome-plated light from time to time?

Classes save steps.

At the bottom of the window there are buttons for making the class visible or invisible in previously created **Viewports** and **Saved Views**. This will be great to know once you know what Viewports and Saved Views are, of course.

Do not check **Use Textures at Creation** and click **OK.**

Double-click on the **None** Class to open the Edit Dialog. Change the line weight to .15mm, check **Use at creation** and **Use textures at creation**, set the Fill to Solid and white. Duplicate the Class as *Normal Line Weight.*

Although we are not assigning textures at this point, new classes will be based on this class. The solid fill is critical for rendering. Without a solid fill 3D objects render as invisible: that can cause designer heart failure. Checking **Use textures at creation** saves steps and clicks later.

Click **OK.** A dialog will appear asking if you want to change the Attributes of objects created in this class. If you answer **Yes**, all of your line weights will change to the .15mm thickness. Click **No** to preserve your view of the different line weights.

Remember, you can also select objects and use the Disclosure triangle on the Attributes Palette to **Set all Attributes by Class.**

Right-click on the class Lighting-Spotlight Lighting Device and select Edit from the contextual menu. Change the line weight to .2mm, check **Use at creation** and do not **Use textures at creation**, and be sure the Fill is set to Solid and white.

You have now used three different ways to Edit a Class.

This can get pretty boring. It's more boring to do this in every document. We have computers, we're going to use them. As stated, all designers customize their documents.

From the Organization Dialog, Classes Tab, click **New** or press Command/Control+N to create a new Class. In the following Dialog choose Import Classes and navigate to the file Classes. vwx provided on the Website. With **Show only classes that are not in the current document** checked, the program will do the obvious. Select all of the classes except Section Style and click **OK.**

Feel free to modify the color choices: they exist to help look at the screen and differentiate objects. The D-Centerline and D-PlasterLine Classes have Line Types assigned so that the Centerline is the traditional long dash-short dash-long dash format and the Plaster Line is a dashed line.

Click **OK**, save your file, thank the author for doing this work, and go to the Resource Browser. Those Line Types should now be visible in the Resource Browser. Open the Classes.vwx file, make sure your working file is the top document, go to the Resource Browser, and select the Classes.vwx file from the top drop-down menu. That file includes additional Line Types. Select those, right-click, and select **Import** from the contextual menu.

You also have the option to Reference these Line Types. Referencing keeps a link to the resource in another file. When the original is modified, the resources in files that have Referenced the original are also modified.

Close Classes.vwx and save your file. Right-click on any Line Type and select **Duplicate** from the Contextual Menu: right-click again to select Edit.

You can adjust the spacing by simply adjusting the blue handles, or by adding specific numeric values in the ensuing dialog.

These are simple Line Types. You can also create Complex Line Types that might includes shapes, images, and/or lines. Right-click to create a **New Line Type** and select **Complex Line Type.**

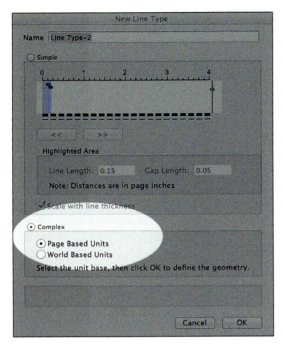

Draw a new line, and with that new line selected, right-click on your new Line Type. Choose **Edit** from the Contextual menu, and then choose **Geometry** from the subsequent dialog. Adjust the object size by selecting the center circle and modifying the size in the OIP, and then adjust the spacing by moving one of the greyed circles. **Exit** the Edit Line Type window to review your changes.

When you modify a Class definition, all of the objects that have been assigned to that class will (generally) change. Class definitions can be over-ridden in Viewports, so if you do not want your dimension to print blue on any specific document, you can change the definition for a specific use.

Your theatre walls may be one color, and your set walls will probably be another color. By using classes to assign these attributes, if the color of the set changes, you can change all of the walls at once.

Design Layers

The design layer is a basic level of organization. Think of layers as sheets of vellum on a table; architects use layers to distinguish floors of a building. Each design layer can have a different scale and can be set to different Z elevations.

Like classes, design layers can be Visible, Grayed, or turned off (invisible) in the Organization Dialog, of the Navigation Palette

This is a basic layer structure:
- Audio
- Light Plot
- Lighting Areas
- Masking
- Scenery
- Audience Seating
- Theatre Architecture
- Trace Layer

Click **OK**, and the screen will change to the **Edit Line Type Screen** characterized by the thick amber border with the **Exit** button at the top right.

Select the **Circle** tool from the **Basic Tool Set** and click and drag a circle from the center of the screen. When you release the tool, you will see three circles. The center circle will be black, the left and right circles will be greyed. Choose the selection tool and move one of the greyed circles. This determines the spacing of the circles on the line.

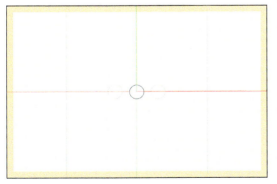

Once again, you will be spared some tedium here. Open the Organization Dialog and Design Layer tab. Click to create a new layer, select import, and navigate to the Classes.vwx file.

You have the option to Import Layer Objects, but there is no content. This option will likely be useful at some point.

Select all of the Layers and import.

A PDF or a JPEG of the theatre, ballroom, or television studio architecture can be imported to a bottom tracing layer. On top of that you may have an architecture layer, it is best not to trace on the same layer as your reference object. By tracing above, you do not accidently click on, and move the trace image.

If importing a DXF/DWG/DWF or a SKP file to trace, do not import into your working file. Create a New Document, trace in that document. Copy the Vectorworks information from there and paste into your working file.

These file types often bring *baggage* data along with important information. That extra data can clutter your resources..

Design Layers can be used to create specific physical elements that may be saved as symbols and placed in the layer with the architecture or the set.

These Design Layers all have a scale set 1/2"=1'-0" (1:24). You can change that scale one layer at a time, or you can Shift-Select all of the layers and change the scale. If you're working using the Metric system, now is a good time to change the scales to 1:25.

In any event, **Edit** one Design Layer and see that you can affect the opacity of the layer, the default wall height, and the Renderworks Background here. We will return to those settings.

There is a general similarity to creating/ editing Design Layers and Classes.

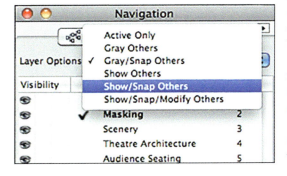

The same choices exist for classes in the Classes tab of the Navigation palette.

Active Only allows you to focus on one layer at a time. Graying the others allows you to see objects in context but pushes other objects into the background. **Gray/Snap** allows you to use the SmartCursor to orient objects in relation to objects on other layers. **Show Others** and **Show/Snap Others** follow the same logic. **Show/Snap/Modify Others** allows you to work in all layers at once. This can often be confusing and lead to mistakes.

There is no one correct choice, and you will find yourself toggling between these options often.

Using different Design Layers for different tasks allows you to isolate details, and create clear, easily read drawings.

Unified View

In Unified View, Design Layers of different scales cannot be viewed a the same time.

In a document with several layers, it is likely that you will need to look at multiple layers at once and will want to switch between views. Simply switching views affects only the active layer unless **Unified View** is activated.

In order to invoke the **Unified View,** simply click the Unified View button in the View Bar. To disable the Unified View, click again. Unified View can also be accessed via the **View>Unified View** command.

So, if you have the lighting design in one Design Layer, and the Set Design in another, you can render the set with the stage lighting visible.

Not all primitive drawing functions will work when Unified View is in use.

Using Multiple Design Layers

In the Navigation palette on the Design Layers tab, there is a drop-down menu of six choices:
- Active Only
- Gray Others
- Gray/Snap Others
- Show Others
- Show/Snap Others
- Show/Snap/Modify Others

Stories

Stories are a function of Vectorworks Architect. You may or may not see this tab. The Stories function creates a number of specialized design layers for each level of a building.

Sheet Layers

Vectorworks has a built-in Desktop publishing system. Sheet Layers are the pages in documents that can then be published or printed. Sheet Layers are where drawings are annotated and arranged for clear viewing and understanding.

Sheet Layers can be created in a number of ways. Most obvious right now is that you can create Sheet Layers as you create Design Layers or Classes. Sheet Layers can also be created when creating Viewports. If you are working in architecture and have the Architect Module, the Automatic Drawing Coordination command creates Sheet Layers as needed for a standard architectural design. Architects have rules.

Sheet Layers are always in a 1:1/Full Size/Actual Scale. Sheet Layer Viewports are placed onto Sheet Layers and the Viewport is in scale, or (possibly) in a reduced size. You can have many Viewports on a Sheet Layer and the Viewports can show different scales.

A Viewport can be a window into a 3D Model.

Viewports

There are two types of Viewports: Design Layer Viewports and Sheet Layer Viewports.

Design Layer Viewports can display design layers from the current file, or one or more design layers that are workgroup referenced from another file.

A Sheet Layer Viewport displays a view of one or more design layers. Sheet Layer Viewports can be annotated or cropped on the Sheet Layer. This does not affect the original drawing. Class and Layer visibilities help to define the look of a Sheet Layer Viewport. Class definitions can be over-ridden in Sheet Layer Viewports, so that magenta Centerline can be black or green.

Saved Views

Saved Views are created from the Saved Views drop-down in the View Bar. A Saved View allows you to quickly revert to a view at any time. There may be an area of detail that you continually need to return to in your plan; a Saved View will allow that. Saved Views can have different layers and classes visible. Saved Views are also very useful for looking at scenes rendered with lights focused, lighting levels set, and gobos inserted as you adjust the light levels.

Referenced Files

When working in a team or just to keep files smaller, develop different elements in different files, and then use the **File Referencing** features to bring all of the elements together.

You also have the option to Reference Line Types and other resources. Referencing maintains a link to the original resource in another file. When the original is modified, the resources in files that have Referenced the original are also modified.

Referencing Files is Teamwork!
Don't be afraid to share.

Referenced resources can be accessed and edited from within the files to which they have been referenced. References can be broken and the result is the same as if the resource had been Imported.

A Few More Settings

This section jumps around a bit to explore a few tools out of context. The mission is to set a few default choices. You may want to add to this list as you delve into the application.

Camera Tool

Go to the **Visualization Tool Set,** select the **Camera Tool,** and open the **Tool Preferences** from the Tool Bar. The Camera Tool is perfect for creating renderings: it can also be used to check sightlines. On film/television projects, you can position a camera and lens in a set and show the Director, Director of Photography (DP), Set Decorator, and others exactly what will be seen in the frame. The camera defaults to an old-school television monitor proportion of 4:3. Change that to either 16:9 or 2:3, which are wider and more pleasing. The 2:3 view is close to the Golden Proportion; 16:9 is the proportion of a modern video screen and gives a wide stage view. Also check **Auto Update 3D View** and **Auto Center 3D View.** These selections help to see the view on your screen, and when editing the camera view. Click **OK.**

Object Properties	
Renderworks Camera	
Camera Height:	5'0"
Look To Height:	5'0"
Top/Plan View	
Display Camera View	
Fine Tune Camera View...	
Projection:	Perspective
Render Mode:	Wireframe
Aspect Ratio:	1.78 (16:9)
Custom Aspect:	1.33
For Film Size of:	35mm
Focal Length is:	31mm
Field of View:	70
For DPI of:	72
Pixel Size is:	800 x 600
Crop Frame Scale %:	100
Left/Right Tilt Angle:	0
Camera Name:	Camera
Camera Display:	2D+Name
☑ Auto Update 3D View	
☑ Auto Center 3D View	
Cancel	OK

Drawing Label Tool

In the **Dims/Notes Tool Set,** locate the **Drawing Label Tool.** Every drawing needs a label so the reader knows what they are seeing. We have already imported the D-DrawingLabel class. Select the tool, and select the tool preferences. Note, and copy the choices below; they give you a place to start to develop your own style. The Margins of 1/8" are approximately 3mm. The 5" Printed Length does not matter as the Line Length Mode is set to Control Point, allowing for the line under the drawing to be set to the width of the drawing. The thick line weight of the class anchors drawings on the page, and the margins give the text room to breath, as seen in the illustration below.

Click **OK** to adopt your settings.

Focus Point Object Tool

From the **Spotlight Tool Set,** select the **Focus Point Tool.** The Focus Point Objects tell Spotlight Lighting Devices where they will be focused, and they can label lighting areas on the Light Plot, or a plan specifically for the Lighting Designer to use when focusing. Open the tool preferences and review the drop-down menu.

There are many choices. The standard 3D leaves an object that looks like a flying saucer in renderings. The others use different objects from the default content to indicate lighting areas. Select **Standard 2D,** which uses a 2D object (that goes away in renderings) with a 3D Locus object. We have turned off the display of **3D Locus Objects** in Vectorworks Preferences.

Lighting Designers will likely change, or modify the default content as they develop a personal graphic style. You have imported a Class specifically for these objects.

The Default shape is a regular octagon with a small alpha-numeric character.

Magic Wand Tool

The **Magic Wand Tool** is a special selection tool. Select the Magic Wand from the Basic Tool Set and click on the Tool Preferences. Deselect what is selected and check **Object Type.** Click the **Save** button and save the setting as *Object Type.* Uncheck **Object Type,** and check **Class.** Save that setting and repeat for **Symbol Name.** Click **OK.**

These Saved Settings now appear in a drop-down next to the tool preferences. This tool is extremely useful for making selections and changes, especially when you have a few settings saved for quick access.

Over time, you should make many adjustments to your template file(s). I keep many different templates for different sheet sizes and for different venues, especially those where I work frequently.

You can save Design Layer Content, Viewport, Sheet Layers, and more in stationery files. If you work in a venue with stock scenery, that content may stay in a template file. Similarly, if one venue has an inventory of Shakespeare lighting units you might want those symbols in a template with the venue architecture and prepared Sheet Layers, different from another venue that stocks ETC Source 4 lighting gear.

Saving a Stationery File

Template or Stationery files work like any other new file, except they have whatever saved settings and/or content you might always use already in place. Go to **File>Save as template**. Vectorworks will save your template file in your user folder in the **Libraries>Defaults>Templates Directory.** Save this template file as *Default.sta*. Vectorworks will add the .sta file extension automatically. The Default template file also affects any new files created without using a template

Every building needs a solid foundation. Every drawing also needs a solid foundation. In each case it's generally the boring part... as I think you've seen. It gets better. I promise.

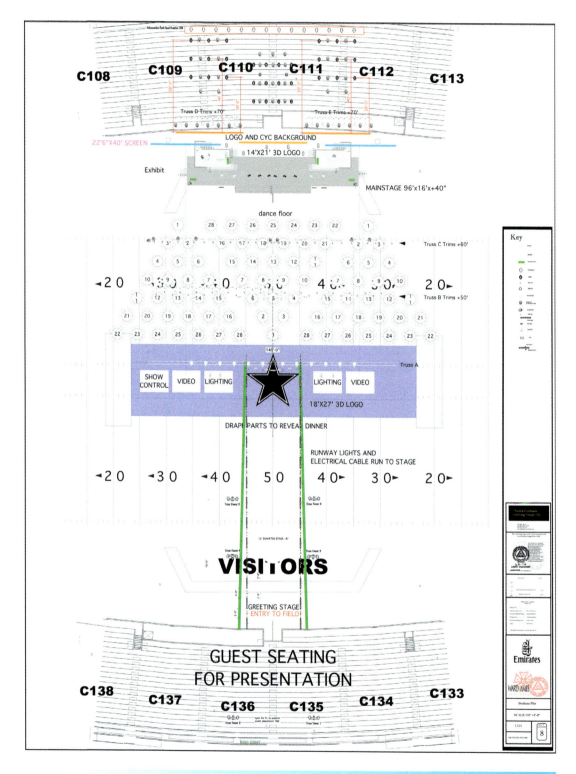

Air Emirates

Air Emirates Dubai to Dallas Route Announcement
Light Plot Overview (left) and production photo.

Air Emirates Dubai to Dallas Route Announcement
Dallas Cowboy Stadium

Scenic Designer: Peter Crawford
Producer: Ward & Ames Events of Houston
Lighting Designer: Herrick Goldman
   Assistant Lighting Designer: Susan Nicholson
Gaffer: Rob Baxter

Air Emirates chose to announce their new Dubai to Dallas route by throwing a dinner for a thousand guests in Dallas Cowboy Stadium. Not exactly a small venue. Peter Crawford designed a 160' tall cyclorama, and the production company wanted a runway effect from the 50 yard line under the scoreboard to the dinner area.

4. Vectorworks Workspaces

Before we started, we made sure that we were using the Vectorworks Spotlight workspace. Now, what is a Vectorworks Workspace? For one thing, it's the next piece of our foundation.

It might be great to just jump in and draw, but that's not a great path to understanding. Take a step back, and get a real feel and understanding for the Vectorworks working environment.

Vectorworks is a fully customizable application. Users may adjust the menu structure and many of the palettes to suit their own particular needs and workflow. Additionally, the program is extensible through Plug-in Objects (PIOs), and scripting. In fact, many of the basic tools within Vectorworks are built as PIOs. Take a look at the directory **Vectorworks>Plug-Ins** and you will see that even the simple Rectangle Tool is a Plug-in Object.

want to organize existing tools, or new tools to suit their own way of working.

As easily as you can add additional tools, you can also remove tools or options that are not used in your personal workflow, or process. In developing your workflow, you may find that you want to continually customize Vectorworks as you work.

Workspaces can be customized, and most professionals have at least one custom workspace. Some users have different workspaces for different parts of their jobs, or different computers. It is proper to rebuild your workspace when the software is updated.

As mentioned, Vectorworks is completely customizable. Adjusting the menu and palette layout is the most readily apparent way that average users can make Vectorworks their own.

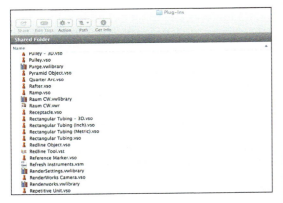

Program Add-Ons like ESP Vision, the Auto Plot Tools, and InteriorCAD are all scripts and/or PIOs. When adding these resources, the Vectorworks interface usually needs to be modified to find the new tools. Some come with their own workspace. Other add-ons or plug-ins need to be added to any workspace where you might want to use them. Either way, users will

Rebuild your custom workspaces with every new release of the software.

First go to **Tools>Workspaces** and look at the choices available. If you have the Designer Suite, you should see the following:
- Architect
- Designer
- Fundamentals
- Landmark
- Spotlight

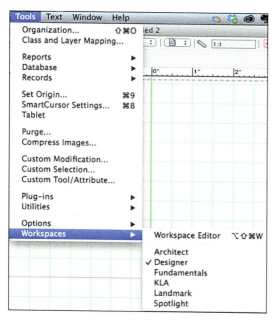

Open each one and see how the menus and palettes change.

Workspace files (with the file extension .vww) are stored in the **Vectorworks>Workspaces** directory, user workspaces are kept in the User Folder. Go to **Tools>Workspaces>Workspace Editor**, and you will have the following choices:
- Edit the current workspace
- Edit a copy of the current workspace
- Create a new workspace

Avoid creating a new workspace as well as editing one of the workspaces that are provided

in the installation process. Creating a new workspace gives you a blank slate, so don't create a lot of unnecessary work. Editing one of the workspaces provided means you may lose that resource.

Making a copy of the Spotlight Workspace gives you an excellent foundation on which to build, and you always have the original to go back to for reference. You can name the copy whatever you like to differentiate your workspace from the original.

From the workspace editor, make a copy of the Spotlight Workspace to see how this is done. You will now have a window with three tabs that allow you to edit the menus, tools, and keys.

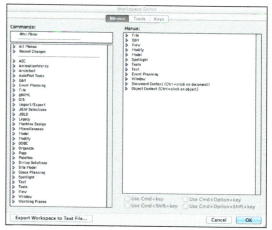

Grab the new menu from the left column, and drag it over to the right column. Name it. Note that you can easily rename the other menus just as you can rename a file. You can also delete a menu by selecting and hitting the delete key. Once you have a new menu, you can drag other items from the left column into your new menu and arrange them as you like.

You can also edit the contextual menus to readily access an often-used tool from the right mouse button.

From the Tools tab, you can modify your palettes in much the same way. You can reorganize the Tool Sets to meet your needs. By clicking and dragging the Tool Sets, you can also change their stacking order to your specific needs.

The Keys tab displays the keyboard shortcuts for the workspace. From here you can modify the keyboard shortcuts, again, to your specific preferences.

If you have the Designer package, examine the tools and commands available with Architect and Landmark, and pay attention to the way these workspaces are organized. You may find that you want to incorporate some of the tools that might not seem to be entertainment based into your workspace and workflow. As you work with the Spotlight workspace, you may find that you would prefer some tools or commands organized differently. Go ahead and make those changes in your personal workspace.

Vectorworks ships with the most current tools. Nemetschek also includes, but does not put in workspaces, many *Legacy* tools. These are items that have been supplanted by newer methods. Sometimes, these tools can be quite interesting. Look for the Torus Object Tool. Still the fastest way to model a donut.

Exporting your workspace as a text file allows you keep a record. This is a good idea, as is backing up your custom workspaces and stock workspaces.

Back-up your Workspaces and the originals as you would any other important document.

2012 Republican National Convention Preliminary Sketch

2012 Republican National Convention Rendering

2012 Republican National Convention
Tampa Bay Times Forum, Tampa, FL

Production Designer: Jim Fenhagen Jack Morton/PDG
    Art Director: Eddie Knasiak JM/PDG
    Sketch Artist: Erik Linton
    Drafting Project Manager: Matt Glaze JM/PDG
Lighting: Steve Brill, The Lighting Design Group
Screen Graphics: James Jackson
Director: Ron De Moraes
Executive Producer: Philip Alongi

Production Designer Jim Fenhagen of Jack Morton/PDG begins by roughing out his thoughts and ideas with pencil on paper. He turns his designs over to his colleagues and staff for the creation of Vectorworks models, Cinema 4D renderings, and then production documents back in Vectorworks.

5. Your Workstation

For our purposes, a **work station** is the place where you do your work, not necessarily a type of computer system. A **Workspace** we have already defined as an arrangement of tools commands within Vectorworks.

Obviously, every Vectorworks user needs a computer, maybe more than one computer. Every designer is different; so is their choice and arrangement of their work station. Thinking through and experimenting with your work area is a part of the designer's life. Except when you're assisting, then you get what you get.

In our studio we work on 15" MacBook Pros. My partner has a second screen attached. I occasionally hook up a Wacom Tablet and stylus, but for the most part, we use the track pad on the MacBook for input. We also have large-scale drawing boards nearby, easels, and portable drawing stations. We use the drawing equipment when we need to think through ideas, and to review large-format prints. We have invested in comfortable chairs; they are critical.

Lighting Designer, Author, and creator of Field Templates and SoftSymbols Steven Louis Shelley works with his laptop and an external monitor, surrounded by books.

We have traditional desk height desks, and drawing table height desks where we can stand and work. Sometimes, it is just a good idea to get up, look away from the screen, and walk around.

Some designers have a laptop and a desktop computer. Some have arrangements with multiple displays so that one screen can be used to fully display the drawing and the palettes can be moved to another screen or screens.

You may be working through this book in a computer lab designed by someone else. Learn from that as you build your own studio. For learning, there is something to be said for a lab, or working in a group, even on laptops in a lounge. The group experience can allow people to feed off of one another. This same experience exists in the professional design studio where multiple designers are collaborating on projects.

Ultimately, you need to create the work station that works for you. Sometimes, a situation will drive some choices. We've all had to draw by the hotel pool at one time or another.

Your computer system, the software, and your work environment should be the best you can afford. It will grow and evolve as your career grows. These are your tools; cheap paintbrushes can be frustrating, as can inexpensive, or under-powered hardware and software.

Your computer or computers should be as fast as possible, and have as much RAM installed as possible. Most software is updated annually (like Vectorworks), some software is updated more frequently (like the Adobe Creative Cloud). Software updates take advantage of the latest available computer hardware. It is fair to say a computer system will last about three years before it becomes too slow to operate the latest software, so plan accordingly.

Tony-Winning Scenic Designer Beowulf Boritt uses his drawing table for many things: model making, sketching, and computer work.

Art Director Martin Fahrer works at his personally custom-built water-cooled PC. The system is driven by an Intel Quad core processor, sports two 23"TS series HD Monitors, and runs Windows 7. He uses a Wacom Intuos 4 tablet with Vectorworks, SketchUp, Cinema 4D, and Photoshop.

It is important to stay abreast of software updates. Not only do you have access to the latest features, it also helps when collaborating. Software Piracy is illegal. Software, like your designs and ideas, is someone's intellectual property. Just as you do not want others copying your designs (without paying a fee), you need to pay for the use of software.

Learn how to calibrate the color display for your computer system; calibration needs frequent checking. If you use two monitors and one gets out of calibration; it will be quickly noticed; what you see on your screen should closely match your output. What you can't necessarily control is what your colleagues see when you send a

rendering; that is why we still have hard copy, to ensure that everyone sees the same colors.

Hardware

In addition to a computer system, you might also consider some additional hardware like:

- a color, or black and white inkjet printer
- a laser printer
- a plotter
- a flatbed scanner
- a color copier

Like building any other kit, these items can be added as your career grows. Some items, like the

Sound Designer & Composer Scott O'Brien's normal daily work environment includes an equipment rack, three MacBooks (running Windows and Mac OSX), a 32" monitor and, out of the frame, keyboards, controllers, guitars (electric, acoustic, and bass), and drum triggers.

color copier, might be used only on larger projects and rented by a production office. For any of these functions, there is likely a nearby service bureau that can take care of most needs.

Back-Up

It is important to create and evolve a back-up protocol. Save early, save often is important, but make sure there are redundant back ups of your work. Applications crash. Systems crash. You want to lose as little work as possible.

We have seen that Vectorworks has a built-in back up protocol that can be configured in the Vectorworks Preferences, Autosave Tab. Vectorworks will automatically save your file at a specified interval, and back-up your file to a specified location. Consider a dedicated folder so that all back ups are in one location.

Mac users can take advantage of the Time Machine back-up function, which will back up your entire drive to another drive. I use the functionality and have it set to back-up every hour. Hard drives, or other hardware, can fail; Time Machine can fully restore your work.

In addition to Time Machine, I have a Carbonite back up, which is a Cloud-based back up service.

If I am traveling and away from my Time Machine back up, I continue to back up to Carbonite. If something happens to my back up hard drive, the Carbonite back up provides a redundant system.

Services like Dropbox and Vectorworks Nomad provide tools for collaboration; while they also add to your back-up options, back-up is not the main function of these services.

Calculator

Sure Vectorworks does a lot of math for the user, but sometimes you still need a calculator. In general, the calculator on your system or phone will suffice. For more advanced features, and working feet and inches, Calculated Industries makes several models; the Construction Master Pro and the ProjectCalc Plus are good choices. Additionally, Calculated Industries has several apps that provide the same functions on phones and tablets.

There are also specialized calculator apps for rigging and determining the beam angles and/or correct instrumentation for lighting positions.

Build your software kit as you grow as an artist.

Additional Software

Sure Vectorworks is a suite with many integrated functions, but you'll likely also need other software packages to do all of the work required of a designer.

Lightwright

Lightwright is the entertainment industry standard for creating the paperwork to execute the Lighting Design. Vectorworks and Lightwright share data dynamically to keep the plot and paperwork updated.

Show Control
- Isadora
- VNC
- QLab
- VLC

Video Editing and Effects
- Final Cut
- Motion
- iMovie
- Premiere
- After Effects

Graphic Software

The Adobe Creative Cloud Suite of software is a good example of additional software used by designers. Creative Cloud is the Big Dog and it is available on a subscription basis, making it affordable. There is an academic version as well.

Raster Graphics and Vector Graphics

There are basically two types of graphics, raster and vector. A raster (bitmapped) graphic is pixel-based. Vector graphics are mathematically based. Generally speaking, Adobe Photoshop works with raster images and Adobe Illustrator works with vector images, although in both cases, that line is increasingly blurred.

In a raster graphic, pixels are arranged in a grid to represent an image. In a grid format, circles and curves are actually stepped to the grid. To lessen this *pixelation*, many graphic applications *Anti-Alias* the edge, that is they add intermediate colors around the edges to soften the harsh stepping appearance. When rendering a black circle against a white background, the anti-alias function adds squares (pixels) of grey around the black to ease the eye to the white field.

Raster images support a wide range of colors and subtle changing tones; they are well-suited for displaying continuous-tone images such as photographs or shaded drawings.

However, if each pixel is a color, if you double the size, that one pixel is now four pixels. Raster images do not scale well.

This image of the Cape Hatteras Lighthouse was modeled as a vector object in Vectorworks and rendered as a raster object using Renderworks. By the author.

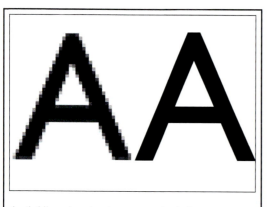

Anti-Aliased raster image on the left, vector image on the right

Vector images, such as those produced by an application like Adobe Illustrator, use mathematical relationships between points, and the paths that connect the points to describe shapes. Vector-based images can be infinitely scaled to any size without degrading the image quality.

No matter how large you make them, the mathematical relationship between the points does not change, and so they are *resolution-independent*.

Adobe Illustrator and Vectorworks both take advantage of Bezier Curves, which are typically defined by three points: an anchor point, and two control points that do not lie on the curve itself but define its shape. The anchor point indicates where the lines pass. The control points are

Create images at a suitable size for the output.

handles that twist the lines from anchor point to anchor point.

Vectorworks creates Vector-based objects and can render those objects as raster images showing subtle changes in tone, light, and shadow. Because of the vector-based geometry, Vectorworks can render the output images to virtually any resolution.

What is Resolution?

Dots per inch (dpi) is a printing term referring to the grid of the print screen. Pixels per inch is the same matrix, referring to a display screen. A typical display screen is 72-96 dpi. A typical color Inkjet printer or plotter requires 125-150 dpi. Printing a book like this is done at 300 dpi. The higher the dpi, the more data or information required.

So, for example, a 40' (12,192mm) object in 1/4" scale would be 10" (3,048mm) printed, so (converting dpi to pixels) the image would need to be 10" by 125-150 pixels across in your image editor, or 1250-1500 pixels to print well on an inkjet printer. The same image would need to be 3000 pixels wide to be printed commercially.

You will need to understand and use resolution when creating image files for use as textures and when rendering Vectorworks files for print.

File Formats

Some raster graphic file formats are compressed. These types of files, typical JPEG and PNG, take samples of color and average areas to keep less data in the file. These files compromise the image, but are more readily sent via email or web. The greater the compression, the less fidelity the file retains of the original image.

Graphic file formats like PSD or TIFF do not compress the data and render more accurately. However, not every user has an application that can read these file formats.

Raster Graphic Creation & Manipulation

Photoshop, or applications like Corel Paint Shop, or Pixelmator, are very useful when creating textures, or cropping/tweaking Vectorworks renderings.

Corel Painter is an application that emulates traditional paint media. It is very useful for creating image files for hand-painted backdrops, or digitally painting portraits or landscapes for use as stage props.

Vector Graphic Creation & Manipulation

Adobe Illustrator, CorelDraw, or Vectormator are useful applications to use with Vectorworks. The AI, EPS, and PDF file formats are vector formats and infinitely scalable. These applications are used to create signs, logos, and clean illustrations.

Desktop Publishing Applications

The Sheet Layers in Vectorworks are a powerful desk-top publishing feature within the application. Sheet Layers and Viewports allow designers to break out information and tell the design story.

It is important to consider the creation of Sheet Layers as a desktop publishing and graphic design

> ## Kevin's First Rule of Graphic Design:
> ## You have to be able to read it.

function. Think of each sheet in your set of drawings as a page in a magazine or other publication.

Adobe InDesign and QuarkXpress are used by graphic designers to create publications. This book was created using Adobe InDesign. Some designers use these programs to create specification documents for their designs, or to compile cut sheets from products needed for production.

Vectorworks publishes and exports to the Adobe Portable Document Format (PDF), which serves many purposes. PDF files can, generally, be universally read by clients, stage managers, and service bureaus. PDF files are high quality and the resolution can be controlled.

The Adobe Acrobat Reader is a free, cross-platform application for opening and printing PDF files.

The Adobe Acrobat software is often useful to designers for marking up or editing PDF files.

Fonts

Fonts are fun. Fonts communicate. Fonts are critical design elements in many instances, not just in graphic design.

It is important here to mention the graphic design element involved in page composition. Fonts are an element of graphic design and the related storytelling, the story of how to execute the various designs.

Fonts can also be designed elements or focal points, such as a store sign or giant icon if part of a set. They can be dimensional, internally illuminated, painted, or spinning, as examples.

So, fonts are important to understand. Remember, if fonts are not used properly and with care, the entire look and feel of your page will change when opened on a different system.

Fonts, like software, are intellectual property. There are many that are free to download and use. There are many that you must pay a fee to license before the fonts can be used. In either case, you have to check the license before you distribute or share the font files.

Fonts are system resources. The fonts on one system are not likely to be the same as the fonts on another. For an application to have access to a font, the font files have to be installed on the system and activated. Many designers keep thousands of fonts, and use font management software to determine which fonts are active at a given time. Arial, a very common cross-platform font, comes in many different flavors, from several different manufacturers. When sharing VWX files, be sure to choose your font(s) carefully, and be sure that your collaborators all have the font files they need. Part of communicating your design ideas is in the design of your page layouts. Every sheet in a drawing package should be as designed as the show, like the pages of a high-end magazine. The page layout should be thought of as part of the means of communication. The choice of font and placement of notes then becomes a design choice. If you share a VWX file with another user and that user does not have the fonts you used, then the page layout will be disrupted. Communication will be damaged, and some information may be completely lost.

Specialty Fonts

You may want to use a specialty font for the title of the show in your title block. Beowulf Boritt told me, *You can't do* **Rock of Ages** *without the Iron Maiden font,* and I do believe he's right. I have the font, but it wasn't activated when I opened Beowulf's files.

If you want a font like Iron Maiden in your title block, use it. Just be sure that you're only sharing PDF files, which keep all of the font information within the PDF format, or go to **Text>TrueType to Polyline** and convert the text to an object. That way your special font won't be substituted with a font that drastically changes your font size and style. Using this same technique, you can also turn fonts and letters into 3D signage, after the polylines have been extruded into 3D.

There is a wide selection of fonts designed for CAD drafting. Some look like hand lettering. Pick one font that is simple, easy to read, and does not distract from communicating your ideas. Use one font for all your drafting on a production. Make that font a system font, or a common font, so that your colleagues will see the page as you intended.

Portable Devices in the Studio

Your phone and your tablet are likely adjacent to your workstation just as they are likely always tethered to your person. They are useful adjuncts to your work station.

In addition to the calculator apps mentioned above, there are many categories of apps that might be useful to every designer's kit:
- Dropbox
- Evernote
- PDF Expert for annotating PDF files
- Vectorworks Nomad
- Magic Plan
- Units (converts dimensions and other measurements)
- A Level/Measuring app

Lighting Apps
- Moire and myGobo
- ETC Datasheets
- ETC Selador
- The Barbizon App
- Lightwright Touch for using and editing your Lightwright Files
- Remote Focus Units
- Gel Swatch Library
- BeamCalc

Sound Design Apps
- AudioBus
- Epic Tunes
- Shazam
- Logitech UE SPL
- Mocha VNC

- Audio Recorders
- Meteor Multitrack Recorder
- Looptastic HD
- AmpliTube for iPad (guitar amp/FX simulator and audio recorder)
- Moog AniMoog

This is by no means a comprehensive list of an every-changing and growing landscape.

All types of stage designers need to be a master of their own specialty, or specialities. They must also be knowledgable about their colleagues' work, and needs. As Robert Edmond Jones wrote in his 1941 book *The Dramatic Imagination: Reflections and Speculations on the Art of the Theatre,* opening a chapter titled *To a Young Stage Designer:*

> A stage designer is, in a very real sense, a jack-of-all-trades. He can make blueprints and murals and patterns and light plots. He can design fireplaces and bodices and bridges and wigs. He understands architecture, but is not an architect: can paint a portrait, but is not a painter: creates costumes, but is not a couturier. Although he is able to call upon any or all of these varied gifts at will, he is not concerned with any one of them to the exclusion of the others, nor is he interested in any of them for its own sake. Those talents are only the tools of his trade. His real calling is something quite different. He is an **artist of occasions.**

Some of these words may now seem to be sexist, but they remain true, just more complicated.

Raster Graphics are pixel-based, and restricted to a specific size.

Vector graphics are based on calculations, and scalable to any size

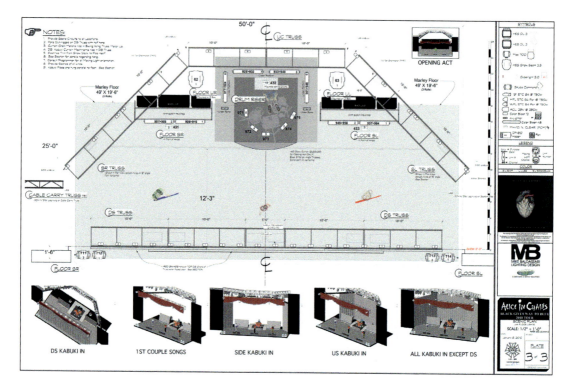

Alice in Chains: *Black Gives Way to Blue* Tour
Overhead Light Plot.

Alice in Chains

Alice in Chains: *Black Gives Way to Blue* Tour
Photo by Mike Savoia

Alice in Chains
Black Gives Way to Blue Tour

Management: Susan Silver
Production Designer: Mike Baldassari

6. Help Files and Resources

It would be terrific if one book could cover every situation you will encounter using Vectorworks over the course of what are or will be long and fruitful careers. That's probably not possible. However, while this book can provide a handy reference and solid beginning, there are places to turn, as you work through the book, and as you work through life.

As you design, you will confront new situations. There is a huge community of Vectorworks users, and resources available to help.

The Help Menu

The Help Menu has many ways to quickly get you additional information.

The **Help>What's This?** Command will change your cursor to an arrow with a question mark. You may then use this cursor to select a Tool, or Command within Vectorworks, and then be sent to the appropriate location within the Vectorworks Help application.

The *Getting Started Guides* are a series of videos created by Nemetschek to help users, well, Get Started. They are always worth viewing; new features are often introduced in these guides.

The search box on a Mac is a nifty feature that finds commands based on the text entered. Pity the still image does not show the animation.

Next, the Help Menu can start the Help application. That might be near the top here, but we'll come back to that, last.

The Vectorworks Knowledge Base is a series of online articles. The Vectorworks FAQ, if you will.

Cloud Services is a part of Vectorworks Service Select and allows the use of the Vectorworks Nomad application.

Nomad offers off-site rendering, and mobile apps for reviewing, sharing and marking up drawings.

Service Select is the Vectorworks subscription service. To begin, Service Select is a monthly fee, rather than paying for upgrades in a large chunk. There are additional benefits to Service Select:
- Tips & Tricks
- How To's
- Tutorials
- Vectorworks 101s
- Video Training
- One-on-One Training
- Support
- Webinars on Demand
- Continuing Education

The content available to Service Select members grows frequently.

Download Content takes you to the Vectorworks website area where the content libraries, like lighting instruments, speakers, and furniture (amongst other objects) can be downloaded and installed on your system. Once installed, these libraries are located in the **Vectorworks>Libraries** directory.

The libraries are an important feature that will take time to explore. Critically, the **Objects-Entertainment** directory contains symbols for nearly all of the lighting instruments available. We have seen that there are also lighting accessories, lighting positions, speaker symbols, and truss symbols.

Forums and E-Mail Lists

The online community (*www.vectorworks.net/community/index.php*) is dynamic and supportive. Join the user forums and e-mail lists.

There are specific lists and forums for theatre, but do not neglect the general areas: they are more active, and confront the same issues. Questions posed to the online community are often answered almost immediately. Vectorworks is widely used internationally. Whenever you are working, there are others working.

Never be afraid to ask for help. Everyone needs guidance from time to time.

The Help Application

Finally, select **Help>Vectorworks Help** to open the Help application. The Vectorworks Help application is easily searchable, and users can modify and adjust the application to their needs.

The Help Application window is divided into two columns. The left column provides navigation, and the right column provides information. Enter search criteria where it says *Enter text to search*. Results will be displayed in the right column. Selecting a search result will display the search topic. Search results can be saved as Favorites by clicking on the star icon. You may also add comments and other information.

Links to the online community and RSS feeds are in the **Favorites** tab of the Help Application. Users may also add their own additional links from within the application.

One day you could be the one providing help. Share your knowledge.

Ben Franklin's Ghost
Rendering by the author.

Ben Franklin's Ghost

Ben Franklin's Ghost

Ben Franklin's Ghost
Philadelphia, Pennsylvania, USA

Designers: Kathleen McDonough & Kevin Lee Allen
    Design Assistant: Edward DeZuzio
Producer: The Entertainment Technology Center at Carnegie Mellon University

Ben Franklin's Ghost was a marriage of new technology and old technology. The image of Ben
Franklin is a simple Pepper's Ghost that responds to questions asked via a touch screen display. The
rendering, mechanics, and engineering were all developed using Vectorworks.

7. Quick Start Overview

You jumped here first, right? Go back.

This is a quick study of how simply and flexibly you can design, and create working drawings or elevations working in 3D. We will create a simple 3D model and then look at and annotate that model in 2D. We'll then modify that model and see how the elevations are automatically updated.

Imperial/metric Conversions are not exact here. Round numbers for approximately similar sizes will be given.

Open a new document using your Default.sta, and change a Layer scale to 1/2" or 1:25. Use either the drop-down menu in the View Bar, or the **View>Standard Views** command, to change the view to a **Right Isometric.**

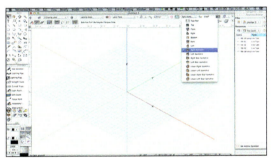

Working in the **Layer Plane,** and using the **Normal Line Weight Class,** click on the Rectangle Tool in the Basic Tool Set; in the Tool Bar, see that the left option, **Corner to Corner Mode,** is selected and that the right option, **Push/Pull Mode,** is also selected. Double-click on the Rectangle Tool to open the **Create Object** dialog. Set the Width and Height to be 3" (75mm), deselect **Position at Next Click,** select the center circle of the **Box Position Indicator,** and set the XY coordinates to 0-0. Click **OK.**

In Vectorworks, you can enter a value in the default measurement unit — for example, inches without including the inches sign ("). To enter feet and inches you must include the feet symbol (') or convert the length to inches. If working in Metric, you can set the default to millimeters, centimeters, or meters.

Create Object		
Rectangle		
Class:	Normal Line Weight	
Layer:	Lighting Areas	
Width:	3"	
Height:	3"	
	X:	0"
	Y:	0"
☐ Position At Next Click		
Rotation:	0.00°	
Ratio:	Square	
Perim:	1'0"	
Area:	.062 sq ft	
	Cancel	OK

Vectorworks will place a square Rectangle in the middle of your page. The object is selected and there is now information about the object in the OIP. You can change the size and/or placement of the object via the OIP. You can also change the object Class, or move the object to another layer.

It is possible to modify sizes in the OIP, either by entering data, or with standard mathematical notation. Dimensions can be changed by adding, subtracting, multiplying, and dividing.

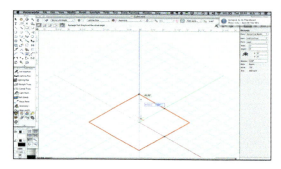

With the Push/Pull tool option selected, the object will turn red when you hover over it, indicating you can extrude. Push/Pull up and down to see how this works. When you Push/Pull, the **Floating Data Bar (FDB)** becomes active and provides an interactive display indicating the depth of the extrusion. Press the Tab key to enter into the FDB and enter 3" or 75mm. If you lose the ability to Push/Pull using the Rectangle Tool, select the **Push/Pull Tool** from the **3D Modeling Tool Set,** and extrude using the **Extrude Face Mode.**

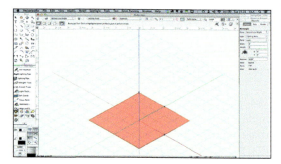

Congratulations! You have a drawn a 3D object. You can now look at the object in the various orthographic and isometric projections available from the View drop-down, or command.

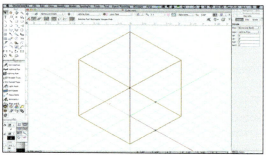

Let's make this a bit more complex, because we can. Go to the **3D Modeling Tool Set** and select the **Taper Face Tool.** There are two modes available in the Tool Bar: **Tangent Faces Mode,** and **Picked Faces Mode.** Select Tangent Faces Mode.

Click on the top of the cube and then the front left side. Pull the side forward. Pressing the shift key should constrain the angle to the 15° we added to the Snapping Preferences. Release and the object should no longer be a cube.

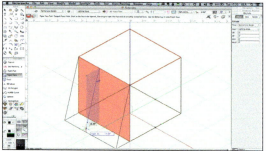

Select the Working Plane Tool from the 3D Tool Set and make the back face of the cube the Working Plane. You will have to press the Alt/Option key to select the rear face.

Double-click on the Rectangle Tool, check Position at Next Click, select the lower-left corner of the Box Position Indicator and set the sizes to make a 1" or 25 mm square. If you are working in Metric, you might insert the Imperial dimension; if you're working in Imperial, try Metric. Vectorworks will do the conversion.

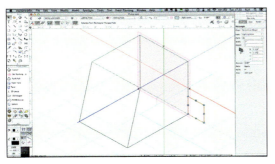

Return to the Taper Face Tool, select the Picked Faces Mode, and again, pick the top, then the right side. Snap the bottom edge of the right side to the square you have just drawn. Adding guides let you specify distance, rather than an angle.

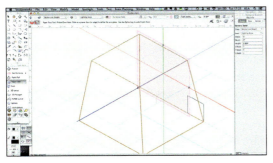

Review the orthographic views and notice how the 2D square appears in each view. Select and delete the square added for snapping. Press Command/Control+5 to return to the Top/Plan view, and go back to the Right Isometric View. Returning to the Top/Plan View clears the Working Plane we created, and the Working Plane is now back to the base.

Return to the 3D Modeling Tool Set and select the Sphere Tool. Note there are three drawing modes available in the Tool Bar. Double-click on the Sphere Tool, deselect **Center at Next Click,** and set the Radius to 1" or 25 mm. Leave the X and Y placement at 0 and set the Z to 1 1/2" or 38 mm. Click **OK.**

Create Object

Sphere

Class: Normal Line Weight

Layer: Lighting Areas

X: 0"
Y: 0"
Z: 1 1/2"

Center At Next Click

Radius: 1"

Volume: .002 cu ft

Surface: .087 sq ft

Cancel OK

This will be your result.

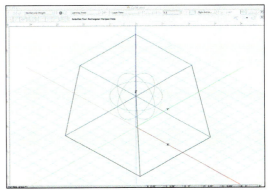

Free Form Modeling is fast and precise.

Go to **Edit>Select All** or press Command/Control+A to select both objects. With those objects selected go to Model>Subtract Solids. Use the Arrows in the dialog to see that the cube-based object is highlighted in thicker red lines and Click **OK.**

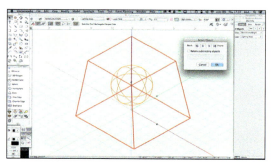

At first glance, it may not appear as if anything has happened, but you have just removed a solid sphere from the solid cubic form.

We have been working and looking at these objects using Wireframe Rendering. Go to either the Rendering Drop-down in the View Bar or **View>Rendering** to select **Dashed Hidden Line** rendering. You should now see the interior objects as dashed lines. Those lines should be slightly grayed.

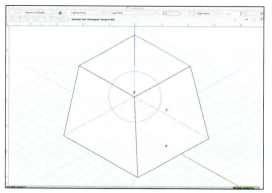

The dash may or may not be the correct dash. This illustration shows a long-short-long dash. Correct for a Centerline. Not correct here.

Go to **View>Rendering** and look at the many available options. Also notice here that you can right-click in the Resource Browser and choose to view the various resources as Thumbnails or a List. Thumbnails has been chosen.

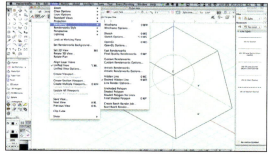

Before we fix the dash take a quick look at the other options available here. The OpenGL and Renderworks modes should show you a basically white form. Artistic Renderworks will add some scribbles. Review the Artistic Renderworks Options; these may be of more value once we have added color to objects. At this point, all you have to work with is your black Pen, and white Fill.

Since we have been, and will be working in Wireframe, open **Wireframe Options.** These choices help to see and see through objects in Wireframe View. You may have noticed the 40% (default) transparency when you added the square for snapping the Tapered Face.

Now to this point, open the **Line Render Options** dialog. Change the **Line Type** to **VW-01 Short Dashed** (which is appropriate for seeing into or under objects), and adjust the dark to light relationship to your liking. You'll have to move in and out of the dialog for Vectorworks to re-render the object to see any changes.

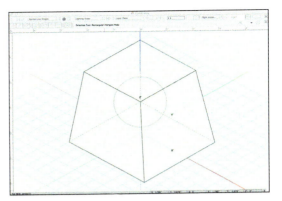

Select the Working Plane Tool from the 3D Tool Set. In the **Planar Face Mode,** select the right front side of the object.

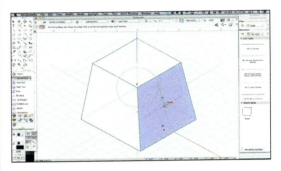

With that Plane selected, open the **Working Plane Palette** and select **Add**, and name the Working Plane. You can close the Working Plane Palette, and will now have that Plane available from the Working Plane drop-down in the View Bar.

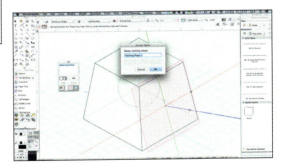

For fun, look at the various **Sketch Options** available. When you render using Sketch, you will also be adding resources to the Resource Browser. Edit some of the Sketch Options to your liking, and return to the correct Hidden Line rendering.

Switch to the Wireframe View. Go to the **Top View,** not the Top/Plan view. You want to look at the object from the top view of the Working Plane. Draw a line as a guide from the center out.

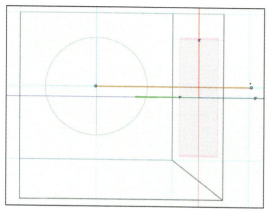

Switch back to the Right Isometric View, and see how the line looks with the Working Plane.

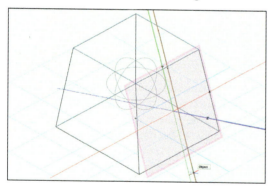

Go to the 3D Modeling Tool Set and select the **3D Locus Tool.**

A Locus, or Datum, is simply a point in space for snapping or measuring. On stage, the intersection of the Plaster Line and the Centerline is often referred to as *Datum*, as that is the point from which measurements are taken for the placement of gear. Similar to the 0-0 point of this document.

Zoom in as needed to place a 3D Locus point at the intersection of your 2D line and the X (red) Axis line. Confirm correct placement by looking at the OIP with the 3D Locus Object selected. The Y should be 0.

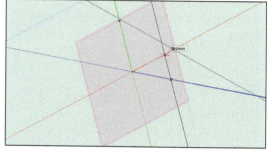

With the 3D Locus Object selected, go to **Modify>Move>Move 3D,** and elevate the 3D Locus Object 1" or 25 mm on the Z Axis with **Working Plane** selected.

Move 3D Selection			
○ Cartesian		● Working Plane	
X Offset:	−.316"	X' Offset:	0"
Y Offset:	0"	Y' Offset:	1"
Z Offset:	.949"	Z' Offset:	0"
		Cancel	OK

Select the Circle Tool from the Basic Tool Set and snap a 1/4" or 8 mm diameter circle to the 3D Locus Object. Go to the 3D Tool Set and select the Push/Pull Tool in the Sub-Face Mode. Select the Circle (here the curve) and then the object. Drag through to the internal opening, tab into the FDB, and enter 1 1/4" or 38 mm, and hit Enter. Release the mouse.

You should now have a small hole bored from the center of the sphere out of the object. The guideline you drew from the Top View provided the proper placement. You could have taken the measurement and done the math to find this location, but Vectorworks did most of the work.

Delete the 2D Line and the 3D Locus.

Double-click on the object, or right-click on the object and select Edit from the contextual menu.

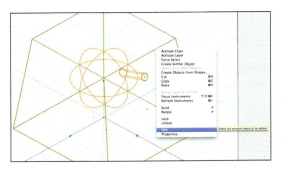

You can now drill back through the process and make changes to the object. Each time you right-click and select Edit, or double-click on the object again, you go back a step in the process.

Viewports and Presentation

Sheet Layer Viewports (SLVPs) are placed onto Sheet Layers for printing, presentation, and producing construction documents. A SLVP is a view of your 3D model converted to traditional orthographic, isometric, and perspective views.

From a Top/Plan view, go to **View>Create Viewport** and create a new viewport. Name it *Object.* Title the drawing *Object.*

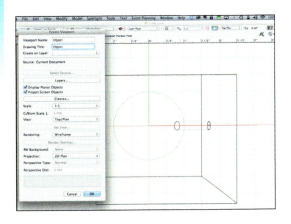

From the **Create on Layer** drop-down menu, select **New Sheet Layer.** When the dialog opens, number the sheet 01 and title the sheet *Object.* Check **Edit Properties After Creation** and click **OK.**

Set the **Raster Rendering DPI** to 125 and click Page Setup. While you have been drawing on either an A4 or Letter size page, you can change the page size when you create a Sheet Layer. In fact, you can have sheet layers of many different sizes.

to **Dashed Hidden Line**. The outline of the viewport will change to a slashed red line, indicating an out-of-date viewport. Select **Update** in the OIP, and the object will re-render.

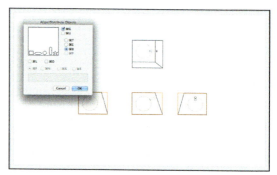

Option/Alt+drag to duplicate the viewport so that you can set-up a traditional Orthographic projection layout on the sheet: Front View centered, with the Plan View aligned above, left and right views in their respective places alongside the Front View.

Click the **Printer Setup** button and make the Sheet Layer either A3 or Tabloid (11" by 17") size. Click **OK** to exit the dialogs.

With a Viewport selected, the View can be changed in the OIP. There's a drop-down for that.

With multiple objects selected, use the **Modify>Align>Align/Distribute** Command to assist. The keyboard shortcut for this command is Command/Control+= and it is one that will save a lot of time if memorized.

Vectorworks will bring you to the sheet layer; this view has a gray border. Your viewport will be visible. The viewport should be selected, and information about the viewport will be displayed in the OIP. Go to the OIP and change the scale to 1:2, and change the **Background Render**

Labeling Sheets

This is a good beginning and a place we can jump ahead to save some time. Go to the **Dims/Notes Tool Set** and select the **Sheet Border Tool.** Be sure that the **Standard Insertion Mode** is selected, open the **Tool Preferences** from the Tool Bar, and:

- Set the Sheet Size to **Fit to Page**
- Check **Lock to Page Center**

Sheet Border Preferences	
Sheet Size:	Fit to Page
Width (in.)	16.5
Height (in.):	10.5
Title Block:	Spotlight Simple Title Blo
☑ Lock to Page Center	
☐ Use As Title Block Only	

Click on **Title Block** and the dialog accesses Default Content. Select the **Spotlight Simple Title Block** and click **OK.**

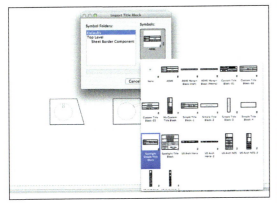

Every drawing needs a Title Block. Yes, that's another rule. The design, content, and arrangement of title blocks vary widely, but this one contains some pretty basic information: the name of the show and the name of the draftsperson. It seriously neglects a place for a Sheet Number, but that won't matter much here.

Click OK and then double-click to insert the Sheet Border with the Title Block attached. You can also click once, rotate the elements, and click to place, but if there isn't a rule against that, there should be one. This is true of most Symbol Insertions, not the rotation; sometimes you need, or want, to rotate. In this case, because Lock to Page Center was clicked, it does not matter where you click to insert. That is not true of most Symbol Insertions.

With the Drawing Border and Title Block selected, you can modify these items in the OIP. Uncheck **Show Grids.**

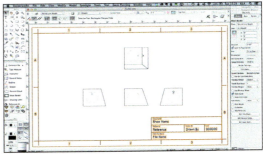

Double-click or right-click on the Drawing Border to edit the content. Add your name, fill in the other information if you like, and click **OK.**

Edit Title Block	
Show Name:	Show Name
Reference:	Reference
Drawn By:	Drawn By
Date:	00/00/00
CAD File Name:	File Name

Cancel   OK

Section Views look inside Objects.

Go to the **Navigation Palette** and right-click on the *Object Sheet Layer*. Select **Duplicate**. Right-click on the new sheet layer and select **Edit**. Change the name of the sheet layer to *Object Isometric,* and notice that you can rearrange the order of the sheet layers by changing their stack. You can also rearrange layers in the organization dialog.

What you've done here is saved making some Viewports, and placing Drawing Borders and Title Blocks.

Annotating Viewports

Return to the Object Sheet Layer. These drawings need to be identified, and they will need dimensioning. First, we'll add a Section View.

Section Views can be created from either the model on a Design Layer, or from a Viewport. When from the Viewport, the command also adds a needed annotation.

Select the Plan Viewport and go to **View>Create Section Viewport.** Snap to click in the center of the Sphere and drag left. Press the shift key to constrain the angle of the cut. Click once to end the cut and then click above the line so that the reference arrow points up to determine the view.

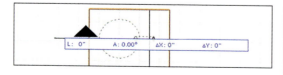

In the following dialog, uncheck **Name the Viewport** and **Create Drawing Label**. Name the Viewport **Section Left,** and call the **Drawing Title:** *Left Section.* Click **OK.**

The Section View should appear in the middle of the page. Use snaps to place the section aligned to the Plan and to the Left Elevation. With the Section Viewport selected, go to the OIP and click **Advanced Properties**. Set the **3D Conversion** to **Very High**.

Vectorworks has created a new Class called Section Style, and it is garish. We also need to class the section line left in the Annotation Space of the Plan Viewport.

Open the Classes Tab of the Organization Dialog and edit **Section Style**. Change the Fill to a Pattern; change the Fore color to black and the Back color to white. Select a diagonal line fill. This is standard for sectioned areas that are being cut through. Depending on the material and nature of the drawing, section fills can be more elaborate and pictorial. Change the Line Thickness to .70 and click **OK.**

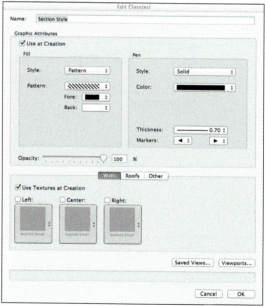

Duplicate and edit the D-Drawing Label Class. Call the new class D-Section Line. Set the fill to the same blue solid as the Pen color. Change the Pen Thickness to .70 and use the **ISO-09 Long Dashed Double Short Dashed** Line Type. Click **OK** and exit the Organization Dialog.

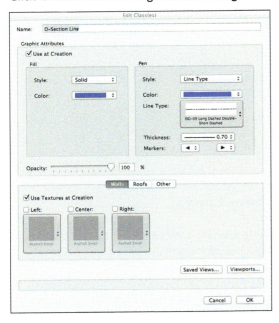

Option-Drag to create a copy of the Plan Viewport to the right of the main Plan. This drawing will be specifically for dimensioning the sphere and its location. Right-click on the main Plan View and select **Edit Annotations** from the contextual menu. Note that if you do not click on a line in the viewport or the edge of the viewport, you will see a different contextual menu.

You have now entered the Viewport annotation space. Sheet Layers are 1:1 scale, and the viewport annotation space is a window into the scale of the viewport as chosen in the OIP. If you dimension on the Sheet Layer directly (outside of the annotation space of the Viewport), your dimensions will not be the dimensions of the object; they will be the real-world dimensions of the scaled drawing.

It has to be assumed that the person doing the drawing will not be available, on a full-time basis, to the person executing the drawing. This is where you give that person all of the information needed to complete the work, as intended. It is a given that using a scale ruler on a print is not a good idea. Prints can be scaled by the mechanical printer. Paper can expand and contract due to weather conditions. Enough, maybe too many, dimensions and notes need to be provided.

First, assign the **D-Section Line** Class to the section line indicator. Call that Drawing E and size to fit over the object.

From within the Annotation space of the viewport, select the **Constrained Linear Dimension** tool from the Basic tool set; note the tool options in the Tool Bar. First you want the second from left mode, **Constrained Chain**. Open the Constrained Preferences, choose **Create individual dimension objects adjacent to each other,** and check **Use collision control when placing chain dimension text**. Click **OK**. Chained dimensions are strings of information, and sometimes those dimensions are too close to be easily read. These choices allow control over the placement of text for legibility.

Chain Dimension the parts of the object and then switch to **Constrained Linear Mode** to dimension the overall size.

The SmartCursor will help you find points and place the dimensions.

Go to the Dims/Notes tool set and select the **Drawing Label tool**. Snap to the left dimension, and place a drawing label under the view; click twice to insert. Grab the **Control Point** and drag the line to the far right side of the section line. Assign the D-Drawing Label Class.

Repeat as needed for the other Viewports, titling each view with the proper Orthographic name of the view. In the Plan View at the top right, use the **Reference Marker** tool for the Dims/Notes Tool Set to indicate which drawing is which side of the object.

Assign those markers the D-Graphic Scale Class, after you have reviewed the options.

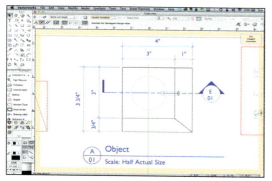

Does this page tell the whole story? Not exactly. We can convert some of the Viewports on Sheet 02 to Isometric Views. That will help, but there are critical elements missing.

First, return to the Design Layer and move to your saved Working Plane. To the left of the Working Plane drop-down in the View Bar, there is a button. Hover over that button and the text **Look at Working Plane** will appear. Click the button, and the view changes to a flat-on view of the angled face that we selected as the Working Plane. Create a Viewport of this view. It is easiest to visualize in **Hidden Line** render mode.

With this view the placement of the bore hole can be accurately dimensioned.

Use the Angular Dimension Tool and the Radial Dimension Tool to add information about the sphere, and the angle of the bore hole. You will need guides. Draw a circle over the sphere in

plan, dimension the circle, then set the Fill and Pen to none.

The same with lines needed to measure the angle of the bore.

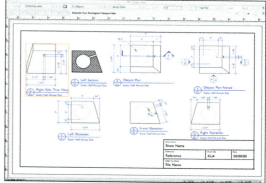

Making Changes

Designs evolve and change. That's a simple fact of life. It's almost a rule.

Save your file as Object.vwx to preserve what you have. Return to the design layer, go to the Top/Plan view, and then to the Left Isometric view.

Before we modify the square edge of the object, we probably need to address the question, *What is a fillet, or a chamfer, for that matter?* First, these things have nothing to do with steaks or fish.

Never leave it to someone else to add up dimensions.

These terms, for softening or easing the edges of hard corners, come from the mechanical engineering world. A *Fillet* is a rounded edge, while a *Chamfer* is a straight, beveled corner. Vectorworks includes 2D and 3D Chamfer and Fillet Tools.

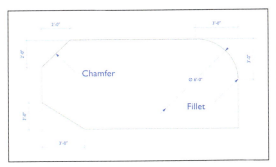

Press Command/Control+6 to fit the object to your window, and go to the 3D Modeling Tool Set. Select the **Fillet Tool** and review the preferences. While you could Fillet every edge, including the angles' edges/faces, by checking **Select All Edges** or shift-selecting (after exiting the dialog), begin with selecting one edge, and setting the **Constant Radius** to 1" or 25 mm. Click OK, and select the vertical edge of the object. That edge will then become highlighted in red.

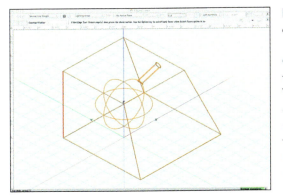

Check the green **Check** in the Tool Bar to execute the Fillet.

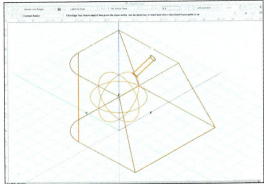

To preserve the original settings, go to the Classes Dialog and **Duplicate** then **Edit** the **Normal Line Weight Class**. Change the Pen Color, check **Use at Creation** under Graphic Attributes, and also check **Use Textures at Creation**.

Textures are, most simply put, 3D paint. Textures can be assigned in different ways, to different types of objects as indicated by the Tabs at the bottom of the dialog. Click the **Other** Tab, check **Texture,** and see that you have accessed the **Default Content**. Choose a texture that you like; you can change the look at any time by editing the Class.

In fact, this is a good time to take a look at some of the different textures immediately available.

Click on the **Viewports** button and be sure that this new class is **Visible** in all of your Viewports. Exit the dialogs and return to the drawing window. Select the Object and assign the new class in the OIP. Vectorworks will ask if you would like to assign the Graphic Attributes of the Class to the Object. In this case you do. That might not always be true.

Render the Object using the different OpenGL and Renderworks styles.

After adding a 3D Fillet or Chamfer to an object, the object must be Ungrouped to Edit. The Fillet or Chamfer will be lost.

It should be now be immediately obvious how working in 3D and using viewports can speed the drafting, updating, and revision process.

Use the Radial Dimension Tool to dimension the Fillet.

The Pen Color might be useful, but also not appropriate for a working drawing. You can redefine the Class, but then you would lose the color in the model. In a complex model, that might be an issue. Select a Viewport, click **Classes** in the OIP. In the following dialog, select the Object Class, and click **Edit**. The changes made only affect the given Viewport. Click **OK.**

On Sheet Layer 02, duplicate the Isometric View.

Return to the Wireframe View, and attempt to edit the object. Due to the Fillet you cannot. You need to **Ungroup** (Command/Control+U or **Modify>Ungroup**) before you can edit. When you Ungroup, you lose the Fillet, but the preceding modifications are available to be altered.

Go to the Sheet Layer 01, Shift-select the Viewports, and click **Update** in the OIP. Your drawings will be updated to show the changes made to the model

Alternately, right-click on the Viewport in the Viewport Tab of the Navigation palette and choose **Update** from the contextual menu.

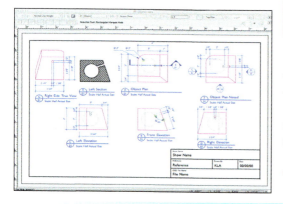

In the new Viewport, set the Background Render to Final Quality Renderworks. This now provides two pictorial views.

Be sure all of your Viewports are properly aligned and labeled on each Sheet Layer.

Go to **File>Publish**, and, select the two Sheet

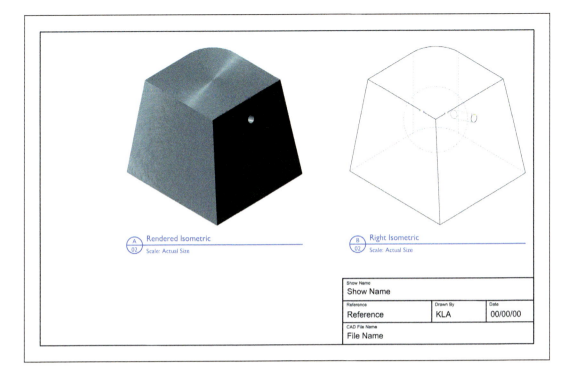

(A) Rendered Isometric			(B) Right Isometric	
(02) Scale: Actual Size			(02) Scale: Actual Size	

Show Name		
Show Name		
Reference	Drawn By	Date
Reference	KLA	00/00/00
CAD File Name		
File Name		

Layers from the left column. Use the arrows to move them into the right column, and select Publish to create a PDF set of drawings.

It is best practice to print, plot, or distribute files

from PDF files.

The Publish Command will also export to DWG/DXF/DWF file formats. It is possible to create and save sets of drawings, and create sets of drawings from multiple files.

That is a basic overview of creating drawings in Vectorworks. From this foundation, it is possible to create increasingly complex objects and document sets.

The zip file called *WorkFiles.zip* on the Website at **focalpress.com/cw/allen** includes this exercise.

Publish sets from one or more documents.

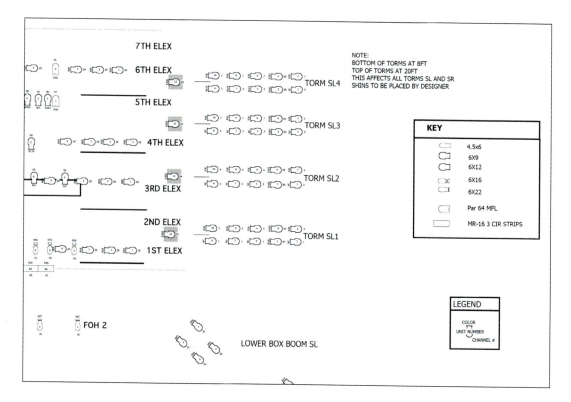

NOTE:
BOTTOM OF TORMS AT 8FT
TOP OF TORMS AT 20FT
THIS AFFECTS ALL TORMS SL AND SR
SHINS TO BE PLACED BY DESIGNER

7TH ELEX
6TH ELEX
5TH ELEX
4TH ELEX
3RD ELEX
2ND ELEX
1ST ELEX

TORM SL4
TORM SL3
TORM SL2
TORM SL1

FOH 2

LOWER BOX BOOM SL

KEY

	4.5x6
	6X9
	6X12
	6X16
	6X22
	Par 64 MFL
	MR-16 3 CIR STRIPS

LEGEND

COLOR
UNIT NUMBER
CHANNEL #

2005 A Chorus Line Tour
Detail of Light Plot

A Chorus Line

2005 A Chorus Line Tour

2005 A Chorus Line Tour

Director: Mitzi Hamilton
Producer: Jerry Lonn
Lighting Designer: Herrick Goldman
    Assistant Lighting Designer: Susan Nicholson

This tour that began in El Paso, Texas and continued on to Honolulu and Maui, recreated the original production as closely as possible.

While Herrick was aware of Tharon Musser's original design, he intentionally strayed away from the ideas that were inherently hers. As a designer he feels it is important to create your own work and not to duplicate the vision of others who have gone before you.

Herrick comments: *Designing **A Chorus Line** gives you a healthy appreciation for mirrors. When I began to play with them, I discovered that when you time it just right, backlight acts as front light and vice versa. This leads to some beautiful moments.*

8. Renderworks Backgrounds and Textures

Renderworks Backgrounds and Renderworks Textures are what paint a 3D model. Certain types of Renderworks backgrounds can also light, and color objects in 3D.

If you have not created a user folder, now would be a good time. You will also need to create a workgroup folder for the *Lysistrata* project that will be the focus of this book. There is a zip file called *WorkFiles.zip* on the Website at **focalpress.com/cw/allen.** That zip file includes the project files and references needed for this work.

In order to accomplish much of what follows, you will need multiple Vectorworks files open at one time, and you will be importing or referencing resources from one file to another via the Resource Browser. When you need to access one file from another via the Resource Browser, select the second file from the drop-down menu at the top of the Resource Browser window. You can **Favorite** files by selecting **Add New Favorite Files** files from under the top left **Disclosure Triangle.** Favorite files then always appear under the drop-down menu, and can be accessed even when not open, from the top drop-down menu. To return the top, or active file, select the home button near the top right of the Resource Browser.

Renderworks Backgrounds and Renderworks Textures are paint in the 3D World.

If you have multiple files open, you can see into the other files' Resources from the active document, by selecting another file from the Resource Browser drop-down menu. Right-clicking on a resource allows you to **Import** or **Reference** the Resource(s). Importing brings the Resource into the active document. Referencing leaves the Resource in the original document, and links that file to the active document. If the Resource is edited in the original file, all instances are updated. If a Referenced Resource is edited in the second file, the Reference is broken.

Resources can be referenced into multiple files. Right now we're going to explore how Backgrounds and Textures can be shared. This idea gets more complex as multiple users share a model of a theatre or other venue.

Renderworks Backgrounds

Renderworks Backgrounds can be added to Design Layers via the Edit Design Layer Dialog. To get to that dialog, either right-click on a Design Layer in the Navigation Palette, click on the Layers button in the View Bar, or go to **Tools>Organization** and select the Design Layers tab.

In the Edit Design Layer Dialog, you have access to Renderworks Backgrounds in the active document and in the Default Content. Remember, different Default Content can exist in two places: first in the Vectorworks Application folder, **Vectorworks>Libraries>Defaults,** and then in the Renderworks Backgrounds folder; second, in your **User Folder>Libraries >Defaults>Renderworks Backgrounds.**

Once you have created, Imported, or Referenced backgrounds, you can also assign a background to

A Renderworks Background can do several things:

- Provide Atmosphere (fog)
- Provide or enhance lighting
- Provide a sense of natural outdoor lighting
- Create a simple day or night sky

Working in an enclosed theatre space, it might appear that we do not need a background, as we have the architecture. However, creating and applying a layer background will allow us to render fog coming from the stage lights. When developing the design for theatre projects, a simple black Renderworks Design Layer Background can stand in for the architecture until the theatre is chosen or modeled. When sketching or designing in Vectorworks, it is often best not to get bogged down in the details and the specifics while simply creating. Vectorworks allows designers to refine the design as it develops.

a layer by double-clicking on the background icon in the Resource Browser.

In the folder **Vectorworks>Libraries> Defaults>Renderworks Backgrounds** you should find several files. The contents of those files will be available by default. If you don't like that content, you can change the contents of those files. Any file you add to either that directory, or **User Folder>Libraries> Defaults>Renderworks Backgrounds** will be always available. This is true of all the **Default Content**.

One reason to have and maintain a user folder is to manage your own resources and content. As a general rule, always back-up and preserve the original files. This is true for Renderworks Backgrounds, it is true for Renderworks Textures, and it is true for every type of resource.

In our studio, in addition to personal User Folders, we have another directory of Vectorworks resources that are not needed every day and that preserve original content. This is separate from folders full of image files to be used to create Renderworks Backgrounds, and Renderworks Textures.

If illustrating an isolated element, like a wine goblet, or a trade show space, you might not want to model an entire world before you render a simple object. In these cases, Renderworks defaults to a white background that you can easily change, if that's not the perfect background.

A Renderworks Background with the **Lit Fog** option checked is required in order to render beams of light.

Let's make a few backgrounds. Open your **Object.vwx** file and save it as **Object-Backgrounds.vwx.** Go to an isometric view of the object and select the **Flyover** tool from the Basic Tool Set. Find a view that you like.

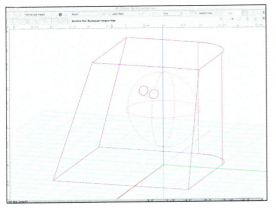

Render as Final Quality Renderworks by either selecting that type from the Render drop-down in the View Bar or going to **View>Render>Final Quality Renderworks**. Vectorworks inserts an invisible light object for renders where no lights have been placed. This is handy as we have not discussed lights yet. You should have some pretty harsh shadows.

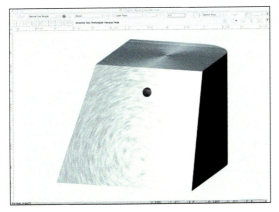

Notice that while executing a Final Quality Renderworks render, Vectorworks displays an OpenGL render as a preview.

Go to **View>Projection>Perspective** to change the view from an Orthogonal to a Perspective view. You can adjust the perspective at **View>Perspective.** Use the **Flyover Tool**, in Wireframe mode, to adjust the view again and render.

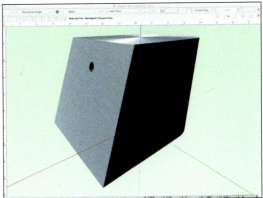

Return to the Wireframe view and go to **View>Perspective>Cropped;** this adds an adjustable frame to your view. Click and drag the corners of the frame to find a pleasing proportion. Use the Zoom Tool from the Basic Tool Set to click and drag so the frame fills your window. You may or may not be able to use Command/Control+6 to get this view. Objects, and points outside of the window view are still included when using the Fit to Screen Command.

With the new view visible go to the **Saved Views** drop-down on the View Bar and create a Saved View. Accept the Defaults, but be aware that if you add Layers or Classes that you want to see in a Saved View you may have to return to this Dialog later to add them. When creating new Classes or Layers, they can be added to Saved Views in the initial dialog. Saved Views can also be modified in the Organization dialog.

Right-click in the Resource Browser to **Create a New Renderworks Background**. Select the Clouds option, name the Background Day Sky and accept the Default settings. Edit the Design Layer and select **Day Sky** from the Layer Background drop-down.

Edit Design Layers	
Name:	Object
Scale:	1:1 Scale...
Stacking Order:	1
Story:	<None>
Elevation:	0" relative to the ground plane
Layer Wall Height:	0"
Level Type:	<None>
Opacity:	100 %
Renderworks Background:	DaySky

Colors...

Saved Views...   Viewports...

☐ Georeferenced   Edit Georeferencing...

Cancel   OK

Render and see the changes.

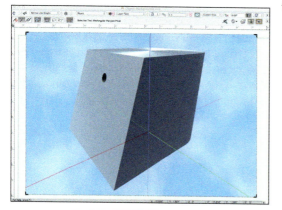

At this point, you can go to **File>Export>Image File,** choose **Current View,** and have Vectorworks create an image, of virtually any size, or file format that you can hang on your refrigerator, or post to Facebook.

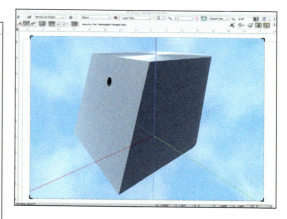

Now, go to **View>Lighting>Set Lighting Options.** First see that there is **Ambient Lighting** in this view. That's fine, but when visualizing a Lighting Design you want to turn that **Off**. Similarly, if rendering an object that you've carefully lit, if there is **Ambient Lighting,** the results might not be as expected.

When Pre-Visualizing a Lighting Design, you can use **Ambient Lighting** to your advantage. Assume you might want a stage wash of R80 and a few bits picked out with specials. You can use Ambient Lighting to create the wash, at least at the very early stages of design.

In the **Environment Lighting (HDRI)** section, check **From Selected Background** and choose **Day Sky** from the drop-down. Click **OK.**

Lighting Options

Indirect Lighting: None

Ambient Info

⊙ On ○ Off   Brightness (%): 35
Color:

Emitter Options

Emitter Brightness (%): 100

White Color Temperature: Indoor (3400K)

Custom (K): 3400

Environment Lighting (HDRI)

○ From Current Background
⊙ From Selected Background
   Renderworks Background: DaySky
○ None

These items control how environment lighting is applied to the layer or viewport. Environment lighting is created by choosing Image Environment for a Renderworks Background.

Cancel   OK

Render again. This Render will take longer, and look different. The object is now being lit by the background image.

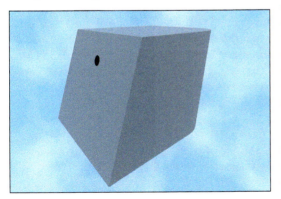

High Dynamic Range Images (HDRI) contain lighting data and are a composite of different exposures that Renderworks can use to

illuminate a view. Some cameras can create HDRI images. Photoshop, and other image editing software packages, can combine different exposures of the same view into an HDRI image. If you're working on an outdoor project, an HDRI image at a certain time of day can help to explore the look of the stage light during, night, or magic hour.

The light data contained in an HDRI image is interpreted by Renderworks, and will cause your model to be lit with the same colors and angles as the background. There are many resources on the Web from which you can download HDRI images. Be sure to verify the licensing and ownership of those images.

HDRI images can also be used in the pre-visualization of stage lighting. Examine and experiment with the HDRI default content, if you are a Service Select member, there is some great additional HDRI content available. With a background like HDRI Sky Night applied, it is easy to quickly see what a certain type of blue wash might do to the colors of the scenery. The backgrounds do not always look like the description, but the light they generate will, and, as seen, you can use the light from one background against another. The larger the image and view in scale, the more background detail will be visible.

This is one of the many cases where you should explore a number of combinations, not just those described in the text.

So, go to the Resource Browser and you will now have two different Renderworks Background Resources available. Right-click to **Duplicate**, and then right-click to **Edit** the **DaySky** duplicate. Change the light blue to a dark blue, right-click to **Apply** the new Renderworks Background, and render.

Throughout, follow this procedure of duplicating resources and editing the duplicates. Name the new resources in a way that works for you.

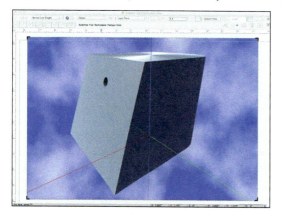

Now, edit the HDRI background **HDRI Day.** Choose **Options**, and try changing the **Brightness** from 100% to 150% or more. View the results, and also try some lesser percentages to see the differences.

In the Resource Browser, right-click and select **New Resource>New Renderworks Background.**

The top drop-down shows the available options:
• Clouds
• One Color
• Two Color
• Image
• Image Environmental (HDRI)
• Physical Sky

It is generally true throughout Renderworks that you are not limited to 100% as an end. It is up to the user to know when and where it might be acceptable to bend the rules of physics.

We have already explored **Clouds**. **One Color** should be self-explanatory and used to create simple colored backgrounds. **Two Color** will allow you to create simple gradient backgrounds.

An **Image**-based, but non-HDRI background allows the placement of image files behind objects or scenes. This isn't a great way to illustrate theatrical backdrops, but it can be used to give exterior context, or to have a really abstract background to any view. The scale of the image can be adjusted in **Page Based Scale** when **Option** is selected. Select **Image>Options** to reveal a standard OS File Open dialog. Select an image that you would like to use as a background, perhaps a landscape, or a photo of your significant other.

That selection takes you to the **Edit Image Background** dialog. The scale of the image can be adjusted in **Page Based Scale**, or sized to the output rather than the scale of the drawing **(World Based Scale)**. Flip H and Flip V are horizontal and vertical. Thus far we have used X and Y. Images can also be inverted for effect.

A **Physical Sky** Renderworks Background creates the realistic appearance of a sky with differing levels of clouds/sun. A Physical Sky can be used in conjunction with the **Heliodon Tool** to render the light and the sky's appearance as appropriate for a specific time, date, and location. The Heliodon Tool can be used to create a solar animation. This is useful for rendering outside events.

For the purposes of working through the projects, create a file in your **Lysistrata Workgroup Folder** with several **One Color; Black** backgrounds with the **Lit Fog** option selected. The Default Fog at 50% might be a little too much, but you won't know until you see. Create backgrounds with these percentages:
- 2.5%
- 5%
- 10%
- 15%
- 20%
- 30%
- 50%

You can modify these, and add or subtract to the list as suits your design style. Name these backgrounds so that the content is easily understood.

Renderworks Textures

Creating great textures that accurately represent the materials and finishes of the set, combined with proper lighting in the 3D world, create great renderings and presentations. The ability to properly plan, and present your ideas is key to success as a designer.

You will need to create a document in your Workgroup folder called **Textures-Lysistrata.vwx**. In that document, model a cube to use for testing your textures. You will also need the folder from the Website called *texture images* and the **Textures_Default.vwx**

file located at **Vectorworks>Libraries>Defaults>Renderworks Textures.** That file needs to be open for our purposes.

Textures can be referenced. In this way, all of the textures for a project can be stored in one location and/or created and modified by one team member who might excel at texture creation. For the *Lysistrata* project, we are now creating that file.

You will need an Image Editor, like Photoshop, for some of the work that follows.

Textures come in basically two flavors: **Image-based** and **Procedural**.

Procedural Textures

A procedural texture is computer-generated using an algorithm designed to produce a realistic representation of natural elements, such as wood, metal, stone, and others. Renderworks includes many options for procedural textures to be created within the application. Procedural effects can be added to **Image-based** textures, just as images can be used to affect **Procedural Textures.**

Properly planning and presenting ideas is key to success as a designer.

Image-Based Textures

An image-based texture has as its primary source an image file, such as a JPEG or PSD file. A logical use for an image-based texture would be to illustrate a painted backdrop onstage. Image-based textures can also represent commercially available products like carpets or patterned plastic laminates.

Images created for use as image-based textures can be designed in one of two basic ways:
- A seamlessly repeating pattern
- Actual size for backdrops, and scenically painted wall surfaces

Images as textures should be kept to a moderate size, and, as a very general rule, should be no larger than a 1Mb file, unless your output dictates a larger size. Create your image files with output in mind. Consider the resolution of the output device, and the size of the final printed or displayed image.

Creating/Modifying Textures

Open both the **Default_Textures.vwx** file, and your **Textures-Lysistrata.vwx** file with the *Lysistrata* file active. Select the **Default_Textures** file from the Resource Browser and **Import**;
- Carpet Dk Red
- Metal Aluminum Brushed Blue
- Metal Gold Polished

Close the **Default_Textures.vwx** file, and **Duplicate**, the **Metal Gold Polished** texture as **Metal Gold Polished modified**, then **Edit** the **Metal Gold Polished modified** texture. Let's look at what we can do here. Textures are defined in Renderworks by adjusting a series of definitions called **Shaders**.

Color is Key.

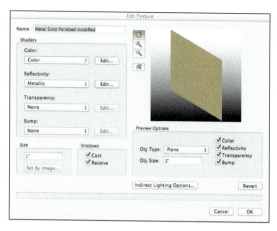

Shaders

Before editing this texture, review the options available. These will not all get used here. **Metal Gold Polished modified** is a pretty simple texture, but it is a pretty good place to start, and we will build up to more complex textures. The more complex the texture, the better the look of the design, but additional rendering time will be required.

The textures we will be creating have all been pre-tested; a lot of time and experimentation has gone into these definitions, or recipes. As always, experiment with your own ideas, and try options not chosen here to see the differences.

The Color Shader

The Color Shader defines the surface color of a texture, which can be a plain, uniform color, an image, or a complex pattern, like wood or stone.

Object Attribute

Object Attribute assigns the object's fill color attribute to apply as a color texture. By creating a texture with the Object Attribute as the color shader, you can assign the rest of the texture shaders to different objects, each with different colors assigned.

Image

The Image option allows importing and sizing of image files. The **Carpet Dk Red** texture is a seamlessly tiling image-based texture. That is going to be used later as the carpet in the auditorium. We will not edit the texture, but you should review how it was created. That image, or any image used in a texture, can be **Extracted** for modifications in an image editor by right-clicking on the Resource in the Resource Browser.

Images used to create Image-based Textures can also be used as **Fills** for 2D forms.

Color

Basic, simple color is defined through the available Libraries or the system color picker. This Shader also allows for the brightness of the color to be modified. The color shader dialog allows access to the stock color libraries shipped with Vectorworks, including:
- Pantone Color Libraries
- Commercial Paint Color Libraries
- Rosco Scenic and TV Paint Color Libraries
- The Lighting Color Libraries can also be made into color textures.

These libraries allow for the realistic rendering of color under given lighting conditions.

The Metal Polished Gold texture is a simple Color Shader. Click on **Edit**, then on the color drop-down, and finally on the **Color Picker** button.

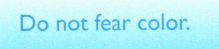

Do not fear color.

Make the RGB values 255, 219, 99 and click **OK.**

You can also access and manage the color libraries here that is adding to the defaults seen at the bottom of the dialog.

Fresnel

Fresnel creates a simple texture that has an overall gradient-like appearance. This can be very useful for glass or Plexiglas. That look can become frosted when combined with a bump map.

Bricks

The Bricks option can create a basic brick pattern based on sizes of the brick and the masonry of the texturesize as defined in the lower-left of the **Create Texture** dialog. Color and size/proportional variants refine and modify the texture.

There is a corresponding **Brick Bump Shader** that creates a matching 3D effect from the texture when rendered with light applied.

Noise

The Noise shader allows access to a huge array of options for creating different painting or natural stone, marble, or granite looks. Don't be constricted by 100% when experimenting with the Noise options.

Pavement

The Pavement Shader creates colored stone patterns and textures. The settings defined in the shader options create realistic and yet random repeats. There is a **Pavement Bump Shader**.

Tiles

The Tiles shader can create many different geometric patterns. The settings in the **Options** allow for a regular or random pattern. There is a corresponding **Tiles Bump Shader**.

The Reflectivity Shader

The Reflectivity Shader defines the amount of light reflected by a surface. Reflectivity is dependent on surface texture properties and light sources.

Note: Increasing the **Blur** of the Reflectivity Shaders increases realism, but it also increases render times. The Blur effect can be used with efficiency, but requires some experimentation. Consider adding Blur as a final touch, late in the design process.

None

Selecting the None option creates a matte surface like a flat paint finish.

Image

Image reflectivity allows a designer to import an image file, that will be then reflected onto objects with this texture assigned. In general, objects with Reflectivity reflect other objects in the model or 3D World.

Back-lit

Back-lit reflectivity will help to properly render things like lamp shades, advertising images, or some cycs. Deselect **Cast Shadows** in the Edit Texture dialog box when using the back-lit shader. When we import **Spotlight Lighting Devices** into a document, the **Default Instrument Texture** will be imported, and that texture has Cast Shadows turned off. Checking **Cast Shadows** on a texture that will

Never be constricted by limiting yourself to 100%. You can have more!

surround a Vectorworks Light Object keeps the light inside the object.

Glass

Glass reflectivity would be appropriate for rendering windows, and adjusting the color options of the shader further defines environmental reflections. The Edge and Center color options allow designers to tint the Glass. These options can be tailored to the other textures used in the same environment or to enhance specific lighting effects.

It is important to remember that everything in the 3D world is not the same as it is in the real-world. Textures and reflectivity can be used to create real-world looks in the 3D world.

Glow

Glow reflectivity creates objects that do not have shadows cast across themselves, similar to a **Back-lit** object that does not require additional Vectorworks Light Objects. A texture with Glow can also emit light, when the **Emit** option is selected. Glow shaders can be an alternative to using Vectorworks Light Objects. When creating an **Image Prop**, the **Choose Constant Reflectivity** option gives the texture a Glow Shader and prevents an object from casting shadows onto itself.

Metallic

Metallic reflectivity options can be used to create realistic metal textures that reflect the colors in the surrounding environment.

The Metallic Shader has three options:
- Metallic
- Brushed
- Turned

Each option creates a different metal look;

changing the color of the Metallic shader changes the reflection.

Edit the Metallic Shader of the **Metal Gold Polished modified** texture, changing the Reflective Color to 255, 231, 152.

Click OK to exit the Texture Definition now that the look has been warmed up and lightened slightly. For this project we will stay away from Earth tones.

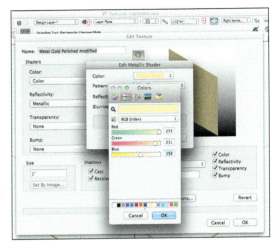

Once you have made this modification, experiment with your cube and other choices with the Metallic finish. Try a pink and then a blue as the Reflective color to see how that changes the finish.

The Metallic Shader can create a cool, and realistic metallic automotive finish.

The image above for a fashion film shoot was created using Procedural Textures in Renderworks. The layers of drapery, created using the Soft Goods Tool, have transparent, slightly metallic textures. The Candelabra lamps have a glow texture, and the chandelier is a Glass Texture. The Figure is a partially transparent 3D Polygon with a black fill and an Obj Attribute Texture. The wall surface is a simple paint Color Texture, and the applied, upholstered panels are a Color texture with a Plastic Reflectivity.

Mirror

Mirror reflectivity can create fully reflective surfaces, like mirrors, or be used at low settings to add a sheen to surfaces. Setting the Reflection to 100% creates a mirror. Using Mirror at lesser percentages adds a sheen to the surface. A lower percentage factor of around 20% creates a shiny surface, like a really glossy paint treatment. As always, experiment, but a more complicated model will be useful to see the variations.

Plastic

Plastic reflectivity offers a subtler set of options than None, Metallic, or Mirror for creating glossy materials like plastic, gloss paint, varnished surfaces, leather, or vinyl. The Roughness attribute, in particular, adds a degree of realism

and control not offered elsewhere. As always, experiment with, and review the options.

Bricks, Noise, Pavement, and Tile

These options work logically with their respective Color Shaders, and possibly, with their coordinating Bumps Shaders. Additionally, these Reflectivity Shaders can be used as an effect on an Image, Color, or Fresnel Color Shader.

However, using a Bricks Color Shader and a Pavement Reflectivity with a Tile Bump might create something quite ugly and a challenge to create in the real-world. This would not be characterized as a definitive statement. There remain, few rules.

The Transparency Shader

The Transparency Shader, as you have likely guessed, defines surface transparency/opacity.

Image Mask

The Image Mask uses either an imported image, or the alpha channel of an image as a pattern or mask. In this case, the mask might work just as a mask, or as a channel works in an image editor, or as traditional masking works in airbrush or scenic painting. Masks created in an image editor can further allow for degrees of transparency. In an image editor, the black area of a mask will be masked, and the white area will be visible; adding in the alpha channel areas of gray or a black to white gradient will produce a partially transparent image in Vectorworks. When rendering the fire in a fireplace, the fire and logs would want to be masked out of the background. However, fire is translucent while logs are not, so if the logs are white in the alpha channel, while the fire is gray, Renderworks will render the final image to show the background of the fireplace slightly visible through the flames.

Image Masks can also be used to create lattice work, or filigree patterns without complex modeling. In this case, the more complex texture will save rendering time, and keep file sizes more reasonable.

This rendering of a small stage for an event uses Image Props for the large-scale Lava Lamps, chrome and black mirror Textures for the stage, and the stage facing is a perforated metal using an image-based transparency map. The figures are a partially transparent Obj Attribute texture with a white fill. The background has 10% fog, and there are gobo textures in some of the Spotlight Lighting Devices.

Image

Image-based transparency masks use an imported image to create transparency. Spotlight Gobo textures, colored or black and white, use Image-based transparency.

Gobo Textures must be square images. To import an image to use as a custom gobo, go to **Spotlight>Visualization>Create Gobo Texture.** That process of creation is very similar to what will follow here.

Color

A Color mask allows the ability to isolate a color from an image-based shader to drop out of the texture. This creates its own mask if an image is against a solid color background.

Glass

The Glass Shader option creates transparency that properly illustrates how glass interacts with the world around. Generally, for clear glass, set the color to white, a pale blue, or light green, and the Index of Refraction to varying degrees, depending on the surface you are modeling:
- 1.1 for architectural glass
- 1.5 for glass like a bottle
- 1.33 for water

Since there are few rules, black can also make an interesting glass.

In order for light rays to bend correctly, Glass requires two surfaces; glass objects should be a 3D Object, not a simple 3D Polygon. Without a second surface, the light will bend as if it is going into glass, but not bend back.

Water in a Fountain provides an exception to the rule; a single 3D polygon bends light going from air to water, and then stays in water until it comes back out at the pool surface.

A 3D Polygon can be created using Tools in the 3D Modeling Tool Set, or from a 2D Polygon (select the Polygon and go to **Modify>Convert>Convert to 3D Polys**. As you will recall from basic geometry, a 3D polygon exists in space and has no depth.

Plain

Plain Transparency is a simple slider and data field that specify different degrees of uniform transparency.

Rectangular Mask

The Rectangular Mask is used to create a **Decal**, and uses the texturesize as a rectangular, transparent mask and is often combined with another shader for a specific effect.

A **Decal** is a special type of texture, created using the **Render Tab** of the **OIP**. A **Decal** can be overlaid on other textures. One example of where to use a **Decal** would be to place graffiti on a brick wall: the Decal will conform to the shape of the Wall and the Bump texture.

Positioning of Decals on objects can be finessed using the **Attribute Mapping Tool**.

Bricks, Noise, Pavement, and Tiles

Bricks, Noise, Pavement, and Tile transparency options combined with the Color and/or bump Shaders of the same type overlay a transparency effect onto a color shader. Of course, these transparency shaders do not have to be used with the corresponding color and bump shaders.

Brick or Tile might be used to simulate a material like glass block or a vacu-form product made with translucent plastic.

The Bump Shader

Bump maps define surface irregularities and bring dimension to objects without the complexity of additional modeling. This is an instance where vector data would create a larger file than a raster adjustment. Proper use of Bump maps will produce files that render faster than fully modeled images.

Each Bump Shader options offers the ability to use a simple Bump or a specified amount of Displacement Mapping. Again, this is something to look at and experiment with as you learn the application. A grass texture used as a bump map with displacement, can yield an effective shag carpeting. Or an unruly lawn, but shag carpeting is more fun.

Bump Maps affect the look of an object, while **Displacement Maps** actually affect the geometry of the object, increasing rendering times.

A Bump and/or Displacement Map is essentially a black and white image. The dark areas recede when rendered and the white areas move forward. The whites are the bumps. Shades of gray add subtlety.

Image

An image-based bump map uses an imported image to be used as the source of the bump and displacement. The image can be either a full-size image or a seamlessly tiling gray-scale of a black and white image.

Bricks, Noise, Pavement, and Tiles

These options can work with their coordinated Color Shaders, or be layered onto a Color Shader for effect.

The Brick bump, used with the Brick Color, can create a specific, and very realistic 3D brick, without modeling each and every brick and the

This render uses a number of bump maps, both Procedural and Image-based. The Bamboo are Image Props with masks. There are gobo textures in some of the Spotlight Lighting Devices.

mortar. A **Noise** bump added to a plain color or a flat image can create stucco.

The Noise Shader can also be used to render curtains, upholstery, or carpet.

Overall Texture Options

In the Create Texture dialog there are several overall options that are not Shaders, as follows.

Size

The size field in the lower-left defines the size of your texture. If creating bricks, the bricks will need a real-world size. In the case of the **Metal Gold Polished modified** texture, that size is quite small, and it tiles. Creating a painted or printed backdrop means that texture will need a real-world size.

Shadows

These Check boxes determine how Objects with a texture assigned will deal with Shadows. As stated, Back-lit textures, and textures on objects that have an imbedded Vectorworks Light Object cannot have **Cast Shadows** turned on; this function inhibits the light from getting out of the object.

If you do not want light or shadows to affect the appearance of an object, like a back-lit translucent image, turn off the **Receive** option.

Indirect Lighting

The Indirect Lighting Options button in the lower-right allows you to over-ride document choices made with the **View>Lighting>Lighting Options** Command. The more indirect lighting used, the more realistic the render, and the longer the render time. Since we're assuming both a controlled environment and a desire to complete our work in a timely manner, we will not be using Indirect Lighting, but, as always, you are encouraged to experiment with simple models.

Preview Options

These are pretty straightforward. Choosing the type of object onto which the texture is displayed helps to visualize the final results. The size of the Preview Object should relate to the size/scale of the texture.

When making adjustments to the various Shaders, it often helps to see just that Shader or a select few, rather than the finished product. Use the check boxes to adjust visibility. Of course, always go back and review everything, before clicking **OK.**

Seamless Textures

Seamless textures are repeating, or tiling, textures that show little, or no, visible pattern. However, not all images repeat equally. For some patterns this can be worked out in the geometry; for others, like marble or granite, the image must be modified.

Create a new Vectorworks document and set the Design Layer scale to 1/2" or 1:25. And go to the Right Isometric View. Click on the 0-0 point to reveal the XYZ handles.

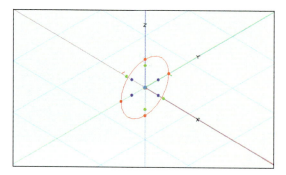

Grab the top red handle and rotate forward 90° so that you have changed the Working Plane from the Top to the Front view. If needed, press the shift key while moving to constrain the angle.

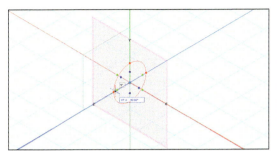

Select the Rectangle tool; make sure that the Corner to Corner Mode and the Push/Pull Mode are both active. Then double-click on the tool to place 4' by 8' or 1m by 3m rectangle, and Push/Pull to a thickness of 1' or 350mm. These are not exact conversions; approximate sizes will work for this purpose.

Press the Alt/Option key to click and drag a Duplicate. While dragging, press the shift key to constrain the plane of the new objects. You must press the Alt/Option key alone first, or Vectorworks will think you want to select multiple items. Pressing the shift key allows you select more than one object.

Repeat to have three slabs.

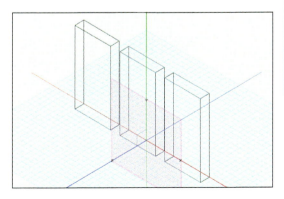

Create a new Renderworks Texture in the document. Accept the default name, from the Website content, import the file Gold.jpg to use as the Color Shader. Set the size of the Texture to 36" or 1m, and the size of the Preview to 72" or 2m. Notice Immediately that you can see the hard edges where the texture repeats in the Preview.

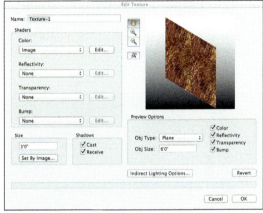

Apply this Texture to the left-hand slab, and render using Final Quality Renderworks. Again, notice the hard edges; zoom in if that helps.

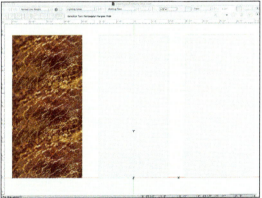

Open Gold.jpg in Photoshop, or another image editing application. What follows is based on a workflow using Photoshop. The process may vary in other applications.

Save the file as Gold.psd. Go to **Image>Image Size** and change the size and proportion of the image to 3500 pixels by 3500 pixels. You have to unlink the Width and Height dimensions or Photoshop will not want to change the proportions. You may also have to change the units using the drop-down menu.

Now go to **Filter>Other>Offset** and offset the image 1750 pixels in each direction. This does not have to be an equal number. From time to time, different proportions will work better. Click **OK.**

Now that doesn't really look too good at all, but while there are now hard lines crossing in the middle of the image area, the corners are set up to tile seamlessly. Use this image to create Texture-2 in Vectorworks using the same specifications as earlier, and map to the middle slab. The repeats are more frequent and more obvious.

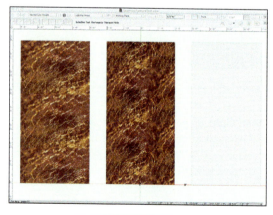

In Photoshop use the **Clone Stamp tool** to work those seams into the surrounding areas. The Clone Stamp picks up bits of an image from one area, and stamps them onto another. In order to begin you must Alt/Option-click to select the source.

In the upper-left of the Photoshop window you can adjust the size and the relative softness/hardness of any active Photoshop brush. If you are not proficient, or used to working with Photoshop, experiment with these settings. The harder a brush setting, the more obvious the edge of the brush will appear. A softer edge blends better, but too soft will produce a blurry area.

Set the size of the brush to a medium relationship to the size of the artwork. In this case, 300-500 pixels is probably a good place to begin.

Save the file as Gold1.psd and create a texture using the file. Apply that texture to the third slab and render to see how seamlessly it is tiling. Use the rendered view to plan your next steps in Photoshop.

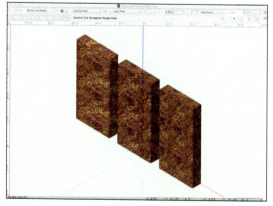

As you update the file in Photoshop, you will have to edit the texture in order for the texture to update. Right-click to **Edit** the texture, Choose **Edit** next to the **Color Shader,** and then **Change Image,** even if you are simply re-importing the same file, saved after it has been modified.

Repeat as necessary, until you have a clean, seamless tile.

Finally, save the file as Gold2.psd. Change the image size to 36" (914.4mm) wide by 24: (609.6mm) tall and 25 DPI. The proper conversion does matter now. This file will be used again.

Creating Textures

The Lysistrata Project will require a considerable number of textures, some very simple, some fairly complex. The process will provide a detailed overview of the Shaders and how they work.

The sub-heads below name the textures.

Black-Gloss

We'll start with a simple Procedural Texture. Go to the Resource Browser and right-click to create a **New** Renderworks Texture.

Choose Black as the **Color,** accepting the other defaults. Choose **Plastic** as the **Reflectivity,** and **Edit** the **Reflectivity** to add **35% Reflection,** and click **OK** to exit the dialogs.

Black-Matte

Duplicate and **Edit** the Black-Gloss texture. Change the Reflectivity to None. Done.

Black-Velour

Duplicate and edit the Black-Matte texture. In the Color Shader, set the **Brightness** to 50%. and add a **Noise** Bump with the **Noise** type selected from the drop-down menu visible after choosing to **Edit** the Shader. Change the **Heights** to 25 and 100. Change **Global Scale** to 5%. Change the **Dimensionality** to **3D Solid** and the **Detail** to 4. Click **OK.** This will make a very dark black velour, the Bump may barely be seen due to the Brightness level.

Use the names of the textures as listed. The sizes in the text are specific.

Acropolis Block

Create a **New** texture, set the size of the texture to 24" (609.6mm), and the size of the **Preview** to 8'-0" (2,438.4mm). Select **Bricks** as the **Color Shader** and press **Edit**. The following dialog has four panes. Accept the Default in the **Color Pane.**

In the **Bricks Pane,** change the colors to RGB 237, 98, 255, and RGB 255, 231, 152. **Choose** the image Sparkle2.jpg from the Texture Images folder and set the **Image Blend** to 70%.

Leave the other settings as they are in the Pane.

In the **Gaps Pane,** change the colors to RGB 92, 179, 150, and RGB 175, 217, 188, and **Choose Image** Turquoise.jpg from the Texture Images folder. Set the **Image Blend** to 25%, the **Size** to 1/2" (12.7mm), and the **Noise** to 25%.

As an aside, the image Sparkle2 is the same image as Sparkle, but has been modified using the **Image>Adjustments>Hue/Saturation** command in Photoshop. Sparkle is also included in the Texture Images folder for your reference.

The **Alt Bricks Pane** allows for the creation of various patterns in the coursing of the brick work. We will not modify this pane. Keep **Reflectivity** and **Transparency** set to **None**. Choose the **Brick Bump Shader** and press **Edit**.

In the **Bumps Pane**, set the **Scale** to 100%, the **Strength** to 150%, the **Displacement Mapping Height** to 1/4" (6.35mm) with Medium Detail. Check **Self Shadowing.**

In the **Bricks Pane**, set the **Brick Heights** to 77% and 83%. Use **Choose Image** to select the Sparkle2 image and set the **Image Blend** to 70%. Accept the other defaults.

Bumps add depth.

In the Gaps Pane, set the Gap Heights to 1 and 100%. Use Choose Image to add the Turquoise Image, and set the Image Blend to 50%. Set the Size to 1/4" (6.35mm) and add 25% Noise.

Click **OK** to exit the dialogs.

China Silk Hot Pink Austrian

Hot Pink China Silk is a commercially available product. The **Color** RGB 240, 77, 152 is an RGB equivalent of a matching Pantone (CMYK color matching system) color.

Set the **Metallic Shader** to the same color with the **Metallic Pattern** and 20% **Reflection**. Although the fabric is translucent, especially when back-lit, we will assume this drape is lined and has no **Transparency**.

The **Bump,** however, is key. Set the **Bump** to **Image** and import the Austrian2.psd file from the Texture Images folder and set the Bump Strength to 1000%. That's not a typo, one thousand percent.

No **Displacement Mapping.**

In the **Edit Texture** window set the **Size** to 10'-0" (3,048mm) and the **Obj Size** to 20'-0" (6,096mm).

Glass Blue

Set the Color Shader to RGB 2, 170, 234. Choose the Glass Reflectivity Shader and set the Edge Color to White, and the Center Color to RGB 0, 111, 186. Use Glass Transparency with 85% Transmission, a 1.5 Index of Refraction and accept the other defaults.

Voila.

Glitz-Gold

Set the **Size** to 3'-0" (914.4mm) and the **Obj Size** to 6'-0" (1,828.8mm). Go to the **Image Color Shade**r and import the Sparkle.jpg file from the Texture Images folder.

Add a **Mirror Reflectivity** set to 50%.

Gold-Rough

Set the **Size** to 8'-0" (2,438.4mm) and the **Obj Size** to 16'-0" (4,876.8mm). Go to the **Image Color Shade**r and import the Gold2.psd file from the Texture Images folder.

Add **Mirror Reflectivity** set to 25%, and change the default **Color** to RGB 255, 191, 0.

Add a **Noise Bump**. With the **Pezo Pattern**, Set the **Strength** to 20%. Change the **Global**

Scale to 4%, use the **Dimensionality** drop-down to assign **3D Wrapped,** and change the **Detail** to 5.

Edit Noise Shader

Pattern: Pezo

Bumps

Strength (%): 20
Heights (%): 0 | 100

Scale

Global (%): 4
Relative (%) U: 100 | V: 100 | W: 100

Options

Dimensionality: 3D Solid
Detail: 5
Cycles: 0
Low Clip (%): 0
High Clip (%): 100

Displacement Mapping

Height: 0"
Detail: Medium
☐ Self-Shadowing

Cancel | OK

Gold-Key Pattern

Begin by **Duplicating** Gold Rough, name the duplicate as above, and **Edit.** Keep the settings the same, except for the **Bump**. Change the **Bump** to **Image**, and select the file Key Bump. psd. Set the **Bump Strength** to 500% with 1" (254mm) of **Displacement**, with **Medium Detail,** and check **Self Shadowing.**

Leopard

Use the file Leopard.psd as the **Color Shader.** This file is an edited version of Leopard-Old.psd; the color and shape have been changed. Set the **Size** to 2'-0" (609.6mm) and the **Obj Size** to 4'-0" (1,219.2mm).

Leave **Reflectivity** and **Transparency** set to **None**.

Use the same image as the **Bump Map,** set to 150%.

Lysistrata Floor

This Texture uses a **Tiles** Color Shader with no **Bump**, and no **Transparency**. The **Size** should be 4'-0" (1,219.2mm).

The **Grout** color defaults to black and can be left that way, as can the default **Tile Color 3.** **Tile Color 1** should be set to RGB 255, 111, 207, and the **Tile Color 2** is RGB 255, 207, 116. Set the **Grout Width** to 0% and uncheck **Bevel Width**.

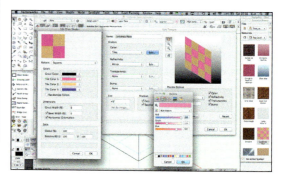

Choose the **Mirror** Shader and set the **Color** to RGB 254, 206, 143 with 62.35% **Reflection**.

Metal Gold Polished Modified

This texture was created/modified earlier in the chapter.

Neon Blue

Another simple Procedural; choose RGB 2, 170, 234 for the **Color**, and **Glow** at 125% with **Emit Light** checked for the **Reflectivity**.

Sparkle

Readers will be shocked to learn that this texture uses the image Sparkle2 as the **Color Shader**. Set the **Size** to 6'-0" (1,828.8mm) and the **Obj Size** to 12'-0" (3,657.6mm).

Add 25% **Mirror Reflectivity.**

Topiary

Set the **Size** to 4'-0" (1,219mm) and **Obj Size** to 8'-0" (2,438.4mm). Use the file grass.psd (a color modified version of grass02.jpg) as the **Color Shader**.

Use the same image for the **Bump** set to 250% with 1" (254mm) of **Displacement, Medium Detail,** and **Self Shadowing**.

Wallpaper

Obviously, this uses the Wallpaper2.psd as the **Image Color Shader** set to a Size of 3'-0" (914.4mm). **Transparency**, **Reflectivity**, and **Bump** are set to None.

Keep textures you will use frequently in your defaults, or stationery files.

Whites

Like the black textures, having some white color textures handy is always useful. In the Textures-Lysistrata.vwx file provided there are a matte, gloss, and Glow white. Set up the same variations for your own use.

Consider the blacks and whites for your own default textures. If you work in film or television, you should have chroma key blue and green always available; also your favorite fabrics: velours, silks, brocades. Certainly much of what is here is project specific, but the glass, and metals should have future use. Why reinvent the wheel?

Zebra

The Zebra.jpg file is there for use as the 12" (304.8mm) Color Shader. This one is very simple. Always get the hardest work out of the way first. Hopefully we eased in and eased out.

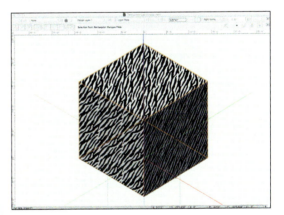

Review

As always, experiment with these settings and texture definitions. These are designed to create the cover image, but you may want to make the designs your own. Duplicate the texture resources before experimenting so you save these resources.

There are options not discussed here. Try adding a color over an image Color Shader to see what that does. Use the **Set by Image** button to size some textures.

Favorite your **Textures-Lysistrata.vwx** file in the Resource Browser. If you do this before closing the file, you save steps, and clicks. With the file saved, click on the Disclosure Arrow in the top right of the Resource Browser and choose **Add Current to Favorites**.

The textures created will be Referenced into other files. The objects created in the new files will then be Referenced by other files. If you decide to modify these textures, and you should make this work your own, you will have to check that each file updates the Reference. Most of that process should be automatic, but check the work.

Vectorworks provides a large number of predefined textures. As always, you'll find them, if you haven't already, in the Libraries. If you have not explored the available content, now is a good time for that review.

Mapping

Texture Mapping happens in the OIP Render Tab.

Sphere, Cylinder, Plane, Perimeter, or Roof mapping types are used to control how a texture is projected onto different types of objects. There should be a large object in your Textures-Lysistrata.vwx file. Apply a texture to that object.

On the previous page there is an image of a cube with the Zebra texture applied. In that rendering, the **Auto Apply Plane Map Type** is used. Create the same view and look at the different options with various textures.

Each **Map Type** creates a different appearance. That appearance may vary with how the object

was originally modeled and from what plane the object was modeled.

Here is the same object with **Plane Mapping**. Not so good.

In the Render Tab of the OIP there are options to change the scale, placement, angle, and repeat of the assigned texture. It is also possible to change the texture on some surfaces, by selecting the **Part** from the drop-down, and changing the Texture from the **Texture** drop-down.

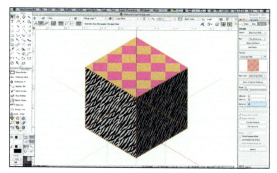

The **Attribute Mapping Tool** allows specific placement of textures on Objects. The Tool will not modify Perimeter or auto-aligned Plane Map Types. Choose the Attribute Mapping Tool from either the Basic Tool set, or the Visualization Tool Set.

You may modify either the Overall Texture, or the Top Texture from the **Part** drop-down in the Tool Bar. Once that choice is decided, the tool allows you to interactively scale, rotate, and place the texture, while viewing the texture in **Non-Repeating Mode,** or **Original Repeat Mode**.

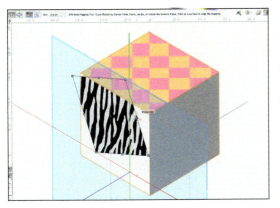

Decals

Decals allow you to apply multiple textures, possibly layered on a single object. Decals are created in the same manner as Textures with a Transparency Mask. Adding a decal allows you to either create a new decal or to use one that you have created residing as a Texture in the Resource Browser. Decals are great for adding graffiti to a wall, a logo to a set, or a corporate logo on a floor. In the case illustrated here, a Decal allows placement of a sign on a curve without a lot of modeling work.

Decals are imported via the OIP Render tab, using the **Add Decal button**. The import process is as familiar as creating a texture. Decals will initially appear in the lower-left corner of the object onto which they are applied

Once created and applied, the **Decal** can be manipulated and placed with the **Attribute Mapping Tool**. Decals or textures can be positioned with absolute positioning on 3D surfaces using either the OIP or the Attribute Mapping Tool.

So, a quick experiment. Use the Sparkle texture with the Sphere Map Type.

With **Overall** selected from the drop-down, press the **Add Decal** button and choose the Gold-Key Pattern Bump image. Name the texture and set a size, which can be changed.

Choose **Image Mask,** then **This Decal's Color**, and then **Transparent Color,** where the **Eyedropper** can be used to choose the white area, adjust the mask as needed.

Edit the **Decal Texture Color Shader** so that the Decal **Repeat Horizontal** is checked.

Manipulate the Decal using both the OIP and the Attributes Mapping tool to see how it appears and can be adjusted.

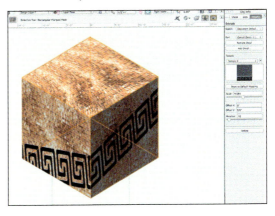

Textures are infinitely versatile and make your designs unique.

Rotary International Convention
Rendering by Peter Neufeld of Limelight Lighting Design Pty Ltd

Rotary International Convention

Rotary International Convention
Production Photo

Rotary International Convention
Copenhagen, Denmark, June 2006

Producer & Creative Director: Paul Haines of Inspiring Events International.
Production Designer, Management, and Lighting Designer: Peter Neufeld of Limelight Lighting Design Pty Ltd

A major international event celebrating the great work of Rotary International with 7,000 delegates attending from 170 countries. There were nine performances of five separate shows in four days.

9. Drawing and Modeling

This is a general overview of the many design tools available in Vectorworks. You'll need multiple documents, or certainly multiple design layers, to experiment and practice the techniques that follow. It's up to you how you want, or need to organize, and archive your work.

Draw along with the text, venture off on different paths, make things. Whether in 2D or 3D the only way to learn the tools is to work the tools.

It is possible to create many objects from simple 2D lines, curves, and arcs by using **Smart Points** to **Snap to Edges**, then the **Edit>Select Connected Objects** command followed by the **Modify>Compose** command. That is not always the best core of action in the age of CnC Routers and 3D Printers. If a corner isn't closed, the resulting geometry can wreak havoc with those types of devices.

Corners can be **Closed** in the OIP after creation, however that check box will add sides, rather than repair less than accurate drawing.

There are 2D and 3D **Locus Tools**. Loci are non-printing points in space that can be used for **Snapping**, or aligning objects. Double-clicking either tool will allow absolute positioning of these guides. Locus Objects can be moved in the OIP, or placed/snapped to exiting geometry.

A **Locus Point Object** can be used to indicate a *Datum*: a reference point in space, like the intersection of the Centerline and Plaster Line on stage. Vectorworks also refers to temporary snapping points as Datum.

Work the tools to learn the tools.

As you work, you may need to move around to look at objects, particularly 3D objects, from angles other than the Standard Views. Select the **Flyover Tool** from the Basic Tool set and look at the object in different views. You will see the following options:
- Interactive Origin Mode
- Object Center Mode
- Active Layer Plane Origin Mode
- Working Plane Origin Mode

For now, select **Object Center Mode.** Then click and drag to rotate the view.

Generally speaking, work in the Layer Plane.

Drawing Basics

Select the **Rectangle Tool** to review the options in the **Tool Bar**. Each Mode or option available in the Tool Bar offers a different means of drawing. By hovering over the mode icons, you will see descriptive text appearing for each mode. Text in the Tool Bar also describes the active option. With the Rectangle Tool as an example, the **Push/Pull** option is added when drawing in a view other than Top/Plan.

Typically when freehand drawing, objects can be constrained when you press a key(s). For example, you can constrain a rectangle to a square by pressing the shift key. You can constrain a rectangle to the Golden Ratio by pressing the Shift and Command/Control keys simultaneously while dragging. With the shift key pressed, an oval can be constrained to a circle.

These options will vary with the tool selected. As you explore the application, try every mode available in each case.

Begin to draw by clicking and dragging with the **Rectangle Tool**. As soon as you begin to draw, you will see the appearance of the **Floating Data Bar (FDB)**. Press the **tab key** to select the first field in the FDB and enter a specific dimension. Tab into the next field, repeat, and click with the mouse to create a specifically sized shape. Try each of the different drawing modes, they each have their place in your workflow.

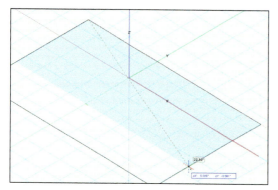

Switch to the **Circle Tool** and try the **Circle by Three Points Mode**. This function also exists for the **Arc Tool** and the **Curved Wall Tool**

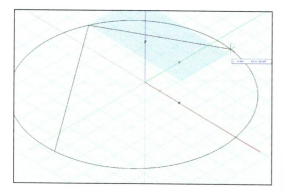

Work your way through the other Drawing Tools in the Basic Tool Set:
- Rounded Rectangle
- Polyline
- Polygon
- Triangle (located under the 2D Polygon Tool,

click and hold the 2D Polygon Tool for the Triangle Tool to fly out)
- Regular Polygon
- Freehand

After drawing with the **Freehand Tool,** select a Freehand object and go to **Modify>Poly Smoothing** and try the various options. Undo between operations.

Similarly, go to the 3D Modeling Tool Set and try those basic tools:
- NURBS Curve
- 3D Polygon
- Sphere
- Hemisphere
- Cone

The Selection Tool

Draw a few objects, and note the highlight color when you hover over a shape and the change in color when you select a shape, these colors can be changed in the **Vectorworks Preferences Interactive Pane**. You can select multiple objects by pressing and holding the shift key or using a **Marquee Selection** (click and drag with the 2D Selection tool). To Marquee select, simply drag around the entire object. You can also Marquee select by pressing the Alt/Option key and selecting any object you partially touch. In addition to the Marquee select, the Selection Tool also has **Lasso** options.

Option-Select
Marquee-Select
Shift-Select
To choose multiple objects.

The **Selection Tool** has a number of modes that should default to the **Single Object Interactive Scaling Mode**, which allows clicking and dragging to change the size of an object. You can turn this off, or scale multiple objects.

Select an existing rectangle and you will be able move it or resize it interactively with the mouse. You can also change its size and location in the **OIP**.

Select the **Rectangle Tool** and hover the cursor near another rectangle. Note the **SmartCursor** hints and the alignments that are indicated. Align with a corner, indicated by the red extension line, and hit the **T** key, if required, to lock in that alignment.

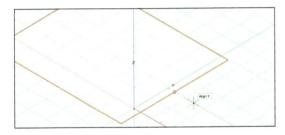

Try this again. When hovering near a snap point, hit the **Z** key to enable the **Snap Loupe**, which allows you to zoom in close until you click the mouse. You can also use the **Snap Loupe** when you want to finish drawing a shape, if aligning to another **Smart Point**.

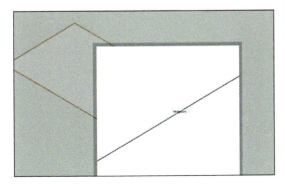

Make use of the different Drawing Modes.

Polygon and Polyline

These tools are for freehand drawing and for intelligent tracing using the **SmartCursor**. The **Polygon** has only straight lines, but the **Polyline** tool allows you to introduce curves. Consider tracing a scanned drawing or placing locus points. You can also use the 2D Line tools and Absolute Positioning to create a set of guides, connecting the dots with the **Polygon** tool.

The **Polyline Tool** (and others) has a **Preferences** option in the **Tool Bar** and six different modes for drawing, including precise arcs and curves. Switch modes in the midst of drawing by reaching into the Mode Bar or pressing the **U** key. This key stroke generally works with similar tools, like the **Soft Goods Tool**.

Polylines are often used in modeling the bodies of **Spotlight Lighting Devices**.

Modifying Objects

Once you have an object or objects, they may not be everything you're after. They can be modified and/or edited.

Reshaping

The **Reshape Tool** is for the editing of 2D and 3D polygons. This tool also focuses **Vectorworks Light Objects** and, in some cases, **Spotlight Lighting Devices**.

The Reshape tool has several modes and options. Reshaping allows users to move points, add points (centered between existing points), delete points, or convert points from corners to curves and vice versa.

Let's assume that you have not been able to make the shape that you want. Draw a rectangle.

Select the **Reshape Tool** from the **Basic Tool Set** and edit. Double-clicking the polygon also selects the Reshape Tool. In some cases, this is not true. If the **Reshape Tool** does not come alive for a **Rectangle**, go to **Modify>Convert>Convert to Polygons**. While you're there make an initial review of the other conversions available. Let's look at the tool options:
• Move points
• Convert points
• Add a point
• Subtract a point
• Hide or show edges

When you select Add or Convert, other options become available. Note also the options for selecting points. This is a very robust tool and is extremely useful for creating sweeping curves.

With the **Reshape Tool** in use, a rectangle (for example) will now show eight points or, more precisely, four points on the corners and four midpoints. Experiment with this tool using a rectangle:
• Select the first option on the left, **Move Polygon Handles** mode. Grab a corner and move it around. Undo.
• Choose the **Delete Vertex** mode, and delete one of the corners so that you have a triangle. Undo.
• Select **Add Vertex**, with the **Corner Vertex** option selected. You can only add and manipulate points at a midpoint. Undo.
• Select the **Change Vertex** mode and then select **Bezier Curve**. Click on a corner and observe the curve. Manipulate this curve with the **Move** mode. Undo
• Convert a corner point to a **Cubic Spine Point**. Manipulate this curve to compare with a **Bezier Curve**. Undo.

Other 2D Objects can be added for alignment and precise snapping.

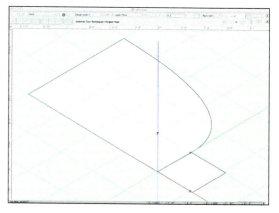

Clip Tool

The **Clip Tool** in the Basic Tool set offers three modes of operation: Exclusion, Inclusion, and Split; then three modes of selection: Rectangle, Polyline, and Circle.

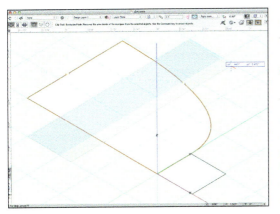

The Exclusion mode subtracts the selection from the original object: the Inclusion mode deletes the area outside of the selection from the object, and the Split mode makes two object from one. The types of selections are pretty obvious.

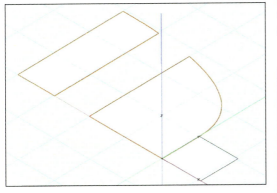

Clip Surface

Like the Clip Tool, **Modify>Clip Surface** is used to subtract one 2D shape from another. Draw one primitive shape over another, larger shape. Select both and go to the command. Only the top object will remain selected. Delete that object, and you will see that piece cut away from the bottom object.

Add Surface

Modify>Add Surface combines two objects into one. Draw two overlapping objects, select

both, and invoke the command. You will be left with one new object.

Combine into Surface

The Combine into Surface command forms a new object from a number of objects. The objects must intersect and form a closed polygon. Depending on objects selected and the location of the mouse click, you can create several different polygons from the same set of objects.

Draw two or more overlapping objects, select them all, and go to **Modify>Combine into Surface**. The cursor changes to a paint bucket. Place the paint bucket inside the area of the polygon you wish to keep and click. A single polygon object is created from the selected objects. The new object uses the current attributes.

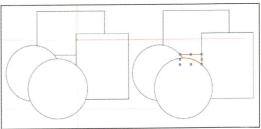

Intersect Surface

Create two overlapping objects and select both. Then, go to **Modify>Intersect Surfaces** and note that the remaining shape is the shape of the area where the two objects once overlapped.

Use the 2D Modifiers to create organic shapes.

Add Solids

Like the **2D Add Surface** command, the **3D Add Solids** command (**Model>Add Solids**) combines two or more overlapping and selected **3D** objects into one larger object.

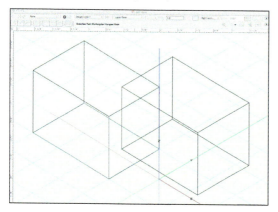

Once joined, the solids, like most other objects can be edited by double-clicking on the combined object.

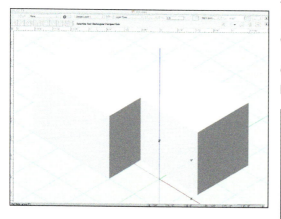

Subtract Solids

Similar to the **2D Clip Surface** command, the **Model>Subtract Solids** command subtracts one or more 3D objects from another. When multiple objects are selected and the command is enacted, a dialog will appear that allows you to choose which object will remain and be modified.

Intersect Solids

Model>Intersect Solids creates an object from the overlapping areas of two other solids.

Section Solids

Model>Section Solids uses an extruded line or 3D Polygon as a sectioning plane to slice another 3D Object in two. One-half of the cut object is left visible. The visible half can be switched in the OIP.

Twist Tool

When you select the **Twist Tool**, your cursor will become a protractor. Select the **Solid Mode**, and click on the top center of a 3D Object. The **Smart Points** will help you find this spot. Drag away and the tool will give you an *arm* to use for the twist. You can precisely place the **arm** in the FDB.

This tool has two modes: Select Solid and Select Face. Begin using the Select Solid, and then experiment.

Click to place and then twist the object. A precise angle can be specified in the FDB.

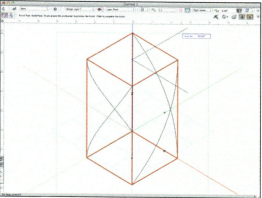

The original geometry has been made much more complex.

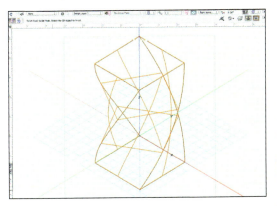

Render, or work, in OpenGL to see the changes more clearly.

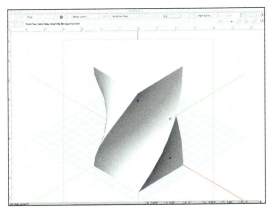

With any of the 3D Modeling tools, pressing the Alt/Option key will allow the selection of a rear or hidden face.

Fillet and Chamfer

There are 2D and 3D versions for these tools. In each case, these tools trim the corner off of a polygon or a 3D Object. A **Chamfer** is a straight line cut while a **Fillet** makes a round corner. Select a tool and trim the edge of a 2D Polygon. First select a mode. The 2D Tools each have the same three modes:

- The first option adds the detail.
- The second trims the lines of the polygon to the detail.
- The third trims the original shape to the new detail and deletes the lines left when using the second mode.

The third, **Trim Mode,** is most often the most useful. Using the 2D tools, **Chamfer** can be an unequal cut, while the **Fillet** is constrained to a radius.

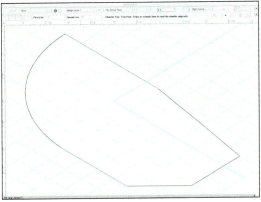

The 3D tools are both constrained to one dimension, however, all edges of an object can be affected. Use the shift key, or the **3D Tool Preferences,** to determine what edges will be modified.

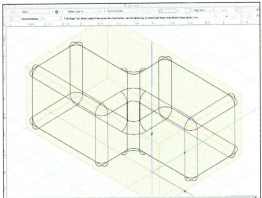

As always, the complex geometry can be seen more clearly when rendered.

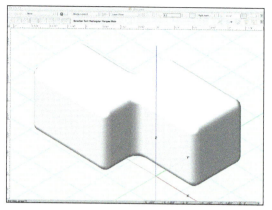

Taper Face Tool

The **Taper Face Tool** from the 3D Modeling Toolset also has two modes: **Tangent Faces** and **Picked Faces**.

Click the top face of a 3D Polygon and then the right-hand side. The top, first click, will stay in place and act as a hinge for the side face. You can then angle the side face in either direction. The tool snaps to other objects, or can be set to a specific angle in the FDB.

Using this tool, you can taper a round tube into a truncated cone, or change the direction of the shaft.

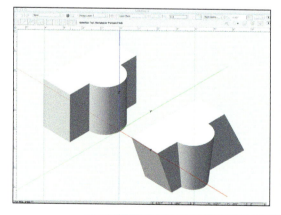

It is possible to select faces from two different objects, 2D or 3D, to move the pivot points.

Extract Tool

The **Extract Tool** duplicates and pulls parts of a 3D object away as a 3D Polygon. The new polygon can be Classed, moved, manipulated, filled, or textured independently from the original.

Extrude a cube, and select the Extract Tool from the 3D Modeling Tool Set. Review and set the options and preferences. Note that when moving around the cube, multiple faces can be extracted. Select a face. Then extract and move the new face away from the cube.

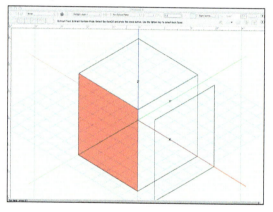

Clip Cube

The **Clip Cube Command** temporarily clips away portions of a complex 3D model to see and work inside that area of the model. Objects inside the cube are visible and snappable in Wireframe or OpenGL. Isolating certain objects makes it easier to locate snap points or to view a specific area of interest.

Select the objects in the area to view, and then **View>Clip Cube**, or the Clip Cube Button in the Tool Bar to isolate those objects. The Clip Cube can be saved as a Saved View.

Modeling

In order to fully utilize the power of computer-aided drafting, there is a need to move 2D objects into the third dimension. Once you have a 3D object, it will often need to be further modified.

There really isn't a linear way to go through each of these processes.

Extrude

Most of your modeling can be most quickly achieved using the **Push/Pull Tool** and the **Floating Data Bar**. However, there are some occasions where the **Extrude** command will be more efficient.

Draw and modify any primitive shape, and with the object selected, go to **Model>Extrude** (Control/Command+E), enter a distance into the **Extrusion** field, and click **OK.**

Create Surface Array

The **Model>Create Surface Array** command duplicates 2D or 3D geometry onto a planar object or a NURBS surface to create free-form surfaces with geometric patterns, or an open framework.

Select a planar object or a NURBS surface to be the base of the **Array Object**, then select 2D or 3D geometry that will be duplicated on the **Surface**, and run the command. Editing the **Surface Array Object** after creation allows the addition, or editing of the array geometry.

Sweep

Model>Sweep creates modeled or sculpted round 3D objects like balusters, finials, martini glasses, and column bases. Begin with a simple 2D primitive form, like a **Polyline** that might be traced. PDF images created as vector files are especially useful for tracing in Vectorworks, as you can snap to points in the PDF or **Ungroup** them to actually use the linework (this might be a place to use **Edit>Select Connected Objects** and the **Compose** command).

Sweep defaults to a .7° **Segment Angle,** which delivers a smooth curve. You can also Sweep to a 60° angle (for example) to create a hexagonal object.

Sweeps revolve around the left-hand side of the Profile. To create a wider Sweep or Object, add a 2D Locus Object and select that as well when using the Command.

One simple profile can create many different objects.

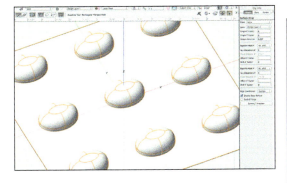

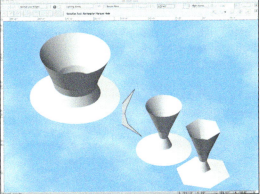

Extrude Along Path

Extrude Along Path can be used to create many objects such as lighting instrument yokes, picture frames, mouldings, or an ornate proscenium arch. Draw a rectangle, and then draw a profile like a solid crown molding, select both, and go to **Model>Extrude Along Path**.

Extrude Along Path extrudes around the center of the profile objects. This small bit of information is important in determining the size of your path. If you want the outer perimeter a certain size, your path needs to subtract the width of your profile.

Working with forms created in different Layer Planes, you can manipulate your extrusions.

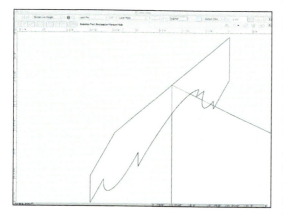

Check the **Fix Profile** box in the **Extrude Along Path** dialog to extrude a form on one Layer Plane perpendicular to a path on another Layer Plane. **Extrude Along Path** extrudes from the top to the right and down, so consider the orientation of your profile.

Double-clicking on an **Extrude Along Path** object offers the choice of editing the **Path** or the **Profile**. If the Profile has not extruded as expected, edit the Profile and manipulate as needed. If the Path is incorrect, it too can be edited, but the path will have been converted to

NURBS and adjusting the size will mean precisely moving the points. It is often easier just to redraw the Path. Keep copies of the 2D geometry until you are well used to using this command.

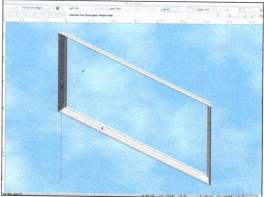

Multiple Extrude

Multiple Extrude creates truncated or tapered objects. Draw a simple 2D primitive and **Offset** a duplicate inside. Select both profiles and go to **Model>Multiple Extrude**. Choose a height, click OK, and use the **Flyover Tool** to study the object. Objects that have been created using the Multiple Extrude command can be edited in the OIP, or by double-clicking/right-clicking on the object. The 2D objects do not have to be centered over one another, but they should be created in a similar fashion. If you drag and draw two circles, and the drag is not parallel, the Multiple Extrude will twist. Try this, it is a mistake to learn to avoid.

Compare **Multiple Extrude** with the type of results that you can achieve using a single primitive and the **Model>Tapered Extrude** command.

A Polygon and a Locus Point can be combined to create a cone or a pyramid using Multiple Extrude.

Chain Extrude

You can create a cornice with **Extrude Along Path**. You can create a cornice with repeating corbels Egg & Dart, or Dental Moulding with the **Chain Extrude Tool** located in the **Building Shell Tool Set**.

Create two simple profiles; one profile to be a continuous object (the back object, or **Modify>Send>Send to Back** Control/Command+B), the other the repeating object. Create the continuous object first. Select the object, and then select the **Chain Extrude** tool, set your preferences for the tool, and draw the line(s) as needed.

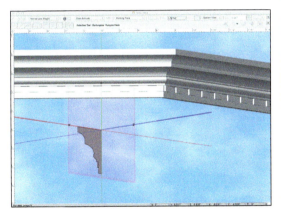

Revolve with Rail Command

This command is challenging until mastered, but very useful for many objects like tents or finials. The **Revolve with Rail** command creates a NURBS surface by revolving a planar NURBS curve about an axis. The revolution is guided by a rail curve on a plane perpendicular to the plane that contains the profile curve and axis.

Create an axis, a rail, and a profile out of NURBS curves. It is generally easiest to work with the 2D tools in the Basic Tool set working in the different Layer Planes, and then select one at a time and run the **Modify>Convert>Convert**

to NURBS command before running the **Revolve with Rail** command. To review:

- The axis must be a linear NURBS curve.
- The profile must be a planar NURBS curve.
- The profile cannot intersect the axis, though it can touch.
- The axis must lie on the same plane as the profile.
- The rail must be a planar NURBS curve perpendicular to the axis and profile.

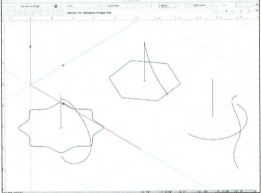

Run the **Model>3D Power Pack>Revolve with Rail** command which will direct you to select, in order, **the axis, profile, and rail**. Once that is completed, the NURBS surfaces are created. NURBS objects are not solids, geometric planes, even curved planes, in 3D space. NURBS have no thickness, but thickness can be added using the **Solid Shell Tool** in the 3D Modeling tool set.

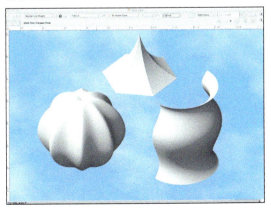

Create Drape Surface Command

The **Create Drape Surface** command creates the contours of a site model in the Vectorworks Landmark package. In the entertainment industries, this functionality can be required when designing landscapes, amphitheatres, tablecloths, furniture covers, or outdoor events.

Model a simple table; the Z height of the table top can be set in the OIP or using the **Modify>Move>Move 3D** command. Select the tabletop and duplicate (option drag, or **Edit>Duplicate Array**) slightly higher and slightly wider. With the new table top selected, go to **Model>3D Power Pack>Create Drape Surface.**

In the next dialog you can specify the number of control points on the **U (X)** and **V (Y)** axes. The more control points, the more editable the **Drape Surface**, but also the more detailed and more complex.

The bottom **Z** value is above, or below the floor, or at zero **Z** from the top of the object selected. Set the bottom **Z** below the floor, or the zero **Z**.

The portion of the tablecloth below the floor line (or any trim length desired) can be removed using an extrude and **Model>Subtract Solids**.

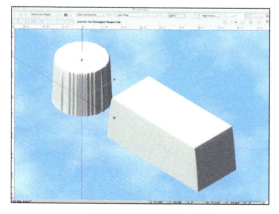

Create Helix-Spiral

The **Create Helix-Spiral** command creates a helix-shaped or spiral-shaped 3D object from one or more path objects. Those paths can be 2D objects or NURBS curves. The **Helix-Spiral** object can be used as a path object for the **Extrude Along Path** command. **Ungroup** a **Helix-Spiral** to create a NURBS curve.

Loft Surface Tool

The **Loft Surface Tool** can create complex shapes from two or more NURBS curves, whether drawn as NURBS or converted, with no **Rail**, with a **Rail** and one or more cross-sections, or with two **Rails** and one cross-section. A **Rail** is a guide: a NURBS curve that helps to determines the result in the one-rail mode. In **Birail Sweep** mode, **Rails** do not need to intersect the cross-sections.

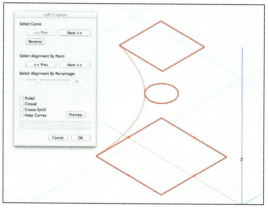

These objects are similar to those created with the **Multiple Extrude** command, but with curves. The **Loft Surface Tool** creates a 3D object (as a **Generic Solid**) from a series of NURBS curves. The cross-sections do not need to be equally spaced.

Loft with one or two **Rails** allows for the modeling of complex handrails on custom stairs, or complex sculpted forms.

A Rail is not required, but checking that the NURBS Objects are going in the same direction is, unless you desire a twisted object.

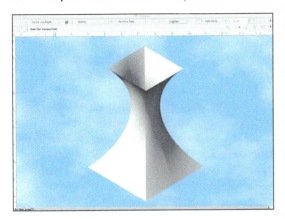

Manipulating Objects

Once you have any object or objects, they may not be placed where you need them be, but there is no need to redraw.

Align/Distribute

You will need a number of 2D and 3D objects on a page to experiment with this tool. Select the objects and go to **Modify>Align>Align** (Command/Control+=).

You can align objects on centers, horizontally, or vertically. Objects can also be distributed to equally space the distance between them. To align/distribute in 3D space, go to **Modify>Align>Align 3D** (Shift+Command/Control+=).

While this command can also be used with **Spotlight Lighting Devices**, there is also a tool specifically for Lighting Design in the **Spotlight Tool Set**. The **Align and**

Distribute Items Tool works as described along a guide line and as specified in the dialog.

Grouping

Multiple objects can be grouped together for simpler handling with the group command **Modify>Group** (Command/Control+G). Groups can be edited by double-clicking, or right-clicking on the group to enter the Edit Group mode, and can be ungrouped by selecting the group and going to **Modify>Ungroup** (Command/Control+U). This can be useful for keeping a furniture arrangement, or set of audio speakers together.

Move

The Move command (Command/Control+M) or Move 3D (Command/Control+Option/Alt+M) **Modify>Move>Move** or **Modify>Move>Move 3D** allows the movement of objects along the XY or XYZ axis of the drawing. In general, Move 3D is the most efficient command when working in 3D.

Let the computer and the software do the work.

Scale Objects

Modify>Scale Objects offers a number of options. **Symmetric** and **Asymmetric** are obvious. **Symmetric By Distance**, not so much.

When importing an image file or a PDF of an object or a venue, it is often necessary to use **Scale Object, Symmetric By Distance** to properly scale the import. All you need is one dimension.

Choosing **Symmetric By Distance** and pressing the **Dimension** button returns you to the drawing. Use the activated **Dimension Tool** here to *measure* an object in the drawing. You must be certain to know the proper dimension of this object. Once completed, you will be returned to the Dialog. Enter that length in the **New Distance** field, and click **OK.**

It is always important to include a **Graphic Scale** on exported documents, if only to provide the next person down the line something to use with this command.

Always include a graphic scale in your drawings.

Always be aware of the **Entire Drawing** check box. This should generally be unchecked. When unchecked, **Scale Objects** affects only the currently selected objects.

Offset

The **Offset Tool** duplicates or modifies the size of a surface within or outside of the object. Select the tool and go to the Tool Preferences in the Tool Bar to set the Distance, or placement of the offset; whether you want to affect the original object, or duplicate; smoothing of corners; and whether to **Close Open Curves**. If you have a complex shape and will use that shape as a platform with nosing, you will need to allow for the thickness of the reveal and/or the structure. Simply offset the shape rather than redraw the smaller, interior size.

Using the **Offset by Point** option means the object will offset to the next click.

If you have created a **Polyline** that might be the outside of a vase, choose the **Close Open Curves** option to create a closed **Polyline**. The **Sweep Command** can then be used to create the object.

Creating Repetitive Objects

You have a computer, use it! Draw once, then let the machine work.

Duplicate Array

Often there will be a need to reproduce several of any 2D shapes or 3D forms. Go to **Edit>Duplicate Array** and note that at the top left drop-down menu you have access to three modes:
- Linear Array
- Rectangular Array
- Circular Array

The options for each mode are different, but they do allow you to offset in different ways and to rotate the object(s) that you are duplicating. This command allows Lighting Designers to populate electrics and for Scenic and Lighting Designers to create patterns.

One object can create many.

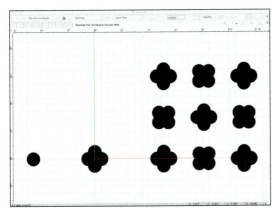

Move by Points

The **Move by Points Tool** combines functionality from the **Duplicate** Command, the **Align** Command (Modify>Align), and the **Move** Command (Modify>Move). The Move by Points Tool is precise while still allowing for free-form drawing. Objects can be moved, duplicated, and distributed along a specified distance by clicking with the Move by Points tool. This tool also moves symbols, like doors and windows, within walls. Use guides, Datum, the FDB, or other geometry for placement and accuracy.

Mirror

The **Mirror Tool** has two modes in the **Tool Bar**: **Mirror** and **Mirror and Duplicate**. Select your objects, select the **Mirror Tool**, the preferred mode, and click and drag. Hold the **shift key** down as you drag if you want to

constrain the angle of the mirroring. Use the **Command/Control** key to select objects while the tool has been activated. This is true of many tools.

It is not a good practice to **Mirror Lighting Position Objects** and **Spotlight Lighting Devices**.

Duplicate Along Path

The **Duplicate Along Path** command creates and places several copies of an object or objects along an existing path by selecting the objects, and the path, and navigating to **Edit> Duplicate Along Path**.

If a 2D object and 3D path are selected, the 2D object is projected onto the path.

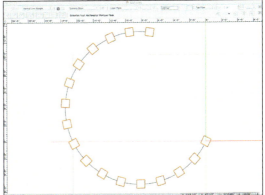

Rotate

Double-click on the **Rotate Tool** and selected objects can be rotated to a specific angle, with precision of up to 1/100 of a degree. Freehand rotation is achieved by clicking on a point on an object, then clicking on another point, and rotating. Vectorworks will indicate horizontal or vertical. Rotate and duplicate is available as an option in the Tool Bar. Press the **shift key** while freely rotating to constrain the rotation angle.

Rotate 3D

Modify>Rotate>Rotate 3D invokes the Rotate 3D command. There are some objects that cannot be rotated in space with the Rotate tool.

A Few Words about NURBS

NURBS is an acronym for **Non-Uniform Rational B-Splines.** NURBS use rational Bézier curves and a non-uniform explicitly given knot vector. Degree, control points, knots, and an evaluation rule are needed to specify a NURBS curve. That sounds awfully complex, doesn't it? NURBS were originally developed for engineers to model automotive bodies, in the 1950s, when American cars had fins.

In the entertainment business, we have to draw some pretty squirreling objects. NURBS may not always be the right choice, but they are an important option to know, and know how, and especially when to use.

Remember, NURBS always draw curves, so if precise straight lines are crucial, be careful of your choice to use NURBS, as they can be manipulated in many ways. Even if NURBS aren't the right choice, they may offer you some unique options for layout and plotting 3D locus points, that can be used to model with 3D polys.

> Make the choice to use NURBS carefully, with the end product in mind. NURBS can be oddly seductive.

> Test yourself. Visit the Library of Congress website and find the drawings from the Historic American Buildings Survey. Model one or some of these structures. Once you have, no theatre or piece of scenery will ever be daunting.

Other modeling tools create solid objects. NURBS objects are not solids, they are defined, pure geometric planes, even curved planes, in 3D space. They have no thickness; this is pure geometry. NURBS objects uniquely combine ease of drawing and precision. Thickness can be added to NURBS surfaces using the **Solid Shell Tool** in the 3D Modeling tool set. The **Solid Shell Tool** works much like the **2D Offset Tool**.

Here is one general and very important note to remember: Every NURBS point can be absolutely positioned in 3D space from the OIP. This precision allows for the creation of some very elegant objects.

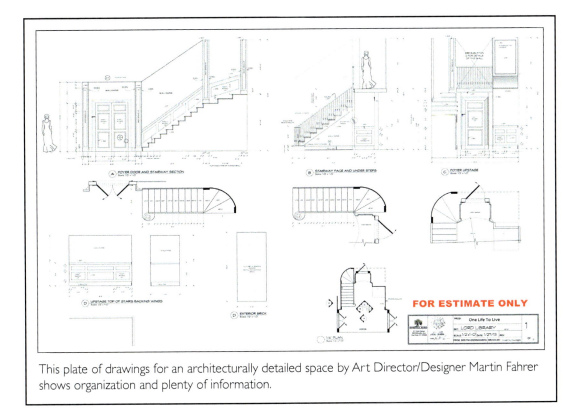

This plate of drawings for an architecturally detailed space by Art Director/Designer Martin Fahrer shows organization and plenty of information.

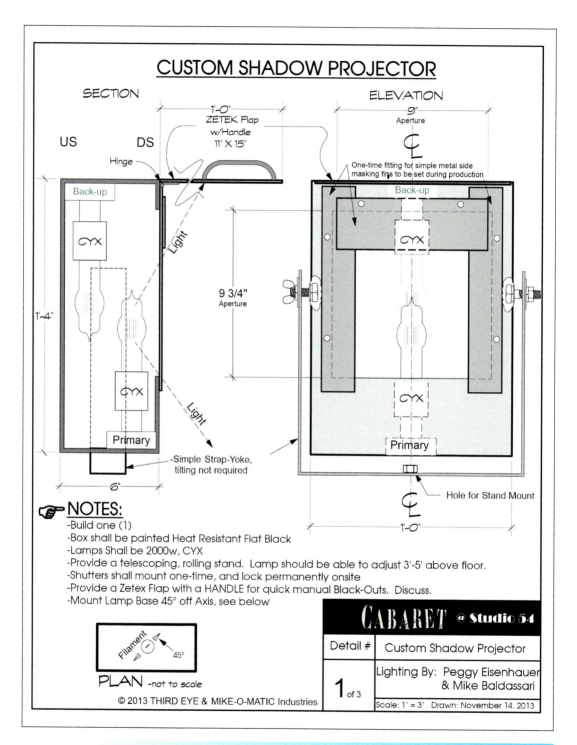

CUSTOM SHADOW PROJECTOR

SECTION

ELEVATION

1'-0"
ZETEK Flap
w/Handle
11" X 15"

9"
Aperture

US   DS

Hinge

One-time fitting for simple metal side
masking fins to be set during production

Back-up

Light

Back-up

CYX

CYX

9 3/4"
Aperture

1'-4"

CYX

Light

CYX

Primary

Primary

-Simple Strap-Yoke,
tilting not required

6"

Hole for Stand Mount

1'-0"

NOTES:

-Build one (1)
-Box shall be painted Heat Resistant Flat Black
-Lamps Shall be 2000w, CYX
-Provide a telescoping, rolling stand. Lamp should be able to adjust 3'-5' above floor.
-Shutters shall mount one-time, and lock permanently onsite
-Provide a Zetex Flap with a HANDLE for quick manual Black-Outs. Discuss.
-Mount Lamp Base 45° off Axis, see below

Filament
45°

PLAN -not to scale

© 2013 THIRD EYE & MIKE-O-MATIC Industries

CABARET @ Studio 54	
Detail #	Custom Shadow Projector
1 of 3	Lighting By: Peggy Eisenhauer & Mike Baldassari
	Scale: 1" = 3" Drawn: November 14. 2013

Cabaret 2014 Broadway Revival Lighting Detail (left) and production photo by Joan Marcus

2014 Broadway Revival of *Cabaret*
The Roundabout Theatre Company at Studio 54

Directors: Sam Mendes and Rob Marshall
Choreographer: Rob Marshall
Scenic and Club Designer: Robert Brill
Costume Designer: William Ivey Long
Lighting Designers: Peggy Eisenhauer and Mike Baldassari
   Lighting Draftsperson: Kristina Kloss
Sound Designer: Brian Ronan

10. Symbols

Symbols can be repetitive, or one-off geometry. When repetitive, symbols help to reduce file size; the geometry is only stored once. One-off symbols allow for collaboration, or easier editing of an element that might not sit square in a space; the symbol definition can be set square, and placed instances of the symbol can be rotated. Data Records can be attached to symbols. The Vectorworks internal database/spreadsheet can count symbols, and manipulate data attached to symbols.

Symbols can be created in one file and referenced onto others. One team member may create the model of the venue, saved as a symbol, and others can Reference the symbol. When a Referenced Symbol is updated, all drawings that use that symbol are updated.

Any object(s) can be saved as a symbol and will be stored for access via the Resource Browser. Symbols can be edited by right-clicking on the symbol in the Resource Browser and selecting Edit from the contextual menu and choosing what portion, or placement options are to be edited. Symbols can also be edited in context, on a drawing, by double-clicking or right-clicking on an instance.

Elements within symbols can be assigned Classes, and have Attributes assigned to the Classes. Symbol instances can be classed, but the Class will not affect the appearance of the Symbol, only the visibility of the instance.

If a project has moving scenery, multiple instances of the same symbol assigned to different classes can represent the unit on stage, in multiple playing positions, and in storage.

Symbol Geometry

Symbols can be built of anything you can create in Vectorworks: simple 2D geometry, complex 3D objects, and even **Plug-in Objects (PIOs)** like doors or windows. Window objects converted to symbols can be used throughout a design, and then all of the windows can be modified by editing one source. Although symbols generally can be placed into other symbols, **Spotlight Lighting Devices** are not supported inside other symbols.

Although there are variations to be explained, overall there are three types of symbols:
- A 2D Symbol has only 2D Screen Plane geometry.
- A 3D Symbol has 3D geometry and will display properly in all views, rendered as the user dictates.
- A Hybrid Symbol has both 2D Screen Plane and 3D geometry and displays the 3D geometry in all views except Top/Plan. In the Top/Plain view, a Hybrid symbol displays 2D information. Spotlight Lighting Devices must be Hybrid symbols.

> **Spotlight Lighting Devices are symbols that are *not* supported when inserted into other symbols.**

Inserting Symbols

Symbols are inserted using the **Symbol Insertion Tool** in the **Basic Tool Set** after a symbol is made active in the Resource Browser. Double-clicking on a symbol in the Resource Browser will activate the symbol, and the tool. Selecting the symbol (single-click) and pressing the **Activate Button** performs the same function. Some special types of symbols, Spotlight Lighting Devices, Lighting Positions, Plants, and others, have specific insertion tools.

Click once to place a symbol; the instance may then generally be rotated until a second click. Double-clicking at insertion eliminates rotation.

Double-clicking on a **Spotlight Lighting Device** will activate the **Lighting Instrument Insertion Tool**. **Spotlight Lighting Device Symbols** can be inserted with the **Symbol Insertion Tool**, but they will not be identified as **Spotlight Lighting Devices**. **Spotlight Lighting Devices** inserted with the incorrect tool can be made into lighting instruments by selecting one, or more and going to **Spotlight>Object Conversion>Convert to Lighting Instrument**.

Symbols speed work.

Lighting Position Symbols must also be **Hybrid Symbols**. Typically they are a 3D extrusion of a square or circle to represent the pipe, and a 2D line, 2D double line, or rectangle to represent the pipe, in Top/Plan View. That choice is part of the designer's drafting style. Double-clicking on a **Lighting Position Symbol** does not activate the **Lighting Position Insertion Tool**, but rather the **Symbol Insertion Tool**. The **Lighting Position Insertion Tool** is located in the **Spotlight Tool Set**. Lighting Position Symbols inadvertently placed can be converted by selecting, and going to **Spotlight>Object Conversion>Convert to Lighting Position**. When a Lighting Position Symbol is inserted using the Lighting Position Insertion Tool, you will be prompted to name the position. If you do not see the prompt, you have the wrong tool.

3D symbols, like furniture objects, can be inserted onto working planes on a different angle from the ground plane, like a raked stage. Hybrid Symbols are constricted to the Ground Plane, or parallel to the Ground Plane.

Creating Symbols

To create a symbol, select your geometry and go to **Modify>Create Symbol**. The Create Symbol Dialog offers insertion and scale options. It also allows classing of the instances.

A Symbol created from an Auto-Hybrid Object will automatically create a Hybrid Symbol. In other instances, a 3D symbol will have to be edited to create a Hybrid Symbol.

Use the correct Symbol Insertion Tool for the type of symbol.

Symbol Types

Plug-in Objects (PIOs) create customizable objects; these are not symbols. Plug-in Objects are modified in the OIP or other dialogs.

Black Symbols

The most common type is the Black Symbol. Changes made to the Symbol affect all Instances of the symbol.

Red Symbols

A Red Symbol is a saved Instance of a configured **PIO**. Insertions of these symbols can be individually modified in the OIP. An Image Prop Object, saved as a PIO becomes a Red Symbol. Individual instances can have the size adjusted.

Blue Symbols

A Blue Symbol is created when **Convert to Group** is selected in the **Create Symbol Dialog**. Instances are converted to an editable group. Changes made to the symbol later have no effect on the group. Changes made to the Group have no affect on the Symbol.

Green Symbols

Green Symbols have **Page-Based Scale** rather than **World-Based Scale.** These symbols, like a North Arrow Indicator, would be used as annotations; they are scaled relative to the page size.

Modifying Symbol Insertions

Instances of a Symbol placed on a document can be scaled by percentage (symmetrically or asymmetrically), or replaced in the OIP.

Updating one symbol can update an entire project.

Editing Symbols

Symbols can be edited, in context, from the document window, or from the Resource browser. Editing in the document shows objects around the symbol grayed. When editing from the Resource Browser, the symbol is isolated in the Edit Symbol Drawing Window. In either case there is a heavy yellow-orange border around the drawing area with an **Exit** button in the top right of the window.

To create a Hybrid Symbol, edit the 3D component in the Top or Top/Plan View, and trace the 3D in 2D components while working in the Screen Plane. On exiting, Vectorworks will separate the Screen Plane objects into the 2D symbol component.

While usually the 2D geometry matches the 3D geometry, that is not always correct. An Image Prop Object, saved as a symbol, can have pictorial information in the 2D, as well as in the 3D. Image Props are 3D representations of objects made using pictures. Image Props are great for adding people to some renderings, or plants and props that would otherwise add overly complex geometry. If the 3D component, shown as a line or a cross, is a plant, the 2D might be a hand-drawn aerial of that type of plant. Or another picture. While the 2D might not match the 3D, the 2D should be the same size.

Auto Hybrid Objects.

An **Auto Hybrid Object** creates 2D Geometry from selected 3D geometry. With components of an object selected, go to **Spotlight>Architectural>Create Auto Hybrid**. Vectorworks will generate an editable 2D representation of the 3D object that can be modified in the OIP, before or after it is made into a symbol.

Symbol Referencing

Symbol referencing is essential for working in a team environment. To preview, go to **Tools>Organization** and open the **References Tab** on the far right.

Symbols are referenced in the Resource Browser from Favorited, or other open files. Right-clicking on any symbol from a file other than the active document reveals options to **Reference** or **Import** the symbol. Referencing the symbol keeps the symbol stored in the original file while allowing the use of the symbol in the current file. Changes to the original symbol will be updated in the current file and seen in the **Organization** dialog.

Referenced symbols appear in the Resource Browser indicated by italicized text.

The **Settings Button** in the **Organization Dialog, References Tab** opens options for updating changed, Referenced Symbols, which can be **Manual** or **Automatic**. If selected, Vectorworks will automatically check in the background to see if any referenced files have been updated.

Maintain a personal library of symbols.

Referencing allows a team to use the same resources, and keep them updated.

Using Referenced Symbols, different components of a project can be developed simultaneously and the parts can be brought together.

Symbols and Database Information

Information can be associated with a symbol and used to generate reports and worksheets. Information can be attached to either a Symbol Instance, or the Symbol Definition (when editing the Symbol) in the **Data Tab** of the **OIP.**

A **Record Format** must be created first in order to assemble database information in worksheets. To create a Record Format, right-click in the Resource Browser and select New Resource from the contextual menu and Record Format from the fly-off menu.

Spotlight Lighting Devices must be attached to a **Light Info Record,** which contains photometric data for the lens and the source.

Application Resources

On a Macintosh, the Vectorworks application directory should be in the Applications folder on your hard drive. On a PC, this directory should be in the Program Files folder. Go to the Vectorworks application directory and review the many libraries provided with the application. Service Select members have access to many additional Resources.

Files with symbols appropriate for your practice can be **Favorited** in the Resource Browser.

A 2D Lighting Boom Position Symbol

On a Light Plot, booms and ladders may be placed, but the hanging details will be located elsewhere. Open the file s4.vwx in the Exercise Files folder from the Website. This file contains a Polyline that is one-half of the plan view of an ETC Source 4 lighting instrument. This is not a symbol, and certainly not a Spotlight Lighting Device. It has no records attached.

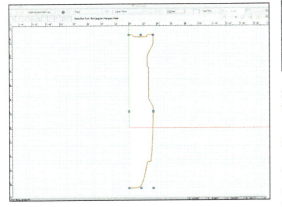

Work in the Lighting-Spotlight Lighting Device class. **Mirror** and **Duplicate** the **Polyline**. Select both and **Modify>Compose** to create one Polyline. You can monitor these changes in the OIP, which identifies what is selected.

Move the Polygon 12" (304.8mm) to the right. Place a 24" (609.6mm) diameter circle at the 0-0 point and **Modify>Send>Send to Back** (Command/Control+B). Place another circle 1" (254mm) radius on the 0-0 point.

Select the Source 4 Polygon and click on the **Fill** drop-down. There are many choices, and this is a good time to see what some do as they access their specific **Default Content**. For this purpose, assign a **Pattern** with diagonal lines. Mirror and Duplicate.

Select All and create the 2D-only symbol **Boom Plan**.

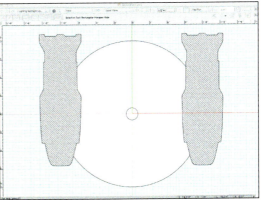

Save the file as BoomPlan.vwx in the **Lysistrata Workgroup Folder**.

A Hybrid End Seat Symbol

The **End Seat Symbol** is a **Hybrid Symbol** comprised of only 2D objects. Draw in the Layer Plane to view 2D geometry as 3D objects.

Create a new document, save as **EndSeat.vwx** in the **Lysistrata Workgroup Folder**, and assign Design Layer 1 a scale of 1/2"=1' 0" (1:25), and then create the Classes:
- EndSeat-Container
- EndSeat-White
- EndSeat-Black

References do not have to be in a Workgroup Folder.

Assign each a line weight of .05 mm. For the White and Black versions check **Use at Creation**. For the **Container**, leave that unchecked. The **Black Class** should have a fill of black and the **White Class** should have a fill of white.

The sizes of the geometry are based on average human and seat sizes.

Go to the **Top/Plan View**, select the **Circle** tool, and place a 16" (406.4mm) diameter circle at 0-0. Assign the **White Class**, **Duplicate**, and assign the **Black Class** to the duplicate.

Use the **Clip Tool** in **Exclusion Mode** and **Clipping by Rectangle** mode, snap to the center 0,0 point, and click and drag to remove the lower-right, and upper-left quadrants of the circle.

Double-click the **Line Tool** to insert a 21" (533.4mm) horizontal line centered at 0-0. **Rotate** in the **Duplicate Mode** to create a vertical line. Assign both to the White Class.

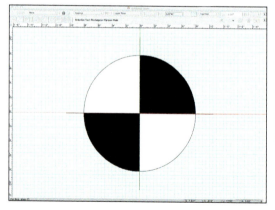

Select All, go to **Modify>Create Symbol,** and create the symbol **End Seat Plan View**. Be certain **Plan Projection Center** is selected as the **Insertion Point**, assign the **EndSet-Container** class, for visibility control, in the drop-down at the bottom, and click **OK.**

To preserve the 2D-only symbol, right-click on the symbol in the **Resource Browser** to **Duplicate** as **End Seat**, and then **Edit** the **End Seat Symbol, 3D Component**.

In the **Front View** and drawing in the **Symbol Definition Plane**, draw another set of circles, 12" (304.8mm) in diameter. Assign the classes, and clip as before. Place the center of the circle at +3' 9" (1,143mm) up on the Y axis. That is the typical height of a person's eyes while seated. Draw a 16" (406.4mm) horizontal line through the center of the circle, and a vertical line from 0 to 4'-6" (1371.6mm) through the circle.

Go to the **Top View**, **Select All**, **Rotate**, and **Duplicate** the objects 90° so they cross. Switch to an isometric view, and go to **View>Rendering>Wireframe Options**. Use the slider to adjust the **Fill Opacity**. This is a universal setting, not specific to any object.

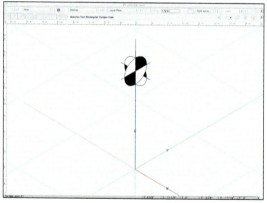

Exit the symbol, and notice how the 2D and 3D symbols are indicated in the Resource Browser.

People Symbols

Drawings require people to illustrate scale in both 2D and 3D. Open a new Vectorworks document and save it as **Figures.vwx** in your **Lysistrata Workgroup Folder**. Open the folder **Figures** from the Website content.

The text will go through several processes once. Those processes should be repeated for each image in the folder.

In the file **Figures.vwx**, create the **Texture Figures-3D** with the color set to **Obj Attribute** and **50% Transparency**. Additionally you will need the Classes **Entourage-2D** and **Entourage-3D**; edit the Entourage-3D class to use the Texture Figures-3D. This texture will allow light to be seen on the figures, and the environment to be seen through the objects.

2D Figures

In the front view, working in the Layer Plane, go to **File>Import>Import Image** file and select one of the images in the Figures folder. Eventually, you will go through all of the files in this folder, so start at the top and work your way through so that you can keep track of the process.

Once the image is placed with the bottom center at the 0-0 mark and selected, go to **Modify>Scale Objects,** choose **Symmetric by Distance**, and click on the **Dimension Button** to be returned to the main document window. Click on the top of the image and drag to the bottom. Press and hold the shift key to constrain the line to vertical.

Click at the bottom to be returned to the **Scale Objects Dialog**. The height of the image will be displayed as **Current Distance**. Enter a typical person's height into the **New Distance Field** and click **OK**.

Scale Objects
○ Symmetric
X, Y, Z Factor: 0.5
⦿ Symmetric By Distance
Current Distance: 132'0"
New Distance: 69
○ Asymmetric
X Scaling Factor: 1
Y Scaling Factor: 1
☐ Scale text
☐ Entire drawing
Cancel   OK

It is a very good idea to vary the heights of the figures.

Move the image back to the 0-0 point and go to **Modify>Trace Bitmap**. Vectorworks will now trace the outline of the figure. When done, delete the image file, or **Move** it out of the way.

Select the trace and you will find you have many small/short lines. With the one line selected, go to **Edit>Select Connected Objects**, and then **Modify>Compose** to create a single **Polyline**.

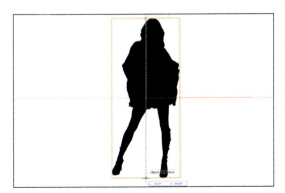

Some of the figures have openings, or holes between the limbs. Those need to be made into polygons in the same way, and then have the **Modify>Clip Surface** command applied to the hole and the original polygon. Use the **Modify>Send>Send to Front** (Command/Control+F) and **Modify>Send>Send to Back** (Command/Control+B) commands as needed.

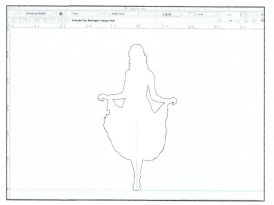

Assign the figure the **Entourage-2D Class**, **Copy** the Polyline, go to the **Top/Plan View**, and make it into a symbol. Use a naming convention like the **image file name-2D** to help keep track of the progress of your work. **Uncheck** *Leave Instance in Place*. When the dialog asks you to choose a destination folder, create the Symbol Folder **Figures-2D**. Store all of the 2D figures within that folder.

Symbol folders are found in the Resource Browser, and help to keep the Resource Browser palette from becoming unwieldy.

> Vary the heights of your figures for a more realistic look.

3D Figures

Paste the copy of the 2D object in place at the 0-0 mark. Select it and go to **Modify>Convert>Convert to 3D Polygon**. Assign the **Entourage-3D Class** and create a symbol as above, changing the default insertion option from **Plan Projection Center** to **Next Mouse Click**. Click the mouse to insert the 3D figure at the bottom center (0-0) mark. These Symbols should be saved in a new **Symbol Folder** called **Figures-3D**.

When complete, you have similar, yet different figure symbols for use in various documents.

Image Props

Image Props have been discussed and defined, but not explained. Here goes…

Image Props begin life, usually, in image-editing software. Image Props help to visualize ideas without adding complex geometry to files. The geometry is supplanted by photos or drawings. Image Props can be used to place costume sketches into renderings. Image Props *do not* illustrate how light falls on objects.

Vectorworks ships with libraries of Image Props. If you have the Landmark package there will be additional plant and tree Image Props in your libraries, as well as the **VBvisual Plant Tool** in the **Visualization Tool Set**. You will have to activate the Landmark Workspace, or Edit your own Workspace to access the Landmark Tools.

These Objects add a lot of geometry to a document, but they also add more detail than an Image Prop. They are great for casting shadows on outdoor installations.

Image Props cast shadows as well.

As always, keep your image files small, as larger graphics files can cause Renderworks to work slowly. In your image editor, you can create images as *actual size* at a low DPI. Generally speaking, keep most image files around 1-2 Mb.

All of the files in the **Figures Folder** have an **Alpha Channel** which acts as a color mask. These figures are simply black, but the process works with full-color images.

From the **Top/Plan View** go to **Model>Create Image Prop** and choose one of the images from the **Figures Folder**. Set a **Height** with **Lock Aspect Ration** checked. The width will then be determined by the image file. Choose **Use Mask** and the **Create Mask** process begins. Choose **Reuse an Image from Another Resource** and select **This Prop's Color** from the drop-

down. The most direct path to completion will be choosing **Alpha Channel**, but you should experiment with the other options. The mask keeps the image prop from being simply rectangular.

In most cases, checking **Crossed Planes** helps to create the 3D illusion. There are times, like when making a sign, or if a figure has a wide stance, that you might not want the crossed planes. The figure below does not use crossed planes. Create and render it both ways to see the difference.

Check **Constant Reflectivity,** which applies a **Glow Texture**. While this keeps light from falling on the Image Prop, it also keeps the crossed planes from casting shadows on one another.

Check **Create Plug-in Object** and **Create Symbol** to have the Image Prop saved as a **Red Symbol**. It is then possible to change the size and proportions of the Image Prop Instances. One figure could become many, or one plant could become many. Within reason, of course.

Check **Auto Rotate to Viewer** to allow the Image Prop to render towards the Perspective View. As above, if you're making a sign that is mounted on a wall, leave this option unchecked, or the sign might rotate into the wall.

The Image Prop will appear as either a straight line, or crossed lines centered at the 0-0 point. It can be moved into a symbol folder from the Resource Browser. Right-click in the **Resource Browser** and select **New Resource>New Symbol Folder**, or right-click in the **Symbol Folders** area and select **New Symbol Folder**.

Right-Click on the Image Prop Symbol and choose **Move** to relocate.

The Human Figure Tool

The **Human Figure Tool** located in the **Visualization Tool Set** inserts a model of a clothed human figure into a document. The figure can be modified in the OIP after it has been inserted.

Human Figure objects can be used to really see how lighting will render on bodies and clothes, however these are complex models. Each **Human Figure Object** adds over 1 Mb of data to a file, and they will slow your rendering process. Consider keeping these objects on their own Design Layer or classing them so you can turn some or all on and off as needed when developing the design.

Insert a **Human Figure Object** and **Render** to clearly review the default look.

Select the **Human Figure Object** and go through all of the options in the OIP. Once the figure has generated, look at it in all views.

There are many configurable options.
• Poses can be customized.
• Clothing can be added or taken away.
• Sex, Age, and Body Type can be established.

The Set Attributes Button in the OIP accesses a dialog that allows further customization.
• Color, and/or texture of the figure can be changed.
• Different parts of the figure can be classed, and attributes such as specific fabric image Textures can be assigned.

Human Figure Objects can be simplified to the form without clothes, and assigned a neutral, or specific skin tone. Don't fear this; they're not anatomically correct, and a simple form requires less data while showing how colored light from different positions will fall on the body and affect the appearance of the body. This is especially useful when designing Fashion Shows, or dance lighting.

Human Figure Objects can be made into **Symbols**, reducing the geometry in the file, and to allow Referencing.

Thoughts on Using Figures

Figures are essential in renderings, elevations, and section views to illustrate scale. Placement of figures helps to illustrate *moments* in production.

Sometimes an Image Prop can overpower a design or detract attention from the structure or the light. Image Props cannot show the lighting design. Simple 3D figures can show the light, but the Transparency or Fill Color may need adjustment to suit a show, a look, a moment, or individual taste. **Human Figure Objects** show light on costume color, and accurate shadows from specific **Lighting Position** angles.

Different directors or clients will prefer one type of figure illustration over others.

However, you have options.

There are many ways to add figures and personal style to your drawings. You need figures; make them your own.

Cabaret 2014 Sound Section

Cabaret Sound

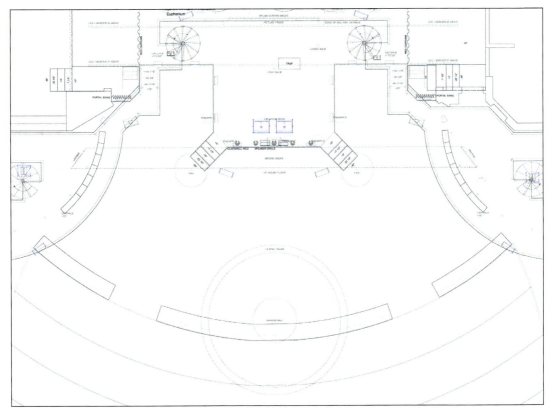

Cabaret 2014 Sound Plot

2014 Broadway Revival of *Cabaret*
The Roundabout Theatre Company at Studio 54

Directors: Sam Mendes and Rob Marshall
Choreographer: Rob Marshall
Scenic and Club Designer: Robert Brill
Costume Designer: William Ivey Long
Lighting Designers: Peggy Eisenhauer and Mike Baldassari
    Lighting Draftsperson: Kristina Kloss
Sound Designer: Brian Ronan

11. Measuring and Modeling the Venue

Typically before beginning to model a theatre, venue, or film location you would need to do a site survey. In some cases you might have unlimited access to the space and can set up to work there. This offers the luxury of being able to double and triple check measurements.

At a university or a repertory company there might be somewhat unfettered access, but not enough time for you to make camp, and work through the process in the space. On Broadway, the survey call requires a crew to be present, and time is limited. This might be similarly true at other venues, like hotels where corporate meetings are staged; the producer is not likely to fly to Hawaii several times to check a measurement, or film locations in active spaces.

You might be given an image file, PDF, or VWX document and need to check the scale to proceed. You must always check and verify any information that is provided to you. Accuracy is critical. The theatre, studio, or ballroom might have been modified since the drawing you were given was created. You don't know how accurate the drawing was in the first place. Scenery must fit into the space. Lighting positions must fit around any physical obstacles.

Many television studios and theatre spaces have limited access; they might be located in an office building and there might be a series of halls and doors between the elevator, and the studio. How big is that elevator anyway? Are there restrictions as to the use of that elevator? Does everything have to fit through a single small door?

Taking a survey requires the designer and assistants to be as accurate and as efficient as possible.

The Survey Kit

You'll need a kit of tools to perform a survey. In your career, you'll likely need many different kits for different jobs. A kit is simply an assembly of tools needed for a certain job function. Kits tend to start small, and grow over time; they are added to as needed, and/or as finances allow.

Camera

Your phone will likely not do for this type of job, but when all else fails, it might have to do. A point-and-shoot is better, but ideally a Digital Single Lens Reflex (DSLR) would be the tool. Multiple lenses and a flash help, but are not necessarily required. Ideally there is enough light without a flash.

To begin to document a space, stand in the middle of the room, using a normal focal length lens (35-50mm), look to the left corner and take a shot. Rotate slightly and take another photo. These images should overlap slightly. Repeat until you have the full panorama of the wall in front of you.

Some cameras will assemble these photos into one view for you. In other cases you may want or have to assemble the panorama in photo editing software like Adobe Photoshop. To do this in Photoshop, open the first image and change the **Image>Canvas Size** to be longer than the width of all of the photos required. Make the **Height** somewhat higher. Check the left, center locator box so the canvas expands from the left to the right. Click **OK.**

Accuracy is paramount.

Sample collage of photographs from a site survey.

Open the additional images, and copy and paste them across. Crop as needed. These images become a collage. They can be artful in their own right.

Repeat for each wall in the space. If you're surveying a proscenium theatre you'll likely want to do this in the house and onstage.

Pixels are cheap; take as many detail photographs as you require. Take too many. Time and experience will let you know what is the perfect amount of information.

Measuring Tools

The Stanley brand 25' tape measure is the most basic measuring tool. The case of the tape measure is exactly 3" long so you can measure into tight corners. The width and quality of the tape mean you can measure vertically without buckling. Even outside. In the wind.

If you only have a 25' tape measure, you will certainly need pencils and/or chalk to mark where you've measured to and from.

It is not really a measuring tool, but a carpenter's snap line or a scenic's chalk line are needed to establish places to measure from.

Longer tapes are also useful, necessary for some dimensions and accuracy. To measure a typical proscenium you would need at least a 50' tape measure. A 100' tape would be more useful, and for some locations, only a 200' measure will do the job. Longer tapes are often Fiberglass. All materials change over time and in different climates.

A Laser or Sonic measuring device, one that also accounts for its own mass, can be very useful. With a tape measure, two people are often required to get the most accurate information. With an electronic device, one assistant can do the work.

Build your kits as you build your career.

A distance measuring wheel, a wheel with a vertical handle attached and an odometer, can be useful for exteriors or large ballrooms. This is not a precise device.

Apps like Magic Plan can stitch together images from the iPad camera, combine them with a few dimensions (you still need the tape measure), and produce simple CAD drawings that can be imported into Vectorworks for modeling. This App is more useful for simple, generally bare, rooms, than a complex theatre.

Notation

You still need a pad and pencil, or an iPad and a stylus, or both.

At some point you will need to write down these many dimensions. How is a matter of personal preference. Some people like lined paper, some like a grid paper, others plain white paper. Pens, pencils, markers, colors? These are personal choices, usually made and evolved over time.

Color is useful. If you draw the architecture in black, perhaps blue or red will help to see the dimensions as they are jotted down?

Clarity is critical. Survey time is usually limited. Light might be limited. The drawings must be simple and clear. The notation accurate and easy to read. Consider that the person doing the survey might not be doing the drafting.

Embrace and experiment with the technology that is available.
Many apps are free, try as many as possible

There are many iPad apps that can be incorporated into the survey process. **Skitch** can be used to annotate existing PDF files, as can **PDF Expert**. **Skitch** and **Morpholio Trace** are the App equivalent of onion skin tracing paper, and they allow text, notes, lines and drawings to be added to photographs. **SketchBook Pro** draws simple geometric forms and text can be readily added for dimensions or notes of important obstructions.

Penultimate and **Evernote** integrate so that if an assistant is in Hawaii doing a survey, the notes can be immediately transmitted back to another assistant, in the home office, who can be putting together the Vectorworks drawings.

There are many different graphic applications for the iPad that can facilitate your design work, and provide information you can integrate with Vectorworks. The few listed are only some of what is available. As with most things, what's right and what works is what is right for the individual designer. Try as many as you can.

Take clear notes.

What Else?

For a rigging call, or to locate the fly lines on a stage, a plumb bob is needed. A plumb bob is a pointed metal weight that is tied with mason's line to a pipe (for example) to determine the pipe's up and downstage position. When the weight stops swinging, a measurement can be taken.

When looking at a location, you might need to match a paint color. Swatch books for the major commercial paint supplies like Benjamin Moore, Pittsburgh Paints, or Resene are useful.

Pantone (PMS) swatch books aren't often needed for a site survey, but they are useful for finding colors off of printed materials. Pantone colors are mixed with CMYK (Cyan, Magenta, Yellow & Black), and it is pretty impossible to create an exact match with paint pigment (Red, Blue, Yellow), or light (RGB) as they are all different pigments/mixing systems. Nonetheless, clients will ask for their logo gobo to be in *their* PMS blue. Matching their Pantone color to an approximate RGB value means you can program the color, or use an App like Gel Swatch Library HD to find the closest, commercially available color.

Apps like Adobe Kuler, and Benjamin Moore Color Capture can also help to identify colors in a theatre or on a location. Of course these apps will be affected by the available light, or lack thereof. The Website easyrbg.com can convert RGB values to commercial paint colors.

At the end of the day, it is not the apps, it is the designer's eye that picks the color.

Speaking of light, you need a light. At least a flashlight. Theatres can be dark. A small flashlight is always useful, even if it is simply a phone app, but you may need to consider having a larger light(s) or lanterns(s) to illuminate the space. The Ghost Light never travels far.

A Profile Gauge is a millworking tool that can be used to *trace* existing mouldings.

A simple torpedo level or framing level is often also useful.

Surveying a Proscenium Theatre

The 0-0 point in a Vectorworks document is the logical place for the intersection of the **Plaster Line** and the **Centerline** of the theatre. All of your survey dimensions come off of that point.

Determine the 0-0 point, or **Datum**, by snapping the chalk line across the proscenium opening at the plaster line. Bisect that line with your tape measure or by drawing arcs to determine 0-0 in the physical space.

The **Centerline** must be perpendicular to the **Plaster Line:** using three tape measures, create a **3-4-5 Triangle**.

A 3-4-5 triangle is a simple way to create a right angle. If the base of the triangle is an increment of three, the vertical an increment of four, then the hypotenuse will be an increment of five. Remember A squared plus B squared equals C squared? In lieu of three tape measures, use the tape and a pencil as a compass to strike arcs.

Create as large a triangle as possible, for the most accuracy. A right triangle of 12' by 16' (with a 20' hypotenuse) would generally be about right. In metric, 3m by 4m will provide a 5m hypotenuse. Once the triangle has been created, you have two points to use to snap another line and create the Centerline.

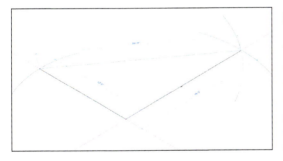

Measurements upstage of the Plaster Line are noted as plus measurements. Measurements from the Plaster Line toward the orchestra are minus measurements.

You may need to establish other right triangles to determine locations like the center of the end seat positions. These seats, the extreme right and left audience seats in the front row of the orchestra determine the visible area onstage. The end seats are used to determine the stage masking, and playable areas.

Much of what we do requires basic geometry and basic algebra, with a dose of trig. In the field, we have to do the math.

Measuring a Curve

Your theatre might have a curved walls, or a curved front edge to the stage. To measure any curve, work from the **Plaster Line**, or the **Centerline,** and take a series of three perpendicular measurements at measured distances. In Vectorworks, you can plot the curve using either the **Circle Tool,** the **Curved Wall Tool,** or the **Arc Tool** using the **three points modes**.

The Theatre Space

Though we don't think of Broadway as small, a Broadway theatre might not have as much room as a show needs. It is best practice for designers, who often do not know what theatre will be used for the production, to design to the smallest possible Broadway house. This is often the case. That would be a theatre with a proscenium opening of 40' (12,192mm) wide, by 20' (6,096mm) high, 29' (8,839.2mm) deep with 15' (4,572mm) wings, and a 45' (1,3716mm) grid.

Modeling the Theatre

Open a new document using your Default Stationary. Go to the Right Isometric View and then **File>Page Set-up**. Check **Choose size unavailable in printer set-up** and select **US Arch E** from the drop-down menu. Uncheck **Show page breaks** (when checked, this adds lines showing how the sheet will print usually on letter or A4 size paper), and click **OK**.

Create and work in a new **Class** called **Guides**.

Save this file as **TheatreSpace.vwx** in your **Lysistrata Workgroup Folder**.

If we had drawings, not measurements, they could be placed in the Trace Layer, and scaled with the **Scale Objects Command**. If placed in the Layer Plane, the plan, section and elevation can cross at the 0-0 point.

Work in the **Venue Architecture Design Layer**, press Command/Control+4 to view the entire page, and go to the **Basic Tool Set** and double-click the **2D Locus Tool**. Place the first locus at 0-0, and click **OK**.

This **Locus** identifies the intersection of the **Centerline** and **Plaster Line** of our theatre space. Using the 0-0 point of the page aids in absolute placement of objects on the stage.

Place additional **Locus Point Objects** at
* -35' (10,972.8mm) X and -15" (381mm) Y
* -35' (10,972.8mm) X and 27'9" (8,458.2mm) Y
* -25' (7,620mm) X and -15" (381mm) Y
* -25' (7,620mm) X and -2'-9" (838.2mm) Y
* -30' (9,144mm) X and -15'-9" (4,800.6mm) Y
* -33' (10,058.4mm) X and -28'-9" (8,763mm) Y

Select these Loci and duplicate them with the **Mirror Tool,** snapping to the first **Locus Point**. These are the snapping points for the theatre and deck.

Reference the **Carpet Dk Red**, **Black-Gloss** and **Black-Matte** textures from the Textures-Lysistrata file with **Path relative to the current document** checked.

Create the classes:
* Venue-Walls
* Venue-Deck
* Venue-Auditorium Floor
* Venue-Balcony

The Walls should use the Black-Matte Texture, and have a solid Black fill. The others should have a solid white fill. The Deck should use the Black-Gloss texture. The Balcony is Black-Matte, and the Auditorium Floor is the Carpet Dk Red. It might help if you assigned different colored strokes to the Balcony and the Auditorium Floor.

In the **Venue-Walls Class**, the texture must be assigned to all of the **Wall Parts** as these will be used on elements made with the Wall Tools. In the other Classes, use **Other**.

Draw in the **Venue-Wall Class** and select the **Wall Tool** from the **Building Shell Tool Set**. Experiment with the different **Drawing Modes**, tap to begin, tap to create a corner, and double-tap to end a wall. With the **Left**

Wall Objects, and Roof Objects have special places to assign textures in the Class Definition.

Control Line Mode selected, tap and drag in different directions. Drag to the right and the Control Line is the top of the wall. Drag to the left and the Control Line is at the bottom. Drag up and the Control Line is finally on the left.

The Center Control Line Mode should be obvious, and the Right Control Line Mode works in the reverse of the Left Control Line. If you have the Designer package, choose a Wall Style (from the drop-down in the Tool Bar) like Ext-2x4-Brick Veneer, to help visualize the way Walls draw; the Diagonal Line Fill indicates the Brick Veneer, or the outside of the wall.

Note that the Starting Point and the Direction in which the wall is drawn determine a wall's *sides*. Imagine walking along the top of the wall: one side might be an interior, one side might be an exterior, or each side might be an interior of a different room. Left Side and Right Side designations are critical when different textures are applied to the different sides of a Wall Object.

No matter the Control Line orientation, Walls drawn Up have the exterior/left side on the page/sheet left. Walls drawn Down have that side on the page/sheet right. When any one Wall Segment is selected there is a directional arrow which indicates the direction in which the wall was drawn. Left and Right are oriented to that arrow.

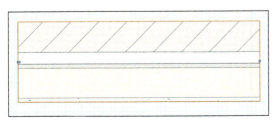

To reverse the wall direction, tap Reverse Sides in the OIP.

Even when drawn as connected, each Wall Segment is treated as a separate Wall Object. Walls can be joined together when drawing or after drawing by using the Wall Join Tool.

Like other 3D Objects Walls can be edited, and peaks can be added or deleted to create Gabled or Stepped Structures.

Use the Magic Wand Tool in the Object Type Mode you have previously saved to select your experimental Walls and Delete.

Open the Wall Tool Preferences and set the Overall Thickness to be 9" (228.6mm) in the Definition Tab, and Height to be 45' (13,716mm) in the Insertion Options Tab.

Be aware that the downstage wall is actually three walls in a row. Choose the Left Control Line Mode, and begin to draw from the downstage right Locus {-35' (10,972.8mm) X and -6" (152.4mm) Y}. Connect the dots.

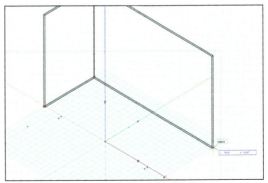

Once you have a box, with the downstage wall in three pieces, select the center section of that wall, the proscenium wall, and change the **Thickness** in the OIP to 24" (609.6mm) and the height to 48' (14,630.4mm). Go to **Modify>Move>Move3D** and **Move** that wall -7 1/2" (-190.5mm) Y and -3' (-914.4mm) Z so that the upstage stage side is flat and the wall is lower then the others.

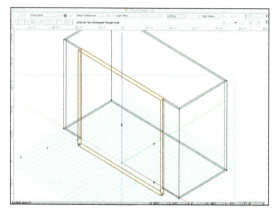

In the **Venue-Deck Class,** click and drag a rectangle from the outside edge of the upstage right wall to the outside edge of the downstage left wall. **Add** a 3' (914.4mm) by 40' (12,192mm) wide Rectangle to the downstage center of the original. Select the Polygon and go to **Spotlight>Architectural>Floor** and set the Bottom Z to -36" (-914.4mm) and the Thickness to 36" (914.4mm). Send this object to the **Back**. A Floor Object is a Hybrid Object.

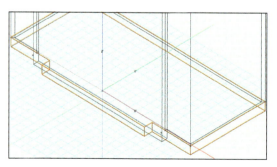

Activate the Door Tool from the Building Shell Tool Set and insert a door at center, in the proscenium wall. With the door selected, look at the door in different views and then, in the OIP, change the width to 40' (12,192mm) and the height to 20' (6,096mm). The **Height** will have defaulted to -36" (-914.4mm) and will need to be changed to 0 so the opening is on the deck. Although the huge **Simple Swing** is funny in the **Top/Plan View**, change the **Configuration** to **Cased Opening**.

Add a standard size Simple Swing Door up left. Review the Door Settings in the OIP to see the flexibility of this tool.

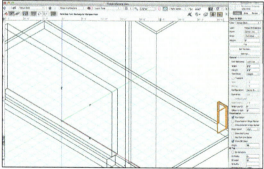

Using the **Round Wall Tool,** in the **Venue-Walls Class** change the **Insertion Options** so the next wall is 48' (14,630.4mm) tall with the **Bottom Offset** -36' (-914.4mm). Use the **Left Control Line Mode** and the **Three Points Mode**.

Snap another Rectangle above the top left point of this polygon 33" (838.2mm) by 20' (6.096mm) wide, and **Add** the two polys together. Use the **Reshape Tool** to delete the top right **Vertex Point**.

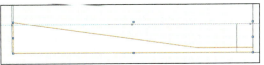

Tap from the Locus at the downstage right of the Proscenium Wall, and connect the dots on the left side of the auditorium. Mirror the new Wall Object.

Extrude this object 35' (10,668mm).

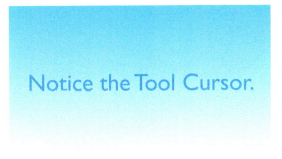

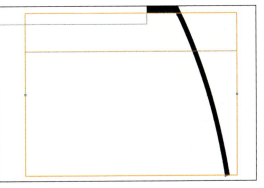

The black fill might be nice for Scenic Designer drawings, but Lighting, and Sound designers will probably want the venue architecture less prominent in their drawings. That's easy to fix with a **Class Override** on a **Viewport** placed on a **Sheet Layer**.

Go to the **Right Isometric View** and change the **Working Plane** to the bottom of this Object. Use the **Arc Tool** in the **Three Points Mode** to draw an arc along the base of the wall object. Once drawn, use the **Selection Tool** to extend the **Arc** in each direction.

Switch to the Right Side View and work in the Venue-Auditorium Floor Class. Click and drag a rectangle from the inner edge of the curved auditorium wall to the face of the proscenium wall, 6" (152.4mm) tall.

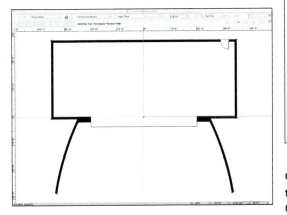

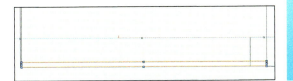

The **Selection Tool** will show two different **cursors** as you hover over the end points of the Arc:
- A Cross which will move the object.
- A Diagonal which will move the end points of the object.

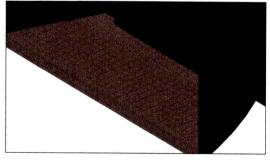

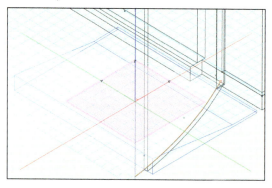

Use the **Push/Pull Tool, Sub-Face Mode** and the **Arc** to **Pull Away** the outside section of this object. First, using the **Push/Pull Tool**, in the **Sub-Face Mode**, select the Arc. Then select the 3D Object. Hover over the area to be deleted, and it will become highlighted. Click and drag that away.

Duplicate Array the **Auditorium Floor** 12'-6" (3,810mm) on the Z Axis and change the Class of the new Object to **Venue-Balcony**.

Turn off the **Visibility** of the **Venue-Auditorium Floor Class**, and go to the **Lower-right Isometric View**. Set the **Working Plane** to the bottom of the Balcony Object. Save the Working Plane. Go back to the **Top View**, and strike an **Arc** by **Three Points** using the center of this Object, and the middle Locus points used to make the auditorium walls. Extend the curve and Trim as before with the **Push/Pull Tool**.

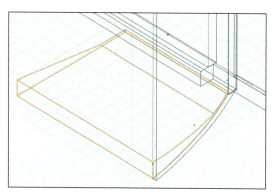

Mirror and **Duplicate** this object from the 0-0 point and use the **Model>Add Solids Command** to make one object.

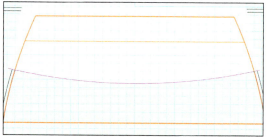

Once again, select the **Round Wall Tool**, and open the **Tool Preferences**. In this case, we will want a 6" (152.4mm) thick wall 54" (1,371.6mm) tall with the **Bottom Offset** 9'-6" (2,895.6mm) to make a railing along the edge of the balcony.

Use the **Three Points Mode** to trace the edge of the balcony object.

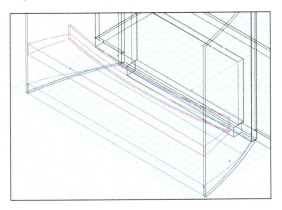

All that is left now are the Smoke Pockets for the fire curtain, and to determine the Plaster Line.

The term **Plaster Line** dates to before the existence of fire curtains. Since the upstage side of the Proscenium was finished with plaster (dry wall didn't exist either), the name made sense. It is really hard to get your hands into a smoke pocket, so the Plaster Line is now typically snapped on the upstage side of the smoke pocket.

Zoom in on the stage right side of the proscenium. **Snap** the lower-left corner of a 12" (304.8mm) wide by 6" (152.4mm) tall Rectangle to the onstage stage edge of the arch opening. **Duplicate** that Rectangle 1/4" (6.35mm) X and

-1/4"(-6.35mm) Y, **Clip**, delete the Clipping Object and **Extrude** to 35'(10,668mm). Assign the Venue-Walls Class and **Mirror** and **Duplicate** to create the stage left smoke pocket.

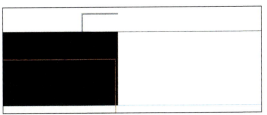

Soft Goods Object Tool

The **Soft Goods Object Tool** in the **Spotlight Tool Set** defines and models Hybrid Objects that can represent many different types of stage and Trade Show drapery. Entire Environments can be created with this Tool, Textures, and Lighting. Select the Tool, and review the drawing modes and Preferences. Draw a **Curtain** and a **Border** using the default settings. Switch to a side view, select one, and change the object type from Curtain to Border, and back. Note how the different objects hang.

Draw a complex shape, and adjust the settings in the OIP. Click to begin, press the **U** key to switch between modes, double-click to end the **Curtain Object.**

We will need the House Curtains, which would be limited. We will assume only a Fire Curtain, and a Grand Drape.

On the **Venue Architecture Design Layer**, in the **Normal Line Weight Class**, using the **Line Tool** from the **Basic Tool Set**, snap a line for the fire curtain from the center of one of the smoke pockets to the center of the other. In the OIP, make that line slightly shorter.

Right-click on the line and select **Create Objects from Shapes**. Choose **Soft Goods** from the drop-down and check **Show Properties Dialog** and **Delete Source Shapes**. Click **OK**.

In the **Soft Goods Dialog**, choose **Curtain**, set the height to 22' (6,705.6mm), the **Pleat Width** to 2' (50.8mm) and the **Pleat Depth** to 1" (25.4mm). Press the **3D Curtain Options** button and choose **Opaque** for the drop-down, and then a light gray color. Click **OK**.

In the OIP, set the Z of the object to 22' (6,705.6mm).

When using an image, the **Soft Goods Object** will stretch the image to fit the size of the object. Consider this when creating texture, like backdrops, to be applied to a Soft Goods Object.

Soft Goods Objects are not Classed in the same way other object types have been assigned classes. In the Preferences, or the OIP, Soft Goods Objects can be assigned to specific sets

of classes that the tool will create. Once created, those classes and assigned attributes can be edited in the **Organization Dialog**. When updating Soft Goods Objects in the OIP, be sure to tap the **Update** button.

Duplicate the fire curtain 12" (204.8mm) on the Y axis, change the color to a red, the Pleat Width to 3" (76.2mm), and the Pleat Depth to 2" (50.8mm) to create the Grand Drape.

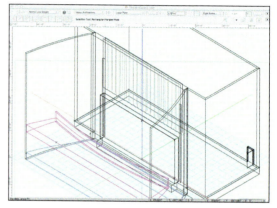

If you want to personalize this project you can begin to consider options:
- Change the shape of the Door Object (the proscenium arch).
- Add a decorative moulding around the arch using Extrude Along Path, assigning a texture already made or a new one of your own.
- Add Grand Valance using the Soft Goods Tool to fill in the top of the proscenium arch

Audience Seating

Go to, and work in the **Audience Design Layer** and the **Normal Line Weight Class**.

This section is about the use of these tools. In general, when drawing a proscenium theatre, it is necessary to plot the end seats, but it is not necessary to know exactly here every seat is located. These tools are most useful in planning theatres, working in unconventional spaces, or

> Share the work load; one survey of the performance space can work for the entire production team.

when other special layouts are needed. How the seating layout might be organized using Classes or Layers is project driven.

There are three different ways to create audience seating in Vectorworks:
- The Seating Layout Tool located in the Furn/Fixtures Tool Set.
- The Spotlight>Architectural>Create Seating Layout Command
- The Event Planning>Create Event Seating Command

They are all variations on a theme and some approaches work better for different users.

When taking a site survey, it is critical to plot the positions of the end seats to determine sight lines. In this case we will use the **Create Seating Layout Command.**

Snap a rectangle to the downstage center of the stage, and the far house right **Locus. Soft Goods Objects** have been classed, and their **Visibility** set to **Off** to speed the drawing.

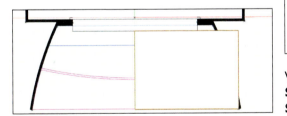

Use the **Reshape Tool** to Snap the top right corner to the auditorium wall.

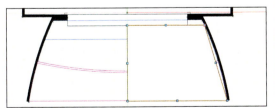

This object will be the **Bounding Box** for the house right seating area: there will be two seating areas, and three fire aisles; select and go to the OIP. Use the **Box Position Indicator** to let Vectorworks do the following math.

The fire aisles must be 5' (1,524mm) wide by building code. The **Seating Layout Command** will inset the seats by about the amount of the **Seat Spacing**, which in this case is 1'-8 1/2" (520.7mm).

In the OIP check the bottom right circle in the **Box Position Indicator** and add -9 1/2" (-241.3mm) in the **Delta X Data Field**, and hit **Return/Enter**. Then choose the lower-left circle in the **Box Position Indicator** and subtract 39 1/2" (1,003mm) from the **Delta X**.

Some of this math has been provided, but the more complex work was left to the application.

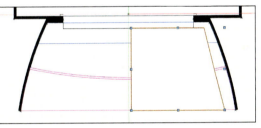

With the Polygon selected, run the **Spotlight>Architectural>Create Seating Layout Command.** Choose the **Padded Theatre Seat** from the **Default Content.** Set the **Focus** to be straight ahead.

In the OIP, change the Row Spacing and Offset First Row to 3' (914.4mm), the Base Z height to -30" (-762mm), and the Rise per row to 4 1/2" (114.3mm).

Mirror and **Duplicate**.

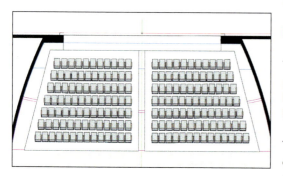

Seats add a lot of geometry to your documents. If you're working in theatre consulting, you probably want to create your own seating symbols. They should accurately represent the products being specified, and use minimal geometry.

Sightlines are critical to masking, and masking is critical to the Audience Experience.

Review this work from a number of different angles. Go though the additional options in the OIP, always reserving one side as drawn.

Of course, these tools can also be used to plan the seating when you're asked to design the opening night party.

End Seats & Sightlines

This is a basic concept for most any kind of production. We do not want the audience to see backstage; what we do is create magic, and seeing backstage gives away the magician's secrets.

This is certainly true of theatre, but also special events, film, television, concerts, and any performance.

Open the EndSeat.vwx file and **Reference** or **Import** the **Hybrid EndSeat Symbol**. Return to the **Venue Architecture Design Layer** and **Insert** an **Instance** of the **EndSeat Symbol** at the center of one of the end seats. Use the Seating Layout to approximate the balcony End Seat.

Turn off the **Visibility** of the **Audience Design Layer,** and locate the Z elevation of the EndSeat symbols, and look at what is visible with no masking in place.

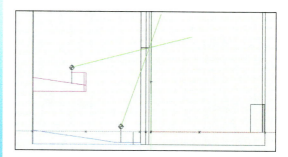

Sightlines on the plan show designers what the audience can and cannot see.

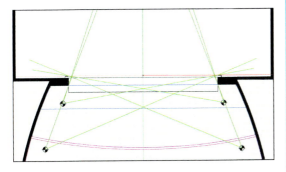

Creating the Theatre Symbol

So, the theatre model is ready to be used by the team. In the **Venue-Architecture Design Layer**, with the **Soft Goods Objects** visible, Select All, and go to **Modify>Create Symbol.**.

Name the new Symbol **Theatre Architecture** and check **Next Mouse Click** as the **Insertion Point.** Tap **OK**, and then tap again at the 0-0 point to use that for placement.

Tools intended for architecture or landscaping can be used for other purposes.

You might also like to make a symbol for the Audience Seating. Be sure to set the **Insertion Point** to the 0-0 point, not the center of the symbol.

Wall Styles

We have been working with **Unstyled Walls**. Vectorworks Designer, Architect, and Landmark include the ability to create and reuse **Wall Styles**. The attributes of an **Unstyled Wall** can be changed by Class, or from the **Attributes Palette**.

Wall Styles facilitate drawing walls by saving the **Wall Preferences Settings** so that they can be applied to other walls. **Wall Styles** are **Resources** and can be imported into other files and shared.

Carefully plot the positions of the end seats.

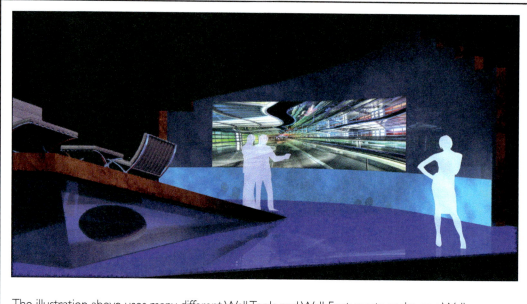

The illustration above uses many different Wall Tools and Wall Features to make one Wall.

Wall Styles allow different portions of walls to have different finishes, depths, and textures. In **Top/Plan** view, these differences can be illustrated with **Hatches**, and/or **Pattern Fills**.

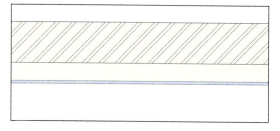

Wall Styles are defined and modified in the **Wall Preferences Dialog**. Walls can also be drawn first, and then modified in the OIP.

The **Wall Tools** are very flexible, they have uses well beyond basic architecture. Roof Lines or the tops of walls can be modified using the **Reshape Tool**. While intended for creating architectural gables and sloped roof lines, they

can be used for those tasks, and other dramatic statements.

Spotlight ships with the ability to modify walls with **Projections** and **Recesses** using simple 2D geometry to configure 3D details. Vectorworks Designer includes the **Stepped Wall** feature from the Architect and Landmark packages, which can be used to quickly model ziggurats, or walls that progress up a series of platforms.

As we did with the proscenium wall, sometimes a wall needs to be more than one wall.

If we had used **Wall Styles**, we could have changed the style of the Wall with the proscenium opening to the different thickness, and not had to move the Wall after changing the thickness. Similarly, Wall Styles would have offered the ability to quickly and easily detail the auditorium in different colors, or patterns, if required.

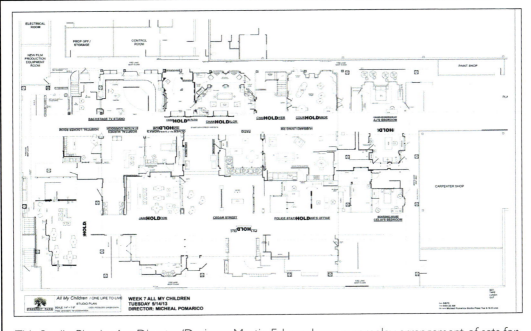

This Studio Plan by Art Director/Designer Martin Fahrer shows a complex arrangement of sets for *All My Children*, the serial drama. A number of different wall types are illustrated..

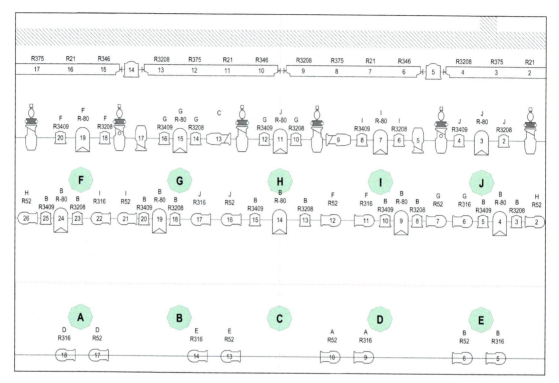

All I Ask of You
Detail of Light Plot

All I Ask of You

All I Ask of You
Michael Padgett, Haley Swindal, Grace Deal, Matthew G. Myers

All I Ask of You: A Musical Tribute to Andrew Lloyd Webber
The Surflight Theatre

Artistic Director: Roy Miller
Executive Producer: Timothy Laczynski
Director: Vincent Marini
Lighting Designer: Kevin Lee Allen
   Design Assistant: Sam Gordon

12. Lysistrata

Every project needs a play. If it's not a theatrical piece, there still needs to be some kind of outline, or program on which the design will be based. For the purposes of this book, we will begin with the Greek comedy *Lysistrata*, and see how far from the text we might divert.

Lysistrata by Aristophanes, an early parody of sexual relations in a male-dominated society, was originally performed in 411 BC, possibly at Dionysia, a festival celebrating the god Dionysus (the god of the grape harvest, wine, ritual madness, and ecstasy). A comedic tale of one woman's efforts to end the Peloponnesian War, Lysistrata persuades the women of Greece to withhold sex from their men in order to force the men to negotiate peace — a strategy that goes awry.

Aristophanes was a comic playwright of ancient Athens and wrote *Lysistrata* as farcical political satire. It is believed that he lived for about 60 years circa 446 BCE to circa 386 BCE. His eleven extant plays are what we know of the genre Old Comedy, defined by political satire and innuendo.

Old Comedy has influenced writers from Cervantes to *Saturday Night Live*. In particular, comedians and satirists continue the technique of disguising a political attack as buffoonery.

Old Comedy's emphasis on real personalities and local issues make the plays difficult to appreciate today without the aid of scholarly commentaries, and even then the text is generally dry. Consider how dated old episodes of *Saturday Night Live* can be without their context being current. Old Comedy is the first example we have of what has become Burlesque, or Neo-Burlesque in current culture.

Burlesque is a variety show (music, dance, striptease, comedic sketches) performance intended to amuse by caricaturing serious works and issues, through ludicrous treatment of the subjects. *Lysistrata*, even in its original form, contained these elements, designed to entertain its contemporary audience. A far different audience than our own contemporary audiences.

Neo-Burlesque is the current revival and updating of traditional American burlesque. Based on the traditional Burlesque art, Neo-Burlesque encompasses a wide range of performance styles; anything from classic striptease to modern dance to drama to madcap comedy.

Lysistrata begins with a series of puns and ends in a metaphorical orgy in song, dance, and feast. It ignores the obvious question: What's a few more days when the men have been at war for years?

Burlesque is a variety show with caricature.

The Conceptual Approach

Lysistrata is a play that satirizes the relationship between the sexes. Our production will update the script into a Neo-Burlesque style performance, more like musical comedy than traditional drama. This approach will make a dated text with an eternal message, relevant to a current-day audience.

Metaphorically, the set will be like a bird cage: an elegant cage that Lysistrata uses to bring her women together and keep them from their men. They are not going willingly.

From a Lighting Design perspective, the guiding image will be that the light will be like fire bursting from cold embers.

The environment requires a few basic necessities:
- The Acropolis, the upper city, the highest point in the settlement.
- An open space for Myrrhine to seduce Cinesias; the same open space for the ending.
- Braziers and possibly The Propylaea

A Propylaea is a monumental gateway.

Greek Architecture

Before we begin to abstract an idea or a period of Architectural Design, we must understand what it is we are abstracting. This short abstract is by no means a substitution for the comprehensive research required of designers.

Historians divide Ancient Greek civilization into two primary eras: the Hellenic period (from around 900 BCE), and the Hellenistic period (beginning with the death of Alexander the Great in 323 BC to 30 AD). During the Hellenic period, substantial works of architecture began to be built. The Hellenistic period saw Greek culture spread, initially as a result of Alexander's conquests, and then as a result of the rise of the Roman Empire, which adopted much of the Greeks' culture. The Peloponnesian War was fought between 431 and 404 BCE, so our architecture must have been built prior to 404 BCE, or during the Hellenic Period.

The basic structure of the architecture of Ancient Greece is of a trabeated or post and lintel/post and beam form. Like most of what the Greeks invented architecturally, this type of construction is still in use today. Vertical posts or columns support horizontal beams or lintels. At the time, wood or stone could be used; now that might also be steel or concrete. Posts and beams divide walls into segments which might be open or filled.

The Golden Ratio

The Golden Ratio or Golden Section is a ratio simplified as 1.618. Also simply, a Golden rectangle would measure 1.618x by 1x. This proportion, mathematically proven, is often considered a most pleasing and beautiful shape. The Greeks built their temple facades to these proportions. The Golden Rectangle is still very important in Japanese design. Vectorworks can create a Rectangle constrained to the Golden

Ratio if Control/Command+Shift is pressed while drawing.

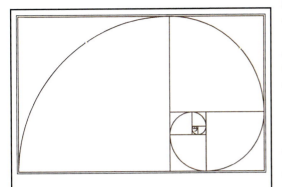

When a rectangle is in the Golden Proportion, and the rectangle is partitioned into a square, the new resulting rectangle is also a Golden Rectangle. Successive divisions create a spiral also known as a whirling square.

The Doric Order

There are three major types, or orders, of Greek architecture:
- Doric
- Ionic
- Corinthian

Given the time frame, it is likely that our temple would be and should be based on the Doric Order. The columns of a temple support a structure that rises in two main stages, the entablature and the pediment.

The *entablature* is the major horizontal structural element supporting the roof and it encircles the building. The entablature is generally about a third of the height of the columns. It is composed of three parts and is usually approximately a quarter of the height of the columns.

Resting on the columns is the *architrave* made of a series of stone lintels that span the columns, and join directly above the center of each column.

Above the *architrave* is a second horizontal stage called the *frieze*. The *frieze* is a major decorative element of the building and often carries a sculptured relief, divided into sections called metopes which fill the spaces between vertical rectangular blocks called *triglyphs*. The vertically grooved *triglyphs* retain the form of wood beams.

The upper band of the *entablature* is called the *cornice*, which is generally ornately decorated on its lower edge.

At the front and back, the entablature supports a triangular structure called the *pediment*. The pediment, like the entablature is about one-third the height of the columns. The triangular space framed by the cornices on the pediment is the location of the most significant exterior decoration. There are decorative enhancements called *acroterion* at the top and sides of the pediment.

The facade of a Doric Temple, excluding the acroterion, fit within a Golden Rectangle.

This model of the Greek temple of Aphaia in Aegina, illustrates the proportions and components of the Doric Order.

The Doric column tapers towards the top and has 20 flutes, and stands without a base on the Stylobate, which is the uppermost step of a platform called Crepidoma. The Doric Capital is a smooth capital that flares (rounds) from the top of the column to meet a square abacus that supports the architrave.

The Roman architect Vitruvius determined the proper height of Doric columns to be six or seven times the diameter of the column at the base. Similarly, Vitruvius determined that the column spacing was determined by the diameter of the column, from 1 1/2 to 3 1/2 column widths. There would generally have been an even number of columns.

Forced Perspective

In order to counteract the perception of the human eye, the Greeks added a slight bit of vertical forced perspective. In truth, the Greek Temples are not square, but they vanish towards a point in the sky, so they are, in elevation, more of a trapezoid. Disney does this in its theme parks, the upper stories of the castles and Main Street buildings are not as tall as the preceding stories.

An illustration of how the Greeks likely used color on a Doric Temple.

The Project Team

It would be typical on any project that one person works out the specifics for the rest of the team. In film, that might be the Art Director. The Art Director is often described as the person who translates the Production Designer's scribbles on bar napkins into executable ideas. In theatre that person might be the Designer or Associate Designer, in each department. This would include working out the sightlines, masking, or the camera shots required.

In this case, that person is the author.

Color

Much of the ancient Greek architecture was colorfully painted to enhance the visual aspects of the structures. Sometimes color was applied to add patterns, sometimes simply to separate elements. Obviously, over the course of thousands of years the paint has faded or peeled away completely. The vibrant blues, bright sunlight, and stark white we generally associate with Greece were not the only colors. Vibrant colors of the time were limited by the available, or invented pigments, or the use of colored stone, like terra-cotta.

Know what you abstract.

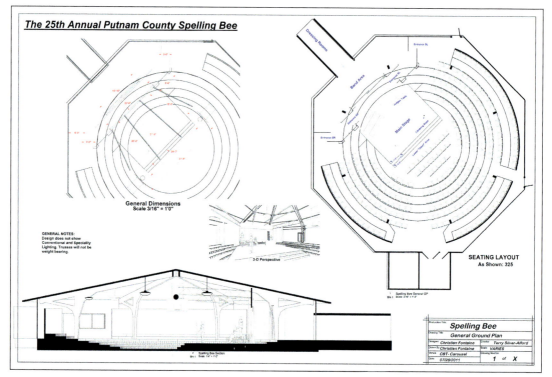

The 25th Annual Putnam County Spelling Bee
General Plans, Section, and Sketch.

The 25th Annual Putnam County Spelling Bee
Production Photo

The 25th Annual Putnam County Spelling Bee
Clarence Brown Theatre, University of Tennessee

Scenic Designer: Christien Fontaine
Costume Designer: Ellis Greer
Lighting Designer: Kate Bashore
Sound Designer: Mike Ponder
Director: Terry Silver-Alford

This design was explored and built out using Vectorworks in 3D.

13. Modeling the Scenery

By now many Vectorworks procedures, like basic drawing, modeling, and creating symbols should be ingrained, if not completely step by step. This chapter walks you through how to combine techniques to model scenery.

The Braziers

Let's begin with something fast and fun. We know we need Braziers, but this is a burlesque production. How historically accurate do they need to be? Not very. Ours will be based on a martini glass.

Open a new document and import the file **Martini.psd** from the Website into the **Trace Layer, Front View**, working in the **Layer Plane** with the bottom left Snapped to 0-0. Use the **Scale Command, Scale by Distance**, to make the image 6' (1,828.8mm) tall.

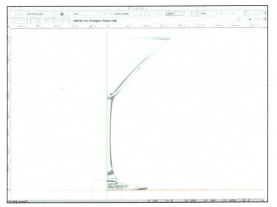

This is an object that will be touched by many departments: it needs to be danceable; Technical Direction will need to weigh in on the thickness; it needs to have fire, another concern for Technical Direction; the Lighting Designer may want to incorporate light below, or some LED tape; the cueing of the fire will need to be coordinated with Lighting Design. We're modeling the Scenic Designer's vision.

Reference these textures from your Lysistrata-Textures document:
- Glass Blue
- Metal Aluminum Brushed Blue

Create the Classes needed for this object;
- Martini-Fire, with **Use at Creation** unchecked
- Martini-Glass using the Glass Blue texture
- Martini-Shaft using the Metal Aluminum Brushed Blue texture

Roughly trace, in another Design Layer, the outline of the martini glass using the **Polyline Tool, Corner Vertex Mode**, or by switching between Modes.

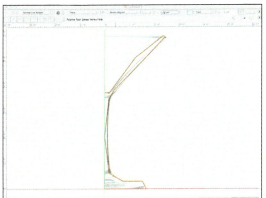

Once you have the initial profile, edit with the **Reshape Tool** until you have an accurate outline.

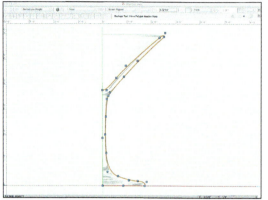

Copy or **Duplicate** the **Profile** to preserve for future use, and **Sweep** accepting the defaults. Assign the Martini-Glass Class.

Paste or **Move** the copy of the **Profile** back to 0-0, on the same Design Layer, and edit the profile to have a 1 1/2" (38.1mm) center shaft (turn off the visibility of the Martini-Glass if that helps edit). This element is the gas feed for the flame. Since this **Profile** will also be **Swept**, that width should be divided by two, so a 3/4" (19.05mm) actual width. Working with the original curve will give you a matching *cup* at the top of 4" (101.6mm); these will double when **Swept**.

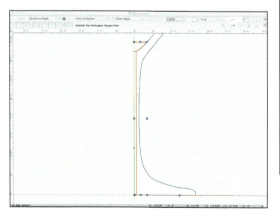

Sweep this **Profile**, assign the **Martini-Shaft Class**, and **Copy** the **Object**. Select both Sweeps and go to **Model>Subtract Solids**, to create a hole in the glass.

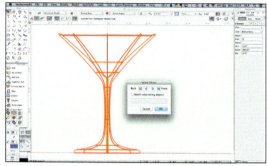

This operation will delete the inner form as it makes that form part of the Glass. **Paste in Place** to add the solid back.

Draw a **Rectangle**, in the **Three Points Rotated Mode** at a 5° angle over the glass object. Extrude to cover the glass; it is best practice to keep the overage to a minimum. You do need some overage.

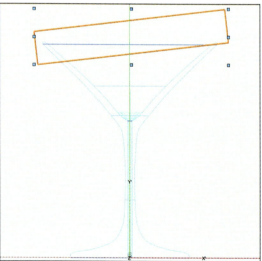

Center the Rectangle Extrude on the glass in the plan view and **Subtract Solids.**

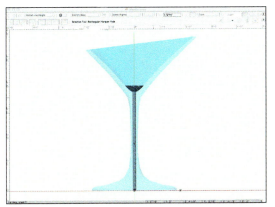

Alternately, the Martini Glass could be trimmed using the **Split Tool** located in the Basic Tool Set. With or without adding Locus Point Objects for a precise cut, drawing a line with the Split Tool in either **Line Split** or **Line Trim Mode** will give the same results as the **Solid Subtraction**.

Add some liquid, an olive, and a toothpick if you like. Class those things so they can be turned off. Go to **Model>Create Image Prop** and import the file Fire1.psd from the Website content. Set the **Height** to 6' (1,828.8mm), and check all of the options. Choose **Use Mask**, and tap the **Create Mask** button. Choose **Reuse an Image from Another Resource**, and **This Prop's Color.** Click **OK.** Select **Transparent Color,** and then tap with the finger cursor on the black area of the image preview. The mask will then be shown on the right side. Use the **Color Matching** and **Mask Contrast** sliders to adjust the **Mask**. Click **OK.**

Find the best ways for *you* to work.

The **Image Prop** is placed at 0-0-0; move it up to the base of the center shaft object. **Select All** and create the **Martini Glass Symbol** with a **Center Insertion Point**. Edit the 2D portion of the symbol to add a simple Screen Plane **Circle Object** at the correct overall size as the 2D component to make the symbol **Hybrid**.

The Topiary

In a new document, **Reference** the **Topiary** texture and create a Class called **Topiary Class** that uses the same. In Vectorworks, you cannot have two resources with the same name, so the Class cannot be called simply *Topiary*. The application also reserves some names, like *Window* for its own use.

This is an opportunity to experiment with the **Bump Map**, **Displacement Mapping**. The greater the **Height** of the **Displacement Map**, the more bold the look of the foliage, the more geometry added, and the longer the rendering time. Working in this file, it is easy to experiment with this feature. When assembled with the rest of the project, large Displacement may slow rendering to an unacceptable speed.

Draw a 12" (304.8mm) by 12" (304.8mm) rectangle and extrude to 7' (2,133.6mm). Duplicate that object -10'-6" (3,200.4mm) on the X axis, change the width to 24" (609.6mm) and the height to 12' (3,657.6mm).

Between these two verticals, draw a 9' (2,743.2mm) by 11' (3,352.6mm) tall rectangle. **Reshape** the **Rectangle** so that you have a trapezoid with the left side 11' (3,352.6mm) tall, and the right 6' (1.828.8mm) tall. Add a **Bezier Control Point** to the top center using the **Reshape Tool**, and pull down to create a gentle curve from higher to lower.

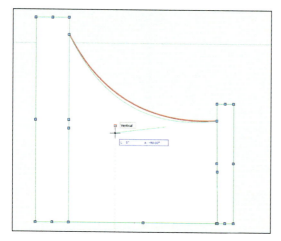

Extrude the center section 6" (152.4mm) and align the three objects on center.

On top of the square column draw a simple finial, about 6" (152.4mm) by 14" (355.6mm) tall. **Clip**

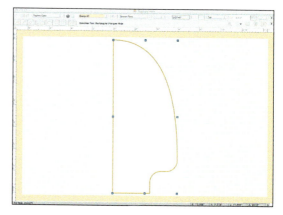

a bit away from the bottom, add an interior and exterior **Fillet**, and **Reshape** to get the top curve.

Sweep, and be sure the finial is centered over the column in the Top/Plan View. Snap centers if required. Save the finial as a Symbol.

This next step can be done in two ways. All of the visible edges now require a 2" (50.8mm) **Fillet**. If you shift select all of those edges with the **Fillet Tool** from the **3D Modeling Tool Set**, the three objects will group together. If that object is **Ungrouped**, the Fillets will be lost.

The desired end product is two different topiary symbols, one as drawn thus far, and one just the square column with the finial. Add the **Fillet** in multiple steps so that all of the objects do not become one group. Save the left column and finial symbol as another symbol, and then the entire

Don't waste the producer's money on things that are not seen.

unit as one symbol that includes the other symbols.

Fillet the taller column and center object. Do not **Fillet** the rear corner; it will not be seen when this object is inserted into the overall stage composition.

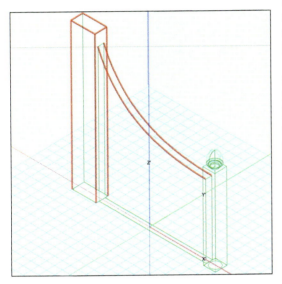

Then **Fillet** the square column. In this case, the rear corner will require a **Fillet**, as some seats will see that edge.

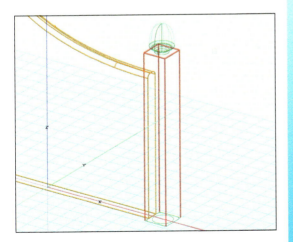

If those placements change, this symbol can be modified and instances in other drawings will be updated.

The Technical Director or constructing shop can fill the voids of these forms with the required structural elements. Given the sightlines, it is likely that the larger column would be only two sided, the center element would be a simple flat, while the square column would actually need to be a column.

Working in the BIM manner allows collaboration between designers, and the craftspeople who bring the designs to life. Sharing files is critical to that collaboration and working in 3D lets everyone on the team see how the components come together.

The Bump Map and the Displacement help to illustrate the greenery, upholstery, and the padding without really complex modeling.

It is likely these scenic pieces would be framed with plywood cores, and pine, skinned with thin flexible plywood, and then upholstered with grass cloth, possibly padding.

Option/Alt Drag to copy the square column, and the finial. Select the first set of objects and create the **Topiary Symbol**, then select the shorter column and finial to create the **Topiary Symbol-2**. Set the **Insertion Points** for both symbols at the center.

Edit each symbol to add the basic 2D geometry required for a **Hybrid Symbol**.

Save and exit the Topiary.vwx file.

The Settee

While Vectorworks ships with extensive furniture libraries, there is hardly a production that does not require the modeling of a custom piece. These techniques are also useful when modeling custom speakers or Spotlight Lighting Devices.

Set up your new drawing document.

The Settee requires three Classes:
- Settee-2D, a duplicate of Normal Line Weight
- Settee-Frame using the Referenced Black-Gloss texture
- Settee-Upholstery using the Referenced Leopard texture.

Save the file as Settee.vwx in the **Lysistrata Workgroup Folder**.

In the Front View, working in the Layer Plane, Import the file SetteeLayout.jpg from the Website. This document provides most of the basic information you will need to create the object as a Hybrid Symbol.

Sometimes you do not have all of the information and have to choose.

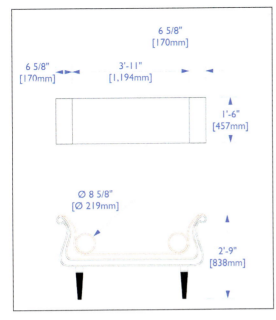

The legs of the settee are not at all obvious. They are 3D symbols named, oh so cleverly, Settee-Leg. Import the file SetteeLegs.jpg from the Website onto a new **Design Layer** and **Scale Objects**.

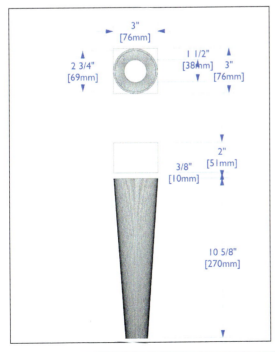

The base of the legs is a **Multiple Extrude Object** made from two **Circles**. The top part is a simple **Extrude** of a **Rectangle**. They are separated by another simple extrude based on a **Circle**.

Assign the Vertical positions in the OIP or by using the **Move>Move 3D Command**.

After modelling, assign the **Settee-Frame Class** and create the **Symbol**.

Return to the view of the SetteeLayout and trace on a new Design Layer. It is best to only trace half, then use the **Mirror Tool**, in the **Mirror and Duplicate Mode**, followed by **Add Surface**.

Begin by tracing and editing the outer profile of the frame. The inner profile of the frame should be created by **Offsetting** the outer frame.

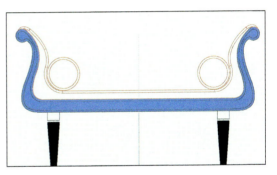

Reserve a copy of the outer frame to use in creating the outside edge of the upholstery. You have the depth of the outer frame, but the inner part of the frame is just trim. It should not be very deep, but it does need to exist on both sides of the settee.

Similarly, the pillows must fit neatly into the upholstery. As you work, be aware of these edges and how they need to be form-fitting for the furniture to look correct when rendered.

The upholstered items have been Filleted with the 3D Fillet Tool. It is alternately possible to use the **Extract Tool** on the upholstered objects and add *piping* using another **Circle** object and **Extrude Along Path**. To reduce rendering times, an octagon, or other regular polygon might substitute for the circle.

A small **Chamfer** on the frame is possible. Chamfers or hard objects catch the light better than Fillets, but for the upholstery a Fillet or piping, or a combination, are more accurate.

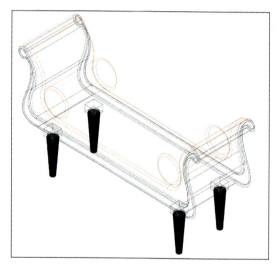

Place the Settee-Legs Symbols, **Select All,** and create the 3D portion of the Settee Symbol. Edit to draw the 2D Content.

This is all much like working from a cut sheet of information provided by a manufacturer.

When drawing the 2D content in the Screen Plane, you have the option of using **Gradient Fills** to add the illusion of shadows and curves in the **Top/Plan View**.

The Portal

The Portal requires the file PortalMoulding.vwx from the Website, referencing the textures Black-Velour and Gold-Rough from the Lysistrata-Textures.vwx file, and of course, a new document. Save the new file as Portal.vwx in the **Lysistrata Workgroup Folder**.

You will need three Classes:
* Portal-2D, a container Class for the 2D components
* Portal-Velour using the Black-Velour Texture
* Portal-Moulding using the Gold-Rough Texture

A Portal or Portals help with masking and provide definition to the end of the stage picture. Portals can be used to change the shape of the proscenium arch.

In an isometric view, click near 0-0 and rotate the working plane from the top to the front view.

Place a 25' (7,620mm) tall by 50' (15,240mm) wide Rectangle centered at 0-0. Extrude to -12" (-304.8mm) thick. Add another rectangle 18' (5,486.4mm) by 36' (10,972.8mm) wide. Use the **Push/Pull Tool** In the **Sub-Face Mode** to create an opening.

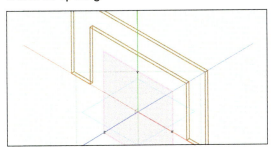

Place another Rectangle, also centered at the bottom 0-0 working in the Front View, 37'-4" (11,369.04mm) by 18'-8 1/2" (5,702.3mm). Use the **Push/Pull Tool** in the **Sub-Face Mode** to create an -8 1/2" (-215.9mm) recess

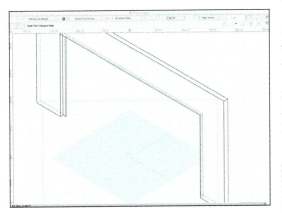

> Profile placement is critical to Extrude Along Path.

Go to the Top View: paste, rotate, and snap the moulding profile to the corner on the stage right side.

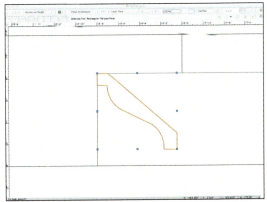

Return to the Front View and trace the opening with the **Polyline Tool**, using the **Corner Vertex Mode**. **Offset** this **Polyline** 4 1/4" (107.95mm) using the **Offset Original Object Mode**.

Move the **Polyline** 5" (127mm) on the Y Axis to center the **Polyline** at the center of the overall size of the moulding profile.

Select the **Polyline**, and the moulding profile and **Extrude Along Path**. Assign the Portal-Moulding Class.

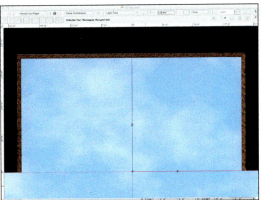

Use the Flyover Tool to navigate around the piece such that the Rectangles can be made to trim away the excess thickness with the Push/Pull Tool in Sub-Face Mode. This unit is 12" (304.8mm) thick all around. In reality there would be 3" (76.2mm) of framing, and the full thickness would only be around the opening and the moulding.

Once complete, create the 3D Symbol *Portal*, and **Edit** to create the 2D content. Set the **Insertion Point** of the Symbol at the center front in Plan View.

The Show Deck

You will need to create the file Deck.vwx in your Workgroup folder. From there, **Reference** the textures:
- Black-Gloss
- Metal Gold Polished Modified
- Lysistrata Floor

Creating a Hatch Fill

Go to the **Resource Browser**, right-click and tap **New Resource**, and then **Hatch** from the **Contextual Menu**.

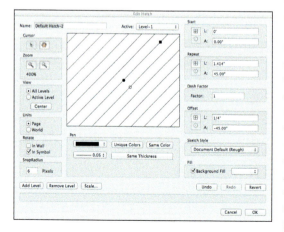

Hatch Fills can be applied to 2D objects, and walls. Hatches are visible in the Top/Plan View.

There are two types of hatches: **Associative** and **Non-Associative**. Their appearance is determined in the **Hatch Pattern Definition**.

Associative Hatches are resources and can be selected from the **Attributes Palette**, or assigned in a **Class Definition**. There are many standard architectural Hatches in the **Default Content**. The appearance of a **Hatch** can be modified using the **Fill Hatch Setting Button** in the **Attributes Palette**, or by using the **Attribute Mapping Tool** to move, rotate, or scale the hatch.

Non-Associative Hatches are placed on selected objects with the **Modify>Hatch Command**. **Non-Associative Hatches** obtain most of their attributes from **Hatch Definitions**, but they do not use the color definitions for the lines that make up the hatch, rather they obtain color definitions from the current **Default Attributes**. **Non-Associative Hatches** have no background color. **Non-Associative Hatches** overlay other objects; space between the lines is empty; portions of objects behind the hatch are visible.

Non-Associative Hatches are groups and not associated with any object. They do not rotate with the object, or act like a fill. They can be broken down into their individual elements with the Ungroup command. For a Non-Associative Hatch to become part of an object, it must be grouped with the object. It is generally *not* a good idea to use Non-Associative Hatches, as they greatly increase file sizes.

Name your new **Hatch** as **Lysistrata Floor Hatch**. The **Lysistrata Floor** texture is a squared, checkered 2' by 2' (609.6mm by 609.6mm) pattern; when applied the texture will be rotated 45° for a slight diamond effect. The **Hatch** will use lines to illustrate that appearance in the Top/Plan View.

Begin by changing the scale from **Page Based** to **World Based,** so that the **Hatch** appears correctly sized in the drawings.

Assign a light gray color to the **Pen,** and a .05mm **Line Weight**. Set the **Dash Factor** to **1** in order to create a solid line.

The **Start Position** should be at 0-0. Set the **Repeat Length** to 48" (1,219.2mm) and the **Repeat Angle** to -45°. **Offset** the **Length** the to 2' (609.6mm) and set that angle to 0. You can make interactive changes by dragging the control handles.

Tap the **Add Level Button**. The new Level will have the same **Attributes,** but will be slightly offset. Change the **Repeat** to 4' and 45° with the Offset at 2' (609.6mm) and 0°. Set the **Start** back to 0-0.

Now we can create the Classes required for this element:
- Deck-Deck using the Lysistrata Floor Hatch and the Lysistrata Floor Texture
- Deck-Face using the Black-Gloss Texture
- Deck-Trim using the Metal Gold Polished Modified Texture

Place a 19' (5,791.2mm) tall by 50' wide (15,240mm) Rectangle with the bottom center at 0-0. At the top center, **Add** a 54" (1,371.6mm) tall by 21' (6,400.8mm) wide Rectangle.

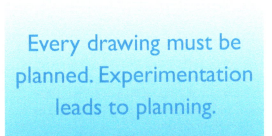

Every drawing must be planned. Experimentation leads to planning.

Place **Locus Objects** at 18' (5,684.4mm) either side of center at 0 Y, and one at 0 X and -3' (-914.4mm) Y. Use these points to draw a **Circle by Three Points**. **Clip** away the excess and add the downstage arc.

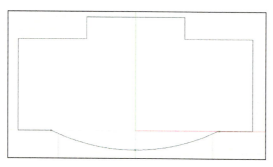

As you work, reserve the 2D geometry for later use both in modifying polygons, and to create the 2D portion of the symbol.

Open the file DeckGeometry.vwx from the Website. Copy the object from the **Center Component Design Layer** and **Paste in Place** above the deck just drawn. **Clip** that object away. **Retain both Objects**.

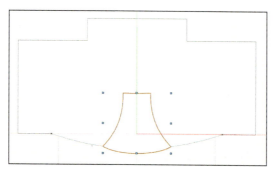

The center section will have an elevation of 1 1/2" (38.1mm) and the overall deck will have an elevation of 7 1/2" (190.5mm). The visible edges will have a simple 1 1/2" (38.1mm) by 1 1/2" (38.1mm) trim.

Offset and Duplicate the large polygon 1 1/2" (38.1mm) inside. **Add** Rectangles so that the **Offset** is only along the downstage and center sections.

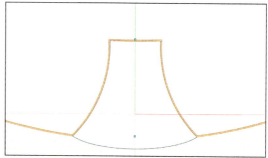

Extrude this element to 1 1/2" (38.1mm). Then in the OIP set the Class to Deck-Trim and the Bottom Z to 6" (152.4mm). Extrude the other portion to 6" and assign the Deck-Face Class. Use **Duplicate Array** to create another object the same size +6" (152.4mm) on the Z axis. Change the **Extrude** to 1 1/2" (38.1mm) in the OIP. Assign the Deck-Deck Class and go to the **Render Tab** of the OIP. **Rotate** the Texture 45°.

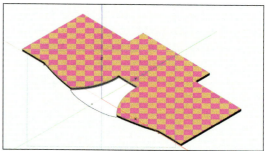

Keep in mind that for the 2D potion of the Hybrid Symbol, we will want the geometry of the outer perimeter.

Offset the center area 1 1/2" (38.1mm) to the outside of the shape. The new shape's edges should conform to the inner edge of the facing. The downstage edge is the edge of the trim.

Use the **Oval** and other geometry in the Deck Geometry file as well as the other geometry you have reserved in this file to create the trim.

Paste in Place is your friend, here and often.

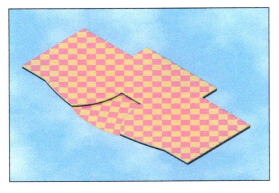

Select All and create the 3D Symbol **Deck** with the **Insertion Point** at 0-0.

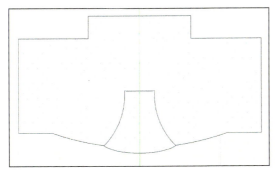

The Gates

Gates.vwx will only require one Class named *Gates* that will use the Referenced Black-Gloss Texture.

Begin in the Front View with a Rectangle 5'-9 1/2" (1,765.3mm) by 7'-10 3/4" (2,406.65mm) with the bottom center at 0-0. This size is specific to fit within the door opening and trim.

Offset the Rectangle by 1" (254mm); with that smaller Rectangle selected, go to the OIP and tap one of the left circles on the **Box Position Indicator** and type **/2** next to the width. Hit **Return**, and Vectorworks will divide the width in half. The OIP uses standard mathematical notation to act as a calculator.

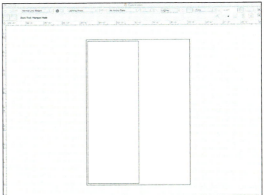

Use **Duplicate**, or **Duplicate Array** to create another **Rectangle**, same size, same place. In the OIP, using the **Box Position Indicator** as before, change the width to 1" (254mm). Repeat, or mirror, to create a similar size Rectangle on the right.

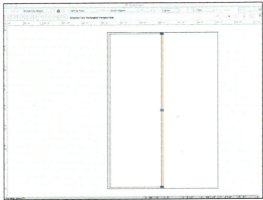

Select the right-hand skinny Rectangle with the **Reshape Tool** (remember you might have to **Modify>Convert to Polygons**), and add **Corner Points** to the verticals. Using the **Change Vertex Mode**, convert these points to **Bezier Curves**. Then in the **Move Polygon Handles Mode**, **Marquee Select** those points and drag the handles to the left. While dragging, tab into the Floating Data Bar and enter 6" (152.4mm) and maintain the 180° Angle.

Use Duplicate Array to make a copy of this object -6" (-152.4mm) on the X axis. Repeat the selection and drag the Bezier Points. Repeat this process until you have four curved objects.

Use the **Modify>Align>Align/Distribute** Command to space these objects. The command will interact with the **Bezier Control Handles**, so this might take some artistic license.

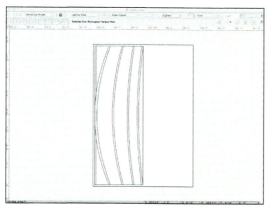

Select the left curved object with the **Rotate Tool** in **Rotate and Duplicate Mode,** connecting the duplicate with the right-hand curved object. **Repeat** with the new object, connecting that from the right-hand object to the second from right. As you work, these objects will need to be stretched in order to have the required length

Use copies of the same, left-hand vertical object to create angled horizontal bars.

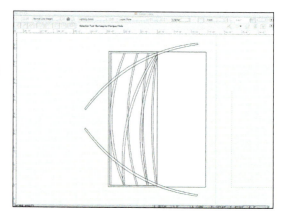

Clip as required to fit within the confines of the second of the larger rectangles.

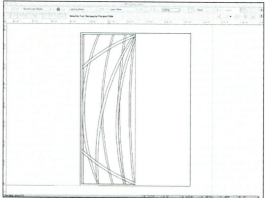

Extrude all of the more vertical elements 1" (254mm), and then **UnGroup** to have individual elements, and extrude the horizontal or diagonal elements -1" (-254mm). If you **Extrude** them all at once, they become **Grouped**, and more difficult to edit. If you have not been working in the **Gates Class**, make sure that the Class and the Graphic Attributes are assigned to all of the pieces.

Select All to make the **Gate Symbol**. It is one of two that make the **Gates**. Set the **Insertion Point** for the center right point. Edit the 2D portion of the symbol to add simple geometry:

- A Rectangle to represent the bars.
- An Arc with arrows assigned in the **Attributes Palette** to indicate this is a **Double Acting Door**.

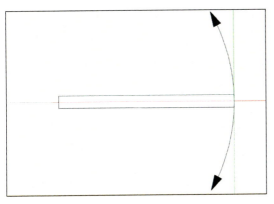

Assign the **Gates Class** to the 2D components.

The Acropolis

As always, create a new file. Save as Acropolis. vwx in your **Lysistrata Workgroup Folder**. Begin by **Referencing** the Textures;

- Acropolis Block
- Black-Gloss
- China Silk-Hot Pink-Austrian
- Gold-Key Pattern
- Lysistrata Floor
- Metal Gold Polished Modified
- Neon-Blue
- Sparkle
- Wallpaper
- Zebra

Using these Textures, create the Classes:

- Acropolis-Deck-Face
- Acropolis-Deck-Floor
- Acropolis-Deck-Trim
    This floor is treated like the Show Deck; also Reference the Hatch.
- Acropolis-Entablature-Architrave should have the *Gold-Key Pattern* Texture assigned
- Acropolis-Entablature-Trim uses the *Sparkle*
- Acropolis-GoGo Pole finished with *Metal Gold Polished Modified*
- Acropolis-Neon using *Neon-Blue*
- Acropolis-Stone with *Acropolis Block*
- Acropolis-Trim which will be *Black-Gloss*
- Acropolis-Wallpaper using the *Wallpaper* Texture

Give each Class a **Pen Color** that helps to identify the pieces. You can always go back and edit the choice.

A good document foundation yields good results.

Reference the Gate Symbol into the document.

Begin by placing a 2" (50.8mm) Circle, extruding to 16' (4,876.8mm). Assign the Acropolis-GoGo Pole Class and save the object as the 3D Symbol *Go-Go Pole*.

The basis of this unit is a Rectangle 8' (2,438.4mm) deep by 21' (6,400.8mm) wide. Insert the Rectangle and add 3" (76.2mm) to the bottom edge. Insert a **Locus Object** -12" (304.8mm) from the bottom center. Use the **Locus** and the bottom side points of the **Rectangle** to **Snap** a **Circle by Three Points**.

Clip away the excess area of the circle, and **Select All**, then **Modify>Add Surface**, so that you have a Polygon with a curved front edge.

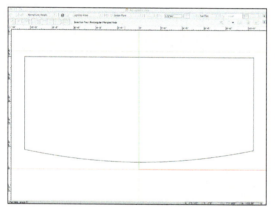

Offset this object 4' (1,219.2mm) and then offset that object 1' (304.8 mm) and, again, **Clip** away the excess so that the left and right edges are all even, but the curved edges move apart.

Clip 3" (76.2mm) by 8' (2,438.4mm) from the left and right of the original Polygon with the curved bottom edge. This allows this piece to sit within the wall to be created. Reserve a copy of this object for use in creating the second level floor and balcony.

Following the instructions used to model the Show Deck, use these Polys to create the base of the Acropolis.

Center a Rectangle 8' (2,438.4mm) deep by 21' (6,400.8mm) wide at the top/back center of the Deck. Offset inside that Rectangle by 3" (76.2mm) and then add the same or more to the back/top to **Clip** away from the original. **Extrude** 17' (5,181.6mm) to make the walls of the Acropolis. **Push/Pull** away from the front to allow this object to sit on the Deck.

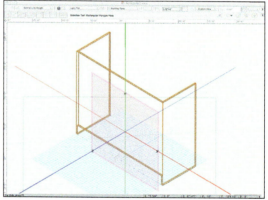

Use Class Visibilities to clearly see what you're drawing, and Snaps.

Assign the **Acropolis-Stone Class** to the object. Review and adjust the **Texture Mapping** in the OIP.

Create the Rectangles needed for the opening in the facade:
- The bottom center opening for the gates is 6' (1,828.8mm) by 8' (2,438.4mm) tall.
- The bottom left and right openings are centered in the space beside the center opening and are 30" by 7' (2,133.6mm) tall.
- The window openings on the second level are 30" (762mm) by 6' (1828.8mm) tall, centered above the base openings and 10'-6" (3,200.4mm) from the base of the object.
- Draw a 6" (152.4mm) by 20'-6 (6,248.4mm) wide Rectangle 9'-9" (2,971.8mm) from the base to allow the second floor to protrude from the facade.

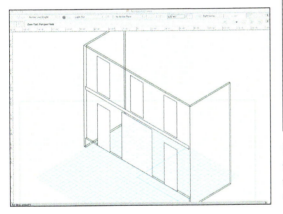

Use the **Push/Pull Tool** in the **Subtract Faces Mode** to create the openings.

In the Acropolis-Trim Class, the smaller openings have a 3/4" (19.05mm) by 6" (152.4mm) casing within the opening. The casing for the Gates is 5/4" (31.75mm) by 6" (152.4mm) deep.

On the upper level, the casings run fully around the openings. On the lower level there is no casing, or *saddle*, at the bottom.

The casings will sit 1" (254mm) in front, or *proud*, of the face of the facade.

Snap to the openings to create the Rectangle, **Offset**, **Clip**, and **Extrude** as needed. Assign these elements the Acropolis-Trim Class.

Within each casing, except for the Gates opening, there is a 1" (254mm) neon tube in the Acropolis-Neon Class.

Trace the openings, Offset the new Polyline or Rectangle by 1 1/2" (38.1mm), and Fillet the corners by the same. Draw the Circles, and **Extrude Along Path**. Center the neon in the openings.

Using the geometry you reserved earlier from the deck, create the second level/balcony area with two differences:
- The entire slab will be Black-Gloss, Classed as Acropolis-Deck-Face. There will be the gold trim on the visible sides.
- **Clip** away 30" by 18' from the top left of the form to allow space for escape stairs and room for actors to move around those stairs.

Once modeled, place these new pieces at the appropriate Z elevation using the OIP. These elements should slot into the long narrow opening in the facade.

The Simple Stair Tool

The **Simple Stair Tool** is located in the **Building Shell Tool Set**. Select the Tool, and open the **Tool Preferences**. Double-clicking on the Tool icon will also access the preferences.

The tight space requires something more along the lines of a ship's ladder than a traditional staircase. We will not be classing the stairs, but you can if you like. It would be likely that the stairs would be painted a flat black or medium gray. Since they will not be seen, for these purposes, they can default to the **Fill Color Attribute** of white.

It is possible to model some interesting stair units with this tool, and the **Custom Stair Tool**, so the tools and classing are worth some experimentation. The Custom Stair Tool can create spiral stairs, useful onstage and off.

Set the parameters in the Simple Stair Tool Preferences:
- Style: Open Riser
- Width 27" (685.8mm)
- Flr-Flr Height 9'-3 1/2" (2,832.1mm)
- Max Riser 7" (177.8mm)
- Tread Depth 3" (76.2mm)
- Tread Height 1 1/4" (31.75mm)
- Nosing Depth 6" (152.4mm)
- Config: Straight
- Landing Tread 5
- Offset 1 - 6" (152.4mm)
- Stringer Width 1 1/2" (38.1mm)
- Check Create 3D
- Check Left Rail
- Check Right Rail
- Set the Rail Height to 2'-5" (736.6mm)
- Set the Rail Width to 2" (50.8mm)

Click **OK**, and click to insert the stairs.

It is not the prettiest thing ever created, but it does communicate to the stage manager the steep nature of the stairs. It also communicates to the shop the very limited space and nature of the stairs.

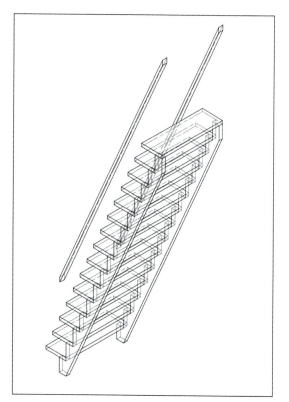

Set the Z of the stair unit to 18" (457.2mm) in the OIP.

The Eyedropper Tool

It took some time to enter all of those parameters. Not as much time as it might have taken to model the stairs, but time nonetheless.

Reset the Simple Stair Tool Preferences, or make a few changes and insert another stair unit, noticeably different from the ships ladder. Choose the **Eyedropper Tool** from the **Basic Tool Set**. Select the **Pick-up Attributes Mode**, and open the **Tool Preferences**.

The **Eyedropper Tool** can be set to pick up many different **Attributes** from **Objects**. Like the **Magic Wand Tool**, you can save specific settings often used for quick choices.

In this case, select all of the options, but the critical choice is **Plug-In Parameters**; selecting all is easier than deselecting many others.

Hover over the first star unit with the **Eyedropper;** when it becomes highlighted, **click**. Switch to the **Apply Attributes Mode**, or press the Option/Alt Key (the cursor becomes a paint bucket) and hover over the new stair. Click to apply the attributes of the first stair case. The second stair should immediately look like the first.

While you may not often need these specific attributes, they may provide a better starting point than the defaults. Save this stair unit, and others in your personal library.

Consider setting the preferences for the **Stair Tools,** and the **Eyedropper Tool** in your stationery file.

The **Eydropper** is also useful for making quick changes to the attributes of Door and Window objects.

Always leave space and access for the other designers.

The Eyedropper Tool quickly moves Complex Attributes from Object to Object.

Above the Walls, there will need to be a 3" (76.2mm) thick element classed as Acropolis-Entablature-Trim. This piece needs to wrap partially around the back of the unit to account for the sightlines. It does not need to wrap a full 360° to complete the illusion.

The inside edge of this element is the inside edge of the Acropolis walls. The TD or shop may change that, but for our purposes, we want to give the lighting designer as much accessibility as possible.

This trim element is 12" (304.8mm) larger than the building on the left, right, and top (upstage). That means a total width of 15" (381mm) including the width of the walls. The back wrap around is the same length.

On the bottom or downstage side this element is 3' (914.4mm) from the wall, or an overall 39" (990.6mm).

Create the **Rectangle**, **Clip** away the inside, **Extrude,** and elevate.

Above the trim is the Frieze (Acropolis-Entablature-Frieze Class). This element is 6" (152.4mm) thick and set back from the edge of the trim by 1 1/2" (38.1mm) and extruded 24" (609.6mm).

Elevate and render. Adjust the texture placement in the OIP or with the **Attribute Mapping Tool** so that the key pattern is centered.

Use **Duplicate Array** or Alt/Option-click and drag the Trim element above the Frieze. If you use **Duplicate Array** the Z distance is the sum of the two thicknesses.

Insert four instances of the Go-Go Pole Symbol between the windows such that actors/dancers can step out of the upper windows and use the poles to drop, or dance to the stage level.

Mask the interior areas exposed by the window openings.

Behind the main bottom opening, use the **Softgoods Tool** to make a floor to ceiling semi-circle. Apply the China Silk-Hot Pink-Austrian Texture.

Behind the other windows model 3" (76.2mm) thick walls, also known as *Hollywood* style flats in the Acropolis-Wallpaper Class. Estimate the sightlines from the audience, to be verified when this symbol is placed in the theatre. On both levels, there will need to be access for the actors to enter and exit the windows.

Approximately one-third of each level is the staircase, one-third is the window acting area, and one-third is rear access. Provide openings or doorways as needed, and mask them with **Softgoods Objects** using the Zebra Texture.

If you prefer the Zebra, or something else, to the Wallpaper, change the design.

Insert instances of the Gate symbol.

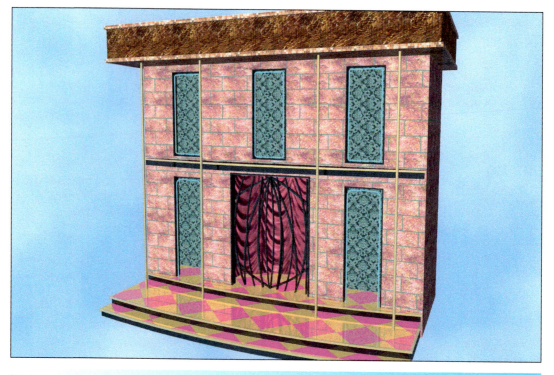

Create Auto-Hybrid

Select the 3D components of the Acropolis and go to **Spotlight>Architectural>Create Auto Hybrid**. The **Softgoods Objects** and the **Stair Object** are already **Hybrid Objects**. The Gate Symbol was created as a simple Hybrid.

If Hybrid objects are selected when you run the command, they will become deselected. Auto Hybrid Objects can be edited and modified after creation in the OIP.

The Auto Hybrid Dialog has three Tabs. In the first, the **Cut Plane**, the Elevation of the Cut Plane should default to 4'-0" in Imperial. Leave that default, and set to the Layer Elevation. Check **Display Cut Plane**, and check **Use 2D Class Attributes** for the Fill and Pen.

Use the Class Attributes **Below the Cut Plane**, and check the **Dashed Hidden Line**, set to a short dashed line, slightly grayed out.

Above the Cut Plane, set the **Fill** to **None**. Examine your results. Be sure the **Display** is set to **2D and 3D** in the OIP.

Consider changing the **Fill** in some of your **Classes** to black, gray, a Pattern, or a Hatch. The beauty of an Auto-Hybrid Object is that as you edit and refine your design, the 2D portion of the Symbol is updated. The drawback is that the 2D may not conform to your personal graphic style. The 2D may need to be redrawn when the design is finalized.

Select All, and create the Hybrid Symbol *Acropolis Symbol*. Set the Insertion Point at the top center of the platform/deck.

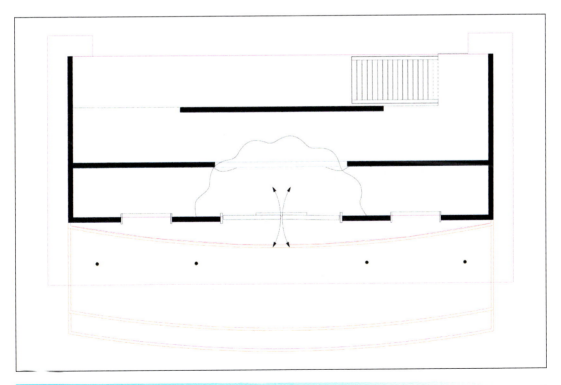

Assembly

Create a new document from your Stationery file and go to **File>Page Setup**. Change the paper size to **US Arch E**. Check the **Use size unavailable in printer setup** box, and uncheck **Show page breaks,** which would break the larger sheet down into smaller sheets visually on your drawing.

Save the file as Lysistrata-Set.vwx in your **Workgroup Folder**.

You will need the other scenic documents from the **Workgroup Folder** either opened, browsed to, or *Favorited* in the **Resource Browser**.

In the **Organization Dialog**, move the Masking Design Layer above the Scenery Basic Design Layer by selecting the layer and clicking and dragging the number in the stacking order.

Reference the scenery symbols into the Lysistrata-Set.vwx file. Since every file will be within the one Workgroup folder, Reference with **Path relative to current document** checked.

Absolute Referencing forces you to keep the links in one location. Relative Referencing means you can move the folder around, and keep the references intact. Vectorworks is not looking for the path to the file; it will only look in the one folder for the referenced file.

Working in the Venue Architecture Design Layer, **Activate** the **TheatreArchitecture** symbol, and insert an instance at 0-0.

Move to the Scenery-Basic Design Layer and **Activate** the **Deck** symbol. Insert an Instance at 0-0. By choosing the **Insertion Point**, these elements become easy to place.

Now, the rest of the scenic elements sit on the deck. They have the Z in the OIP set to 7 1/2" (190.5mm). Alternately, the symbols can be edited and the Z changed in the original file.

If you do not have the file opened, right-clicking the Symbol in the **Resource Browser**, and selecting **Edit** from the **Contextual Menu,** will modify the source document, and then any other documents in which the Symbol has been Referenced.

This is a time to work on creating your graphic style. Modify the work created to suit your taste, as long as clarity of communication is retained.

Add symmetrically:
- The Long Topiary next to the Acropolis, on the upstage edge of the deck
- The Martini Brazier midstage
- Settees downstage left and right

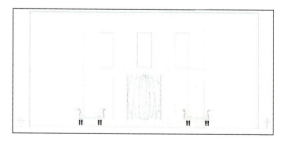

Move to the Masking Design Layer, and insert the first portal with the Downstage edge at 0-0. Use **Duplicate Array** or **Move by Points** to add two more portals each 5' (1,524mm) upstage.

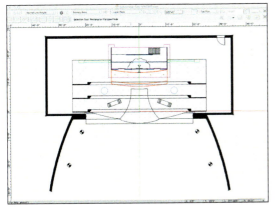

The Portals begin the process of masking the back stage areas as well as providing a frame for the stage picture.

Masking and Sightlines

The end seats and the portals give you a basic framework to determine the horizontal and vertical masking requirements. Sightlines tell us what is visible to the audience. Scenery needs to be placed onstage such that the audience can see the action. At the same time, the backstage needs to be hidden from view, lights and onstage audio gear included.

The importance of sightlines and stage masking cannot be stressed enough.

While typically the responsibility of the Scenic Designer, final placement of masking is often a collaboration with the Lighting Designer. In dance, the Lighting Designer may be solely responsible for the stage masking.

Begin by snapping an **Unconstrained Line** from the center point which is also the **Insertion Point** of the House Right EndSeat Symbol to the most onstage point of the most downstage Portal.

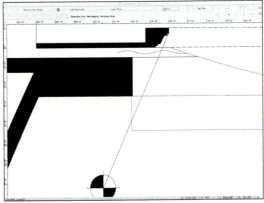

Grab the onstage handle of the line and press the **shift key** to **Constrain** the angle of the line. Typically, this will constrain the angle to those specified in the **Snaps Preferences**. In this case, the angle will be constrained to the angle of the line already drawn. Use this line to be sure that all of the scenic elements are visible to the audience.

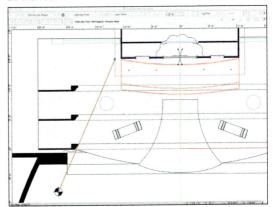

When designing a traditional box set interior, this line determines the angle, or *rake,* the walls require so they can be seen.

Now, draw lines from the same end seat to the portals on the opposite side of the stage.

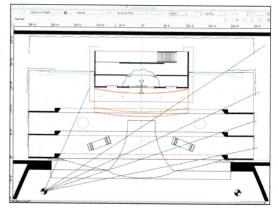

It should be immediately obvious that the audience can see all kinds of backstage.

Use the **Softgoods Tool** from the **Spotlight Tool Set** to add a set of legs just upstage of the Topiary. These legs should be about as wide as the Portals, and 25' (7,620mm) tall.

The masking drapery for the show would be hung **Flat,** or without pleats, or **Fullness.** Set the **Pleat Width** to 4' (1219.2mm) and the **Pleat Depth** to 1" (254mm) just so you get a wavy line which helps to indicate a curtain.

Draw with either **Softgoods** drawing modes or using the **Line** or the **Polyline Tool.** Lines not drawn with the Softgoods Tool can be converted when selected, by either going to **Modify>Create Objects from Shapes,** or right-clicking and selecting **Create Objects from Shapes** from the contextual menu.

At 26'-6" (8077.2mm) from the Plaster Line, add a full stage black drape 25' (7,620mm) by 50' (15,240mm).

Use your sightlines, and others you may require to add *Tab Curtains* to finish the masking. Legs run parallel to the Plaster Line. Tabs run perpendicular to the Plaster Line.

It would be ideal to run the Legs straight off, but there just is not the space available. The Tabs are an acceptable solution. They might all be rigged on the same pipe.

Once the horizontal sightlines have been masked, the vertical sightlines must also be examined. Use the same principles, follow the same steps, draw similar lines to determine where masking *Borders* will be required and add them. Create them as Curtain Objects using the Softgoods Tool. The Border option hangs the curtain forward and down. That choice is applicable when hanging legs and borders on the same pipe.

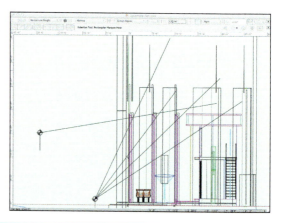

The LED Screen Tool

The Set needs an end, that might typically be a *Cyc* created with the **Softgoods Tool,** but we have a high-tech solution available within Vectorworks.

A Cyc might have curves on either end. Consider changing your upstage black to a conventional Cyc shape when done adding the LED Screen Object.

Go to the Spotlight Tool Set and select the **LED Screen Tool**. Use the **Standard Insertion Mode,** and **Center Insertion**. The LED Screen will be placed 25'-6" (7772.4mm) on the Y Axis, and 0 on the X Axis.

Open the LED Screen Tool **Preferences**. Set the **Module Shape** to **Tile Flat**, 2" (50.8mm) square. Check **Overall Dimensions and Spacing**. Set the **Array Width** to 50' (15,240mm) and the **Array Width** to 25' (7,620mm). Check **Simple 3D** and accept the other defaults. In reality, this screen would not have the high definition required for a theatrical production, but it will give the desired rendering results.

The LED Screen, Blended Screen, and Television Tools can be used to illustrate projections and motion.

The **LED Screen Object** can be adjusted to the specific parameters of commercially available LED Screens. We have a Hybrid Object that indicates the position of the screen, and the **Simple 3D** option allows fast rendering.

Place the **LED Screen Object,** which will now show you a huge Vectorworks logo. With the object selected, go to the OIP and press the Edit *Array Image* button. There is a variety of default content available. Check it out, and close the window without changing the image.

Go to the **Resource Browser** and locate the **Vectorworks Logo Texture**. Right-click to **Edit** and click **Edit** at the **Color Shader**. Choose **Change Image** in the next dialog.

You will need the file Sky.psd from the Exercise files on the Website. Replace the logo with the sky. Don't alter any of the other **Shaders** or parameters here.

It is possible to assign a texture like a **Chroma Key Blue** or **Green** to an **LED Screen, Screen, Blended Screen**, or **Television Object**, and export a still to video compositing software to show moving images that might be a critical design component in a show.

Chroma Key Green is a simple **Color Shader** with the **Green Slider** in the **Colors** Dialog set to 255, with a 100% **Glow**. Logically, the same is true for blue.

Finishing Touches

Add your figures to the composition. Consider using a new Design Layer for the figures as they may be in the way of the Sound and Lighting details.

The Renderworks Camera Tool

While there are ways we've explored to create perspective views, the **Renderworks Camera Tool**, in the **Visualization Tool Set** is particularly useful.

In theatre you can choose a point of view from a particular seat. You can insert cameras above the end seats to look at, and render the sightlines.

In film and television, you can choose specific focal length lenses and camera placement. Using the Animation Tools (**Spotlight>Visualization >Animate Scenes**) and third-party PIOs, it is possible to create *walk throughs* and video *story boards*.

Double-click on the **Camera Tool** to open the Tool **Preferences**. Check **Auto Update 3D View** and **Auto Center 3D View.** Accept the **Defaults**, except for choosing an **Aspect Ratio** of 16:9 or 2:3. Click **OK**, click to insert the camera position, and drag to the center focus.

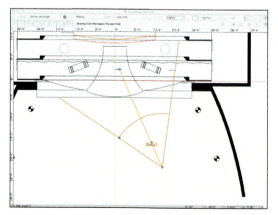

Got to **View>Perspective>Cropped** to eliminate anything outside of the camera frame.

Double-click on the camera object in the Top/ Plan View, or press the **Display Camera View** button in the OIP.

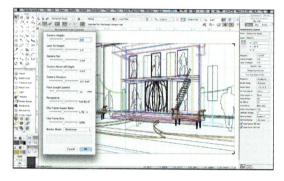

Press the **Fine Tune Camera View** button in the OIP to modify your view. Some parameters can be adjusted in the OIP.

Find several views you like, one from the balcony, and render the progress thus far in Final Quality Renderworks.

Without lighting included in the model, Vectorworks inserts one invisible light object that will flatly illuminate the scene. Once we add lighting, just as in reality, the scene will come alive.

Since the **Camera Object** actually sees beyond the crop, create **Saved Views** of the frame magnified on your screen. If Classes or

Layers are added after a Saved View has been created, those Classes or Layers have to be added to the Saved View at creation, or edited in via the Saved View Drop-down, unless the Class and Layer memory of the Saved View is turned off. A Saved View can be saved with the scene rendered, saving a few clicks.

Once rendered, images can be exported to PDF or Image files by going to **File>Export** and making the appropriate choices. JPEG files are easy to send, share, and view online. Resolutions for those purposes should be kept to the size of a computer screen.

When rendered on screen, your images will retain artifacts from selected items, light objects (if they aren't turned off in Vectorworks Preferences), and XYZ reference lines. Those do not render when images are exported.

Once you establish your Camera Tool preferences, save those settings in your **Stationary File**.

Review your work in different rendering modes to see how they present the design. Try OpenGL, and Custom Renderworks. Fiddle with the settings for each.

Go to **View>Rendering> Custom Renderworks Options**. Turn off **Textures** and **Colors.**

Leave the other defaults at **Low**, and render in **Custom Renderworks** to create a white model view.

The **Image Props** have rendered as crossed planes, but the Class created for the flames can be turned off.

Adjust the **Custom Renderworks Settings** until you have a rendering quality that you like for the white model look.

Right-click in the Resource Browser and select **Create New Renderworks Style** from the contextual menu. The settings will be as you have them. Name this style *White Model,* and review the additional options. You may want to add, now or later, a **Renderworks Background** with **Lit Fog**. Click **OK.**

Go to **View>Renderworks Style** and your new style will be at the top of the list. Render your scene with the Default Styles, including *Realistic Colors White,* to see some of the different ways you can present your design. Most of these styles are created using the **Artistic Renderworks Options**.

Applications like Adobe Photoshop and Corel Painter give designers further options for personalizing presentations.

It is fastest to explore these options before lights are added to the model. Each light adds additional rendering time, although this model has been built for speedy rendering.

Vectorworks Texture creation is a critical part of your rendering style, and optimizing rendering times.

> # Develop and cultivate a personal rendering style, but know that specific texts may require adapting the rendering to the production.

The Hardscape Tool

The Landmark module of the Vectorworks Designer package was created for Landscape Architects, gardeners, and landscapers. It is also useful to Entertainment Designers. If you have the Landmark or Designer package, switch to the Landmark Workspace. As you explore and experiment with these tools, consider adding the tools and Tool Set to your own workspace, as they apply to your practice.

Onstage, there are tools and symbols for creating terrain, and plantings. Just as the **Create Drape Surface Command** can be used to create a simple tablecloth, it can also be used over topography to create an irregular stage surface. Landmark has the ability to expedite this design process.

In film and television, the same is true, but there are also tools and databases to help plan and manage the landscaping of home sets, locations, even entire neighborhoods. Production Designers, Art Directors, and Greensmen can coordinate their work, while creating presentation documents for producers, directors, and crews.

In these instances designers and technicians would be using the tools pretty much as intended.

Working in any entertainment medium, the tools do not have to be used as intended. There are no rules. Well, there are few rules. The Hardscape tool is intended to be used to create exterior patio spaces with a single type of paver (such as brick or stone), or multiple types of pavers in a pattern.

Using the **Landmark Workspace**, create a new document and go to the **Landmark Tool Set**, only briefly described here. Select the **Hardscape Tool**. There are two Modes:

Boundary Configuration Mode, and **Pathway Configuration Mode**. The drawing modes are familiar as they are the same as seen in the **Polyline Tool**, and for creating **Softgoods Objects**. Alternately, you can draw with traditional tools, and Convert any polygon to a Hardscape Object by going to **Modify>Create Objects from Shapes** (which is not, by default, in the Landscape Workspace), or right-clicking and selecting **Create Objects from Shapes** off of the contextual menu.

The **Hardscape Preferences** and the OIP determine the 2D and 3D appearance of the Hardscape Object. The **Hardscape Object** is a **Hybrid Object**. Just as we created a **Hatch** for the Show Deck, custom, and Default Hatches (and other fills) can be assigned to the **Hardscape** and **Border**. Those Fills can be defined by Class, where relating Textures can be assigned.

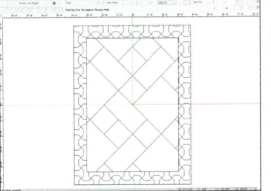

While a Hardscape Object is limited to the Hardscape and Border, objects can be created using traditional 2D geometry and the Clip Surface Command to make complex patterns.

A **Hardscape Object** is not limited to patterns and textures that relate to the outdoors; marbles, other stones, woods, and

The Vectorworks Designer Suite offers many tools that can be adapted for situations other than their original purpose.

wood patterns can be created and assigned to create decorative parquet floors, or complex inlays for a floor, wall, or furniture object.

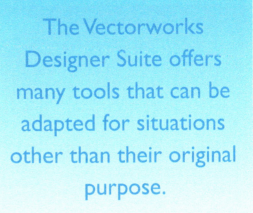

Of course, using the **Hardscape Object** outdoors is great as well, especially if a similar **3D Polygon** is placed over the Hardscape Object with a Texture illustrating puddles of water. No exterior shot really looks well without a wet-down.

With any tool not covered here, search the **Help** files, ask a colleague, or post a question online. As always, experiment, and look at what is available. Tools do not always have to be used as intended. Hammers can be great for adjusting a carburetor.

Transportation Security Administration Studios Rendering

Transportation Security Administration Studios

Transportation Security Administration Studios

Scenic Designers: Kathleen McDonough & Kevin Lee Allen (KLAD)
Lighting Designer: Shadowstone
Systems Integrator: Human Circuit

14. Create the Sound Design

Sharing information is critical to the collaborative process. In lieu of careful planning, scenery and sound can be in the way of lighting the stage. Similarly, lighting and sound gear may change the stage picture.

Sharing documents, the scenic, lighting, and sound designers can work together to ensure that the audio gear is optimally placed, that the scenic design allows for this placement, and that the speakers and/or speaker arrays do not interfere with specific angles the lighting designer might require.

The acting company will require monitors, possibly audio and video monitors. An onstage orchestra or musicians will require monitors. The set designer may choose to modify the set, or add scenic elements to mask those speakers. These issues can be easily addressed when the designers are developing the project together using Vectorworks.

Everyone has to work in the same, limited, space. Compromise is required.

Vectorworks includes the **Speaker Tool**, and the **Speaker Array Tool** in the **Spotlight Tool Set**.

The application entertainment libraries include several files full of symbols illustrating a number of commercially available speaker lines. These symbols do not have the same functionality as **Speakers** created with the **Audio Tools**. They can be used for illustrating physical size, but they do show coverage, which we can do with the **Audio Tools**.

The data content for the **Audio Tools** is located at **Libraries>Defaults>Audio Tools**. Each time a **Speaker Object** is custom configured in the OIP, or in the **Array Configuration Dialog**, custom configurations can be saved in the AudioToolSetData.xml file, accessible to other Vectorworks files. This file exists in both the User Folder, and the Application Folder. The data in your user folder is easy to migrate between application versions.

Plug-In Objects

In the Vectorworks Application Folder, there is a Plug-Ins Directory. Many of the basic functions of the applications are **Plug-In Objects** (**PIOs**), also known as Scripted Command Tools.

Scripting is one way to customize Vectorworks. Scripts can create anything from simple tools that assist with tedious tasks, to sophisticated solutions for demanding design functionality. There are three basic Vectorworks scripting options:
- the Software Developer's Kit (SDK)
- Python programming language
- VectorScript, a lightweight Pascal-like programming language

> Sharing information is critical to collaboration.

Scripts can be created and kept in PIOs. Plug-in Tools and Commands must be installed in a Workspace. Some simple scripting can be done within Vectorworks, and it is not as scary as it sounds, and it's coming.

The parameters which define the appearance of a **PIO** are stored in a parameter record associated with each object instance. A record stores constant data, and default values. Parameters for each Instance can be modified, and often saved for reuse, in the OIP. A Default Parameter Record is created when the first instance of an object is placed in a file. The Default Parameter Record, is distinct from Parameter Records associated with object instances. Subsequent insertions of PIOs can use the Default Parameter Record, so they default back to the initial settings.

The Plug-In Manager

Plug-Ins are created, maintained, and modified using the **Plug-in Manager**, which is accessed by selecting **Tools>Plug-ins>Plug-in Manager**.

Plug-In Objects expand the functionality of Vectorworks.

The Truss Tools and the Audio Tools are Plug-In Objects.

The Truss Tools

The **Straight Truss Tool** and the **Curved Truss Tool** are also located in the **Spotlight Tool Set**. These PIOs create **Hybrid Objects**. The Tools allow for the specification of size to create either custom truss, or objects that match available truss units.

Libraries of commercially available trusses are included with the package, and are located in the Library. These models can be quite complex, and slow rendering times. The geometry can included embossed corporate graphics, and detailed hollow, round tube construction.

The Library Symbols and Objects created with the Truss Tools in the Spotlight Tool Set can be used as **Lighting Positions**. They are not, by default, considered Lighting Positions. To use a **Truss Object** as a **Lighting Position**, select the Object and go to **Spotlight>Object Conversion>Convert to Light Position**.

The lighting and sound departments may share some rigging positions. In a Broadway house, there is typically a truss about 16' (4,876.8mm) downstage of the intersection of the Plaster Line and the Centerline, or 0-0, and 24' (7,315.2mm) above the deck.

In the **Light Plot Design Layer** of your Lysistrata-Sound.vwx file, select the **Straight Truss Tool** from the **Spotlight Tool Set**, choose the **Constrained Line Mode,** and open the **Tool Preferences**. Set the Connection Interval to 10' (3,048mm), the Height and Width to 20" (508mm), be sure that Chord, Ladder Bar, and Lacing Profiles are set to Square (to speed rendering), accept the other defaults, and click **OK.**

Round Profiles are often nicer to look at, but this Truss is not a visual element. Round Profiles take longer to render.

Click and drag a line approximately where the Truss Object is to be located. **Tab** into the **Floating Data Bar** and enter 40' (12,192mm) as the length. Hit **Enter** and click to insert the Hybrid Object. With that new Truss Object selected, go to the OIP and set the XYZ coordinates numerically. If you drew from left to right, the X will be -20' (6,096mm), the Y -16' (4,876.8mm), and the Z 24' (7,315.2mm).

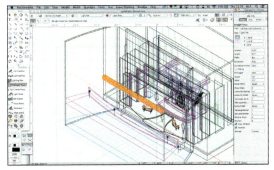

You can modify the placed **Truss Object** in the **OIP** which shows similar settings as the Tool Preferences

Assign the **Truss Object** to the **Lighting-Lighting Positions Class**. Later, when we have imported **Spotlight Lighting Device Symbols, Edit** that Class and assign the **Default Instrument Texture** so all of the Lighting Positions will have matching textures.

> It is imperative that every audience member be able to hear the show, just as it is important that they can see the show.

The Speaker Tool

Create a **Class** called **Audio-Speakers** with a **Line Weight** of **.20**. Switch to the **Sound Plot Design Layer**, and select the **Speaker Tool** from the **Spotlight Tool Set**. Be sure that in the **Navigation Palette** you have the drop-down set to **Show/Snap Others**.

When you first click in the document, the **Speaker Object Properties** or **Tool Preferences** will open. As is generally true, you can also click on the **Preferences** with the **Tool** selected, and you can modify an inserted Speaker Object in the OIP.

From the **Tool Preferences**, select the Yamaha AX_15W speaker from the **Type** drop-down menu. Set the tilt to -15° and leave the other defaults. When you select a speaker Type from the drop-down, the Tool calls upon specifications (such as dimensions, dispersions, and weight) located in the **Libraries>Defaults>Audio Tools> AudioToolSetData.xml** file.

Double-click to insert the front of the speaker at the downstage center point of the **Truss Object**. Go to the OIP and set the Z height of the **Speaker Object** to just under the Truss Object. The X should be zero.

Set the **Listening Height** to the height of the End Seats. Turn on **Show Dispersion Range 1** and see the Vectorworks visualization of where the sound for this speaker can be heard. **Show Dispersions Hatch** also turns on by default. The hatch indicates the coverage shadow for each checked dispersion range. The hatched area (or shadow) indicates what sound actually hits the floor or **Listening Height**.

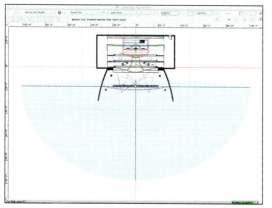

This 3D Geometry of the Dispersion Area is displayed as a wireframe in all 3D views. With the Speaker selected, check **Class Speaker Parts** in the OIP.

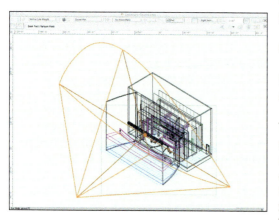

This Speaker is to send general directional sound. The actors and crew will need monitors backstage.

There will need to be four onstage monitors: two upstage (right and left), and two downstage (right and left). Place an Instance of the Yamaha AX_10 Speaker in one position. Set the Tilt Angle to -20° and the Z to 7' (2,113.6mm), with the **Listening Height** at 5'-6" (1,676.4mm). Check **Expand Dispersion Features,** and in **Range 1** change the **Horizontal** to 30 and the **Vertical** to 25. In the OIP, tap the **Save Type to Library Button** and call it *Backstage Monitor*. **Mirror** and **Duplicate** to create the other instances.

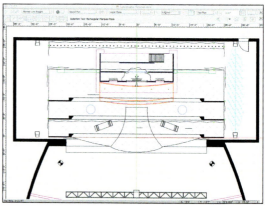

Assign these instances **Backstage Monitors** in the **Purpose Field**, and specify their placement in the **Location Field**.

Class as before.

It is best to have the specifications for the actual speakers you will be using before adjusting Range.

This production will likely have a pre-recorded score. The actors onstage will need to hear and react to the music. **Rotate** and **Duplicate** one of these **Speakers**. Center at the edge of the **Show Deck** between the **Portals**. These Speakers will be hung off of one of the electrics. This is rough placement that will have to be adjusted once the positions of the onstage electrics is determined by the Lighting Designer.

Change the Z to 22' (6,705.6mm), the **Listening Height** to 6' (1,828.8mm), the **Actual Tilt Angle** to -35, and adjust the **Location/Purpose** settings.

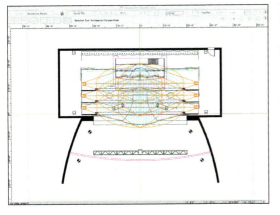

Consider additional **Speaker Objects** within the Temple scenic unit. The Lighting Designer is going in there, why shouldn't the Sound Designer?

The Speaker Array Tool makes fast work of complex object creation and positioning.

The Speaker Array Tool

The **Speaker Array Tool** makes simple work of a complex task. It's not quite as simple as the **Speaker Tool**, but it deals with multiple **Speaker Objects** at one time.

Select the **Speaker Array Tool** from the **Spotlight Tool Set**, open the **Tool Preferences** and **Class the Speaker Array Parts**, name the array in the **Column ID Field** as HL, set the **Location** to House Left, and tap the **Configure Array** button to expose the five tabs of the **Array Detail and Configuration Dialog**.

The **Bumper Tab** defines the hanging bracket for the Array. As with Speakers, you can save custom types and specifications, and reuse those settings later. Choose a **Generic Bumper** of 2' (609.6mm) square and 3" (76.2mm) **Thickness** and **Hardware Width**.

The next three tabs allow you to define the speaker types. You can have multiple instances of any speaker type. If using one type of speaker, **Speaker B** and **Speaker C** can be set to **None**.

For **Speaker A** select the Meyer Sound DS 4P, and set the **Tilt Reference** to **Back**. Check to be certain that **Speaker B** and **Speaker C** are set to **None**.

In the **Array Tab**, you can rock out. With the **Bumper Angle** set to 0, select the Meyer Sound DS 4P speaker in the **Speaker Types to Add** column and tap the **Add/Swap Speaker(s)** button. This will add a speaker to the array.

Tap that speaker in the **Definition** column and set the **Relative Angle to Preceding** to 5. Add three more speakers, the next at 10° and the last two at a 15° angles. These angles are relative to the preceding object.

Click to insert the **Speaker Array** roughly over the **House Left End Seat** symbol. While selected, go to the OIP and set the Z to 32' (9,753.6mm).

There are no speakers, only the Bumper. Tap the **Insert Speakers** button in the OIP, and set the **Rotation Angle** of the Array to 15° and position the Speaker Array so they no longer crash through the walls of the theatre. The Speaker Arrays would be hung with motors and points would have to be spotted for the motors in the theatre. In most instances Absolute Positioning will be required, as those points have likely been established.

Mirror the **Speaker Array** to the House Right Side. Correct the **Column ID** and **Location** in the OIP. Tap the **Insert Speakers** button.

Each Array must have a unique **Column ID.**

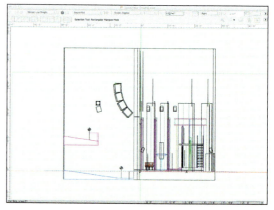

Selecting the **Bumper** selects the **Array Object**. Selecting any individual **Speaker Objects** in the **Array** changes the OIP back to the familiar Speaker View and the Speaker **Dispersion** can be modified.

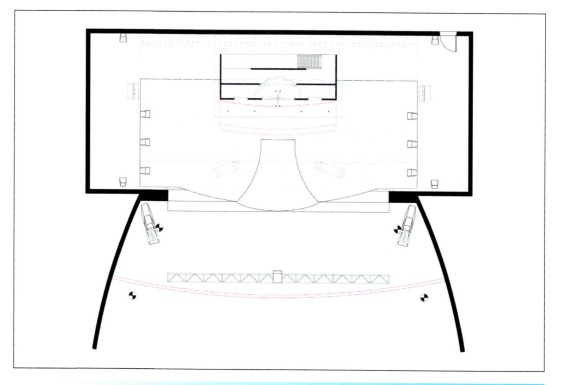

Microphones

There are many useful symbols in the file **Libraries>Entertainment>Audio.vwx**, particularly the microphones. If you have all of these speakers, there has to be a way to get sound from the actors to the speakers. The microphone symbols are not as *smart* as the speakers created with the **Speaker Tools**. However, these symbols can be placed in a document and accounted for using the **Spotlight>Reports>Create Report** command, which can be used to add a spreadsheet view and inventory.

This same file also contains symbols for microphone stands, music stands, and some musical instruments. These can be valuable to all designers at some point or another. Trust me.

connectCAD

There is a PIO for Vectorworks called connectCAD for designing broadcast, audio-visual, lighting, IT cabling, and other connected systems. connectCAD keeps track of large numbers of cables or other interconnected systems in a complex installation. This add-on is ideal for managing a complex audio system.

> Record Formats attach information to objects.

The Record Format

The **Speakers** and **Arrays** created using the **Audio Tools** are **Plug-In Objects**. The **PIO** generates their geometry and associated data on the fly from the XML file. That data can then be modified, and possibly saved via the OIP.

To examine a Record Format, open the file **Libraries>Objects-Entertainment> Audio-Speakers-Atlas Sound.vwx** and copy the SEA-18S Symbol into your file, or a new blank document. Select that Symbol Insertion and look at the OIP, **Data Tab**. The **_ATS_ SpkrModData Record Format** (also now located in your Resource Browser) contains information associated with that Symbol.

Not all of the speaker Symbols in the Entertainment Libraries have data associated.

Record Formats can store a wide range of information including cost or inventory numbers; in this case, information like weight, size, and sound dispersion. A Record Format or multiple Record Formats can be attached to single objects, or symbol definitions.

Like other Resources, Record Formats are created in the Resource Browser by right-clicking and choosing **Create New Record Format**. The data entered and the information is task-specific.

There are a variety of ways to attach a Record Format to an Object or a Symbol. In brief, right-clicking on a Symbol in the Resource Browser and choosing **Attach Record** is one way. Selecting an object and checking an available Record Format in the Data Tab of the OIP is another.

Editing a Symbol, either the 2D or the 3D component, allows access and Editing of the information specific to that Symbol. With the

The Television Tool

Let's give the actors backstage a video monitor or two so they don't miss any cues. Select the **Television Tool** from the **Spotlight Tool Set** and click on the document in the **Top/Plan View** to insert a monitor. The **Tool Preferences** open, and this should be similar and familiar from using the **LED Screen Tool**. Choose a 32" LED screen from the drop-down, and check Add Adjustable Stand. Set the Stand Height to 4' (1,219.2mm). Place one monitor stage right, and another on stage left. As with the LED Screen, the **Screen Image** will default to the Vectorworks Logo. In this case we do not care what is on the screen, but if you like, you can change the image to one of your set renderings. Go ahead, you want to see that.

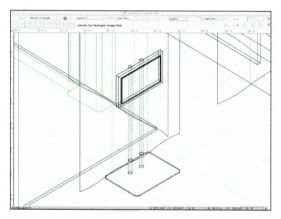

Object Selected, go to the OIP, **Data Tab**, and check the **Record Format**. The Data in that Format can be seen as a **Record Field**, and changed in the **Record Info** area.

Make any changes in a new file. You might want that original again someday.

Data from Record Formats can be used to create reports, spreadsheets, or database records. Go to **Spotlight>Reports>Create Reports**. The **List All** drop-down allows the choice of **Symbols** or **Objects with a Record**. Review the possible columns of information available when *Speaker*, or *Television* is selected from **Objects With a Record**. This is a way of creating an inventory, or schedule of equipment needed for a production.

Saved Reports are Resources, and can be placed into drawings from the, you guessed it, Resource Browser.

We do not need to add the monitors the cast and crew will use to watch the game.

Obviously, for television shows, museum exhibits, corporate events, and theatrical performances that have a heavy multi-media component, the **Television Tool** is invaluable.

Landru Design

C. Andrew Dunning of Landru Design created the Softgoods, Television, Speaker, Screen, and LED Screen Tools for Nemetschek Vectorworks. There are also commercial versions of these tools, and others, available as PIOs to add additional functionality to Vectorworks from Landru Design. They are valuable additions to every designer's tool kit.

Design Layer Viewport

In the **Visualization Palette**, turn off the visibility of all of the Design Layers except for the Sound Plot. This can be easily done if the Sound Plot Design Layer is active, Alt/Option-click in the middle Visibility Column.

Go to **View>Create Viewport** to create the **Design Layer Viewport** to be **Referenced** back to the other design documents. Name the **Viewport** and the **Drawing Title** Sound Design. Select **New Design Layer** from the **Create on Layer** drop-down. Name that Design Layer **Audio DLVP** and click **OK.**

If you forgot to turn off the visibility of the other Design Layers, that can be done in this dialog as well.

As you develop your workflow, this same approach might be used with the stage masking, instead of the **Save As** approach used here. This Design Layer Viewport will be referenced into the Lighting Design document. You might also want to reference it back to your Scenic Design document.

Once you know how and all.

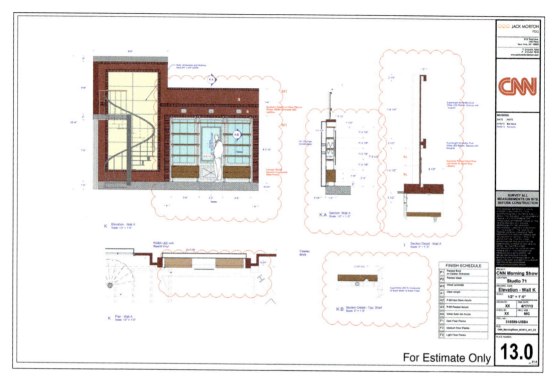

CNN New Day Designer's Elevations

CNN New Day

CNN New Day

CNN New Day
New York City

Production Design: Jim Fenhagen (Jack Morton/PDG)
   Art Direction: Larry Hartman (JM/PDG)
   Assistant Art Direction: Juliann Elliott (JM/PDG)
   Drafting Project Manager: Matt Glaze (JM/PDG)
Lighting Design: Steve Brill & Neil Galen (The Lighting Design Group)
CNN Creative Direction: Guy Pepper & Renee Cullin

Production Designer Jim Fenhagen and his team at Jack Morton/PDG create detailed, illustrated, and annotated Designer's Elevations using Vectorworks after rendering projects modeled in Vectorworks using Cinema 4D.

15. Vectorworks Lighting

Just as textures are not just like paint, wallpaper, or the commercial product they represent, lighting in the 3D world is not always as you expect. The **Spotlight Lighting Devices** that represent theatrical fixtures generally work as you expect, but there are other lighting options available for pre-visualization. Every **Spotlight Lighting Device** that actually lights up includes a **Vectorworks Light Object** imbedded in the symbol, just as these symbols require being attached to a **Record Format**, generally the **Light Info Record**.

Just like using Source 4's, Color Blasts, or Varilites, lighting in the 3D world is complex and takes time to master.

Every light adds math, and increases rendering time, so consider that rendering time when planning your lighting. Renderworks inserts an invisible light when you render an object (we have been working with that light). When you add a light, that invisible light source is removed.

Consider **Vectorworks Light Objects** as either preliminary tools, part of another object, or ways to add accent lighting. Remember that if you want the accent lighting to be included in your **Lighting Design Paperwork**, it must be made into a **Spotlight Lighting Device**.

Sound Designers can create a simple basic lighting set up to review the model of a new speaker. Scenic Designers can use **Vectorworks Light Objects** with or without **Spotlight Lighting Devices** to indicate lighting ideas, and add *chiaroscuro* to renderings. Lighting Designers can use **Vectorworks Light Objects** to rapidly present early visualizations, and to create custom **Spotlight Lighting Devices**. One **Vectorworks Light Objects** can do the work of several **Spotlight Lighting Devices**. Ideas can be presented before committing to drafting the plot.

Exhibits, product renderings, illustrations of props are among the many places where a Vectorworks Light Object would be the right choice.

Vectorworks Light Objects can be included within symbols. Spotlight Lighting Devices are not supported inside of other symbols.

Just as Spotlight Lighting Devices include Vectorworks Light Objects, the realistic lamps included in the files…
- Libraries>Objects-Building Services>Electrical-Accurate Lamps-Imp.vwx
- Libraries>Objects-Building Services>Electrical-Accurate Lamps-Metric. vwx

…also include Vectorworks Light Objects. Those same lamp symbols can be added to fixtures, like those in
- Libraries>Objects-Building Services>Electrical-Lighting Fixtures Int & Ext. vwx

or lights of your own creation.

Lighting in the 3D world takes time to master.

Once the **Vectorworks Light Object** is added, and the **Record Format** attached, a practical lamp onstage can be made into a Spotlight Lighting Device (**Spotlight>Object Conversion>Convert to Instrument**) and included in the Lighting Design paperwork and documentation.

Read through, and work through this discussion. Create files as needed.

Set Lighting Options

Go to **View>Lighting>Set Lighting Options**.

Indirect Lighting is the light that happens when the light from a source bounces off of the surfaces onto which it is directed. This is seen everyday, everywhere. From the sun reflecting off of a glass building, to a simple bare bulb in a dark room. From the drop-down, you can add **Bounces** to a rendering. Each **Bounce** adds calculations, and rendering time. It is best to experiment with these looks on simple files before trying to add **Bounces** to a complex rendering. Learn to estimate rendering time in order to meet deadlines. No one cares how beautiful a presentation might have been, if it had been completed. People only care about what they are shown.

Ambient Light is the extraneous light in any place. When rendering a Lighting Design, turn **Ambient Light Off**. Ambient Light will affect your chosen levels. If you pre-visualize with Ambient Lighting, you may not have enough instruments in the space, or your planned cueing will not be accurate. If you want to illustrate a few spot fixtures piercing an overall wash, you may just want to change the default color and adjust the brightness and/or the color temperature.

Texture Definitions can have their own indirect lighting set to override these settings in order to enhance a scene and reduce the rendering time.

When rendering with **Fast Renderworks**, **Indirect Lighting** is rendered at a *low* quality. **Final Quality Renderworks** set **Indirect Lighting** at *high*. **Custom Renderworks** allows the quality to be selected by the designer.

Emitter Options allow the user to set specific color temperatures and intensity for **Ambient Light**.

An **HDRI (High Dynamic Range Image)** reproduces a greater dynamic range (the ratio between dark and light) of luminosity than possible in standard digital or traditional photographic. Most cameras and monitors can reproduce only a fixed dynamic range. HDR Images can represent more accurately the range of intensity levels found in real life. Whether direct sunlight or a night sky. HDR Images can represent the entire dynamic range of the visible world. All the luminosity of real life is stored in an HDR Image. Changing the exposure of an HDR Image is similar to adjusting the exposure when filming.

HDR Images can be created from bracketed exposures of the same image in Adobe Photoshop. It is also possible to take one image into Photoshop, adjust the Exposure, saving several files: the properly exposed image, an overexposure, and an underexposure, and then Merge them into an HDRI. This is not as effective as actually creating the exposures in the camera.

Vectorworks ships with a number of **HDRI Renderworks Backgrounds**. More are available to **Service Select** Members. Copious HDR Images are available online and can be made into custom HDRI Renderworks Backgrounds.

The **Environmental Lighting (HDRI)** options allow you to **turn on** the light in an HDRI layer background; specify using the light source in a different HDRI Background; or not to use lighting from a background image.

It is worth looking at and rendering with a few of the HDRI Renderworks Backgrounds to see how they impact a simple object, or arrangement of objects.

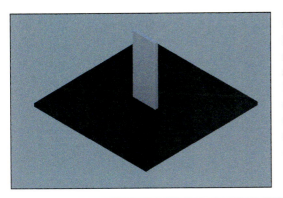

Render outdoor events with the impact of the sun.

The Heliodon Tool

The **Heliodon Tool**, located in the **Visualization Tool Set,** creates sunlight based on the location, the date, and the time. The Tool can also create a **Solar Animation**.

While this tool is of little help to this indoor production, the **Heliodon Tool** can be invaluable if designing an outdoor event, like a concert, festival, or outdoor drama. There is obvious benefit to studying the light on a film location. If you have the Architect or Landmark packages, the Massing Model Tool in the Site Planning Tool Set can make quick work of roughing out an entire neighborhood.

The **Heliodon Tool Preferences** set specific options:
• Time format
• 2D Symbol
• Location from either selected cities, or specific Latitude and Longitude

Click once to insert a Heliodon Object, and then rotate to North on the drawing. With the Symbol selected, the Date, Time, Daylight Savings Time, and Rendering Options can be specified. The **Physical Sky Option** creates the realistic appearance of a sky with varying amounts of clouds. When used with a Heliodon Object, the sky will appear appropriate for the set time of day and can change dynamically when creating a solar animation.

The Light Tools

Go to the Visualization Tool Set and select the Light Tool. There are Options in the Tool Bar for:
- Directional Light Mode
- Point Light Mode
- Spot Light Mode
- Custom Light Mode
- Preferences

Once inserted, Lights can be modified in the OIP. There will be a drop-down to change the Light Type. We have turned off the appearance of the Light Objects in the Vectorworks Preferences, Display Tab; from time to time, you may want to see the lights, and those settings are easily changed. They do not render in Exports, but they can clutter preview renders if left visible.

Directional Lights

The **Directional Light Object** is a general light coming from one direction and indicated by a globe. They are like suns, except they have absolutely parallel rays. Placement of a Directional Light Object and the light they emit is very general. The Directional Light source can be moved interactively with the **Selection Tool** and can be modified absolutely in the OIP. You can change the Z height of the Directional Light Object, but it does not matter.

Color and intensity can be modified in the OIP. The color of light from a Directional Light Object can be changed in the Attributes Palette.

They will not get light into your television studio, sound stage, convention center, or theatre space if the space is fully modeled with ceilings, floors, and walls that would naturally keep the light out. Our theatre does not have a roof; a **Directional Light** will cast broad shadows across the interior space, even if a Directional Light Object was placed inside the theatre. A Directional Light Object can show how light will fall when entering a space through a window.

Use Emitter allows you to specify the light's actual brightness and color temperature. Deselect this to use the light as a simple light source. **Set Light to View** changes the orientation of the light to the current view. **Set View to Light** sets the orientation of the current view to the light.

Spot Lights

Vectorworks Spot Light Objects are the primary Lighting Objects for working in an interior, enclosed space. **Spot Lights** are embedded within each **Spotlight Lighting Device**, at least for stage fixture types. Once placed, the OIP can interactively or numerically dictate the **Spread** and **Beam**. Spot Lights need to be carefully focused and set to a proper Z elevation, with an associated Z Look To Height. In the OIP, you can use **Absolute Positioning** to place and focus **Spot Lights**.

Spot Light Objects can be interactively moved, snapped, and focused using the **Selection Tool**, and/or the **Reshape Tool**.

In the OIP, **Distance Falloff** is the change of intensity moving along the beam away from the light source. **Angle Falloff** specifies the intensity change between the **Beam** and the **Spread**.

Spot Light Objects can have a hard or soft focus, adjustable in the OIP. Every **Spot Light Object** has an adjustable **Beam** and **Spread** angle. These refer to what we in the business of show refer to as the **Beam** and **Field** of a lighting instrument. Those are the area of the beam of light where the intensity is generally nearer 100% (the **Beam**), and the area of the **Beam** where the intensity falls off approaching 50% (the **Field**, or in this case, the **Spread**).

When the Beam and Spread are equal, the edge of the beam is sharp. When the Beam and Spread differ, the edge of the beam softens.

If the **Design Layer** has a **Renderworks Background** with **Fog**, a Spot Light can show as a beam in rendering if **Lit Fog** is checked in the OIP. Spot Lights can have any intensity. Do not be limited by 100%. Spot Lights can have a very wide Beam, so one Spot Light, can do the work of many Spotlight Lighting Devices when roughing out a design idea.

Point Light

Point Lights can serve a great many functions, but they add to rendering time. **Point Lights** are an uncontrolled, unfocused lamp sitting in space. Like the Ghost Light in an empty theatre, the light goes everywhere. There are Point Light Objects in many of the Electrical-Accurate Lamps.

It is not a good idea to simply drop a **Point Light** into a Model and call it done. Point Lights are great in table lamp, or behind a lamp shade that has a Back-lit Shader. Points Lights can be used to create a glow around a floating object.

Line Lights and Area Lights

Line Lights and **Area Lights** are created by Commands, not Tools. These are great sources for creating neon effects, edge lighting, illuminated bars, and the like. To create either, start with a 2D primitive line or shape (either for Line Light, or shape only for an Area Light), and go to **Modify>Convert** and either **Convert to Area Light** or **Convert to Line Light**. You can import an *IES* file to define a Line or Area Light.

It is true, but counterintuitive that a **Line Light Object** is not like a neon, or fluorescent tube. The **Accurate Lamps** do use **Line Light Objects** as the source within fluorescent tubes, but it is the tube object that defines the object. Similarly, we have created Neon just using a Glow Shader on an object.

> Lighting is not always intuitive.

Line Lights and **Area Lights** can also add considerably to rendering time in large/complex models. An **Area Light** can be used as the sole source to quickly render the look, and the light, of a **Silk** used in film and television. Line Lights are great for creating the edge lighting we can easily do with LED tape.

With either Light type, you can choose to show the original geometry, or turn that visual off in the OIP.

IES Files and Custom Lights

What on Earth is an IES file you may have asked? **IES** files contain photometric data. Most manufacturers provide IES files for their lighting products and are available online. When you select the **Custom Light** option in the **Tool Bar**, you can load an IES file and create a light in the 3D world based on commercially available photometric data.

Everything, everyone needs a Key Light, a soft Fill Light, and Back Light..

Using IES files, it is possible to create a table lamp and look at the fixture with different light sources like tungsten or CFL, before manufacturing.

A Basic Lighting Set Up

Any basic lighting set up requires three-point lighting: a **Key**, a **Fill**, and a **Back** Light. This is true in theatre, film, television, environmental design, and when you want a simple way to begin to study light on a set or a set piece.

Open a new document and model a simple floor with a theatrical flat-like object sitting on the floor. The flat should be larger than a human, and there should be space on the floor object to add more flats. For the moment, do not texture the objects; they will render a simple white, assuming you create them in the **Normal Line Weight Class** which has a white Fill.

Experiment, and review. Lighting takes time…

Add lights on other Design Layers so it is easy to control which lights are seen, and which are hidden. Go to the **Top View**, not the Top/Plan: Vectorworks lights need to be inserted and placed in a 3D view. **Spotlight Lighting Devices** must be placed in the 2D Top/Plan View, and they can be focused in either the Top/Plan or 3D Views.

From the **Visualization Tool Set**, select the **Light Tool** and the first **Mode** on the **Tool Bar**, the **Directional Light Mode**. Then select the **Set Direction Mode** (the sixth option in the Tool Bar). Your first light should be about 45° from the straight-on angle of an object. So, click on the object, pull away from the object, and drag to place the light. This is the **Key Light** and can be named in the Data tab of the OIP. In the Shape tab of the OIP, set the elevation to 60° and the brightness to 60%.

The **Fill Light** comes in lower and fills in places missed by the **Key**. Typically this is a softer light, so click and drag this light to be 45° from the **Key Light**. In the OIP, set the elevation to 20° and the brightness to 40% for this light. Turn Shadows **Off** in the OIP.

For the **Back Light**, **Mirror** and **Duplicate** the Fill Light. Set the elevation of the **Back Light** to 45° and the brightness to 30%.

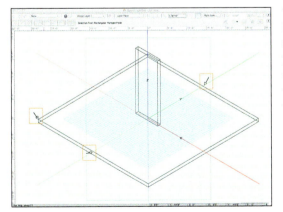

Add a **Camera Object** and **Render** to review.

On another layer, convert these to **Spot Light Objects** to create a similar set up. There will be differences.

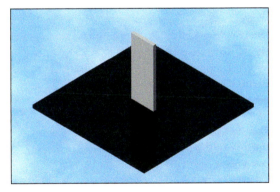

Add color to the lights, and adjust the intensity to compensate, if you feel that makes a better image. There is a drop-down in the OIP that accesses the standard system color palette, but you can also use commercially available Gel colors from the major manufacturers by selecting the **Light Object**, clicking on the fill color in the **Attributes Palette,** and selecting the saved **Color Palette**, or the **Color Palette Manager**.

The Color Libraries are installed with Vectorworks, allowing us to create Renderworks Textures and to color Spotlight Lighting Devices, accessible via the Attributes Palette.

Click on the **Solid Fill Color** swatch in the **Attributes Palette** to open a dialog with four choices across the top:
- Color By Class
- The Color Picker
- Pick a Single Color
- Color Palette Manager

Picking a single color allows you to access any individual color in an installed color library. So if you want a specific Benjamin Moore color or a Rosco Super Saturated Paint color, those are available. All of the Lighting Gel Color Libraries that come with Vectorworks are also accessible.

Selecting the **Color Palette Manager** allows you to **Check** and make any number of entire libraries active immediately in the Attributes Palate. Once active, the libraries remain available across all documents, until deactivated.

Tap the **Utility Menu** (the triangle) at the bottom of the dialog to choose how to display the palette.

When refining a lighting design, you can assign a color to a light object by selecting it and then choosing a color fill in the Attributes Palette.

Experiment with different objects on other Design Layers. Add additional Camera Objects to see different views. Create Spotlight Objects with different degrees of softness and examine how the light changes with different Falloff Settings. Be aware that these looks change with the relationship of the light to the object.

Lighting a Scene

After experimenting with the Vectorworks Light Objects, open the file Lysistrata-Set.vwx, and save that as Lysistrata-Lighting.vwx. Open the Lysistrata-Sound.vwx file and copy the Truss Object. Paste in Place on the Light Plot Layer of the Lysistrata-Lighting.vwx file.

Next, from the Sound Plot Design Layer, reference the Design Layer Viewport created in the Lysistrata-Sound.vwx file. Go to **Tools>Organization** and then to the **Viewports Tab**. Tap the **New** button. Create on the Sound Plot Design Layer and tap **Select Source**. Source a **New Reference** to an **External Document**, tap **Choose,** and navigate to the Lysistrata-Sound.vwx file. Click **OK** to exit the dialogs and the Sound Plot will now be in the Lighting Document. Even though the DLVP is created in 1:1 scale, it will find the appropriate scale.

Create new Design Layers to experiment with the Lighting Design.

As you work here, you may find it necessary to adjust the amount of Glow emitting from the Neon Texture, and the LED Screen Object that is the Cyc. Use the Vectorworks Light Objects to rough out a lighting design, to perform quick color studies, and to look at ideas. It takes fewer Vectorworks Light Objects to light a scene than it does theatrical, or film fixtures.

Eventually the Lighting Designer will be using real lighting positions, so place the Vectorworks Light Objects roughly where the stage lights will eventually be located:

- The FOH Truss already placed.
- The Balcony Rail position directly in front of the balcony.
- The Box Booms are vertical positions House Left and House Right.
- Onstage electrics between each Portal and masking.
- Booms or ladders in each wing.

Generally accept the default settings of the Spot Lights as placed. When using Spotlight Lighting Devices, shuttering can be controlled. With Vectorworks Light Objects, it is more like film and television: you can create Flags to mask the light, or accept it where it lands.

This is all about developing a personal process.

Placing the Light Objects

Begin by creating a new Design Layer called Lighting-Rough. Render often to see your work. Look at the light in the White Model Renderworks Style.

The Balcony Rail offers a low, dead-on flat wash. It's great for fill light. That Fill can also color the shadows created by the higher front light off of the Truss and stage electrics.

Use a Black **Renderworks Background** with **Fog**. A soon as you add a light with lit fog, experiment with differing degrees of Fog.

Over one of the Martini Glass Braziers, place a Spotlight Object with a medium blue color. It should be high enough that it is behind the masking, and focused at the bottom of the glass; at the top of the stem, turn on **Lit Fog** in the OIP. Render and adjust the Fog settings until you have a look you like. Once you have them the way you want, **Mirror** and **Duplicate**.

Work within the confines of the physical space and where the real lights will eventually be placed.

Add some rose-colored front light, and also some warm yellow or amber. See how few lights you can use by giving them a wide Beam and Spread. Use a narrow Beam and Spread when you want to force focus. Add some lighter blue side light from one side. Never forget the backlight. In a show like this, there will be cues that only use backlight.

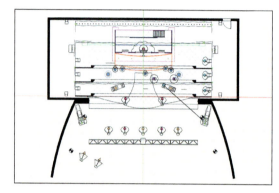

The reflectivity of many of the textures now helps bring this look to life. In the original renderings, with only the single light source, the look was flat. Lighting is everything to the finished look and feel of the presentation.

Look at these colored lights in the **White Model Renderworks Style**.

Duplicate the Rough Lighting Layer, use the **Magic Wand Tool** to select all of the **Vectorworks Lighting Objects**, and change the color to white in the OIP. Now you have two

different looks by toggling the layers on and off. Three if you look at both layers visible.

Render again in the **White Model Renderworks Style**.

These are quick and easy methods to explore different palettes for an entire show or looks for different scenes. Change the colors, change the angles. As always, experiment.

Vectorworks Light Objects do not really support **Gobos**, and that discussion has yet to happen here. There are no rules about mixing and matching **Light Objects**. A Set Designer may not want to deal with the intricacies of drawing a light plot in order to have mood, light, and shadow in a rendering. A DJ might want a model of a typical set-up, showing some colored light, and custom or stock gobos on a dance floor.

There is no reason why you cannot use both **Vectorworks Light Objects** and **Spotlight Lighting Devices** in a preliminary rendering. Once you've learned how to do that, of course.

Render important moments.

Batch Rendering

When Renderworks or any other 3D program renders and exports, it is a two-stage process. First the application renders to the screen, then it repeats the process to render to the export settings. Batch Rendering speeds that process by eliminating a step.

From a Wireframe View go to **View>Render>Create Batch Render Job.** In the ensuing dialog, insert the parameters for the output, size of the image, type of image file, rendering quality, and name the Job. You might want more than one Export of the same image; one for printing a large image, another for e-mailng.

Once you have a Job, or Jobs and are ready to render, go to **View>Render>Start Batch Render** and select the Jobs that you wish to output, and the location where you want the files saved. Vectorworks and Renderworks will then produce the images. You will see a significant gain in speed.

Strong visuals show competency, and help to convince others that your ideas are sound.

Chaplin: The Broadway Musical, Storyboard by Beowulf Boritt

Chaplin: The Musical on Broadway

Chaplin: The Broadway Musical, Production Photograph by Beowulf Boritt

Chaplin: The Musical
Ethel Barrymore Theatre, New York City

Scenic Designer: Beowulf Boritt
    Associate Scenic Designers: Edward Pierce & Nick Francone
Costume Designer: Amy Clark and Martin Pakledinaz
Lighting Designer: Ken Billington
Projection Designer: Jon Driscoll
Director & Choreographer: Warren Carlyle

This design was storyboarded using Adobe Photoshop and then drafted for production using Vectorworks.

16. Crafting the Light Plot

Work in your Lysistrata-Lighting.vwx file, and create another document for experimentation. Before beginning the actual Light Plot there is some additional set-up required to speed the process. Most designers, certainly Lighting Designers, will want to add these settings and resources to their Stationery file.

You may want to delete the **Design Layers** with the **Vectorworks Light Objects**. If so, use Save As to preserve that work. That idea, or ideas, can now be translated into a design that can be executed, and improved upon with theatrical fixtures.

To keep all of the name references in this text consistent, work in the Lysitrata-Lighting file.

Throughout this process, keep in mind what you need to add to your personal Stationery file. Also consider creating your own library files from the available resources. If there are certain gobos you like, and use often, import those textures into a file of your own. Review the available content, particularly the Rosco Colorizer and Prismatic gobos; they can bring a simple environment alive. The same is true for lighting instruments, particularly if you often work in a venue with a fixed inventory.

These files will be easier to search, and keep your Stationery File from becoming bloated.

Without a gobo, a light is just a light.

Vectorworks ships with **Color Libraries** from the major theatrical gel manufacturers. These are accessible through the **Attributes Palette**, and can be assigned to selected Selected Spotlight Lighting Devices in the OIP. In the **Attributes Palette**, you can create a **Custom Color Palette** by tapping the **Solid Fill Color**, then the **Color Palette Manager**. Tap **New**, name your palette, and then tap **Get** to add your colors. This is also a method of organizing, and recalling the colors selected for a specific production. Custom colors to be assigned to units, and that custom color mix can be created and kept in a Custom Palette.

We have already created some **Classes** for working with stage lighting:
* Lighting-Focus Point Objects
* Lighting-Lighting Positions
* Lighting-Spotlight Lighting Devices

Use these as they are named, and where options exist to use additional Classes that will organize your work and communicate your ideas more clearly, create those Classes.

Adding Resources

This file will now require **Spotlight Lighting Devices** from the **Vectorworks Objects-Entertainment Libraries**. A **Spotlight Lighting Device** is a **PIO**, and it will be represented in the drawing by a **Lighting Instrument Symbol**. Spotlight Lighting Devices are typically associated with the **Light Info Record Format**; some devices have additional proprietary Record Formats. There are Lighting Instrument Symbols not associated with the PIO, they are simple 2D Symbols (or Hybrid), but cannot perform the calculations that a Symbol with a Record Format can make.

Open, or add as Favorites in the Resource Browser:

- Libraries>Entertainment>Lighting Positions Imp.vwx
- Libraries>Entertainment>Lighting ETC.vwx
- Libraries>Entertainment>Lighting Martin.vwx
- Libraries>Entertainment>Lighting Varilite.vwx
- Libraries>Entertainment>Lighting Wybron. vwx
- Libraries>Entertainment>Lighting Accessories. vwx
- Libraries>Gobo Textures>Rosco Clouds and Sky.vwx
- Libraries>Gobo Textures>Rosco Image Glass. vwx

Import into both your Lysistrata-Lighting file, and your experimental file:

- Martin – MAC Viper Profile (Hung)
- Varilite – VL2201 Spot, and VL 3000 Spot
- ETC Source 4 – 10°, 14°, 26°, 36°, and 50° units.
- Rosco – R33625 Foam Bubbles, and R77109 Blossoms (Detail)
- Lighting Positions – 20' and 50' Pipes
- Wybron – CXI Color Fusion 4"
- Lighting Accessories – 7.5" Top Hat

Organize your Resources.

Whichever lights you import first will bring the **Default Instrument Texture** and the **Light Info Record** into the document. Instruments can be textured in any way you like as long as you remember one important factor: **Cast Shadows** must be turned **Off**. Any instrument texture with **Cast Shadows** turned **On** *will not allow the light to escape the object.* As you import additional symbols, you will be prompted to import, or not, these resources again. This is not needed.

It is sometimes useful to change the color of the instruments from the default black. For fashion, concerts, and other events, you may want custom-colored, white, or chrome-plated instruments. Consider making the symbols for custom-finished instruments different by duplicating and renaming for clarity, especially if used on a project with concealed instruments with the default finish.

Edit the **Class Definition** of **Lighting-Lighting Positions** to use the **Default Instrument Texture**, or **Duplicate** that Texture with **Cast Shadows** turned **On**. These elements will cast a shadow, which might be important.

Add gobos as you like; a light is just a light without a gobo. If you are familiar with other, similar devices, bring in those resources as well. This is all about process and making choices. Vectorworks gives designers the freedom and flexibility to explore ideas, right up until deadline.

Lighting Instrument Textures *must* have Cast Shadows turned **Off**.

Create **Symbol Folders** for the **Spotlight Lighting Devices**, **Positions**, and **Accessories**. Consider making a folder(s) for the scenic elements, and moving those symbols. Keep your Resource Browser organized.

While the Vectorworks Libraries are extensive, you may not find every unit and accessory that you desire. **ESP Vision** users have access to very extensive libraries, and the commercially available **Soft Symbols** from Field Template can greatly augment your resources.

Lighting Inventory

When working with a house inventory, with or without a limited number of rental units, you can create an inventory of units, once symbols for those units have been imported. Go to **Spotlight>Reports>Create Lighting Inventory**. Highlight the proper name, and enter the proper numerical value. In this dialog you can see that each ETC Source 4 fixture uses a common body symbol.

The **Instrument Summery Tool** can be set up to track the number of each light in use on the plot.

Quick Overview

In your test, or experimental file, double-click on the ETC Source 4-19° degree symbol, and then double-click to insert an instance of the symbol in your file. Clicking once inserts the instance, and the second click sets the rotation. Between clicks, you can rotate the symbol. In the OIP set the Z Elevation to 24' (7,315.2mm).

Choose the **Focus Point Object Tool** from the **Spotlight Tool Set** and place a **Focus Point** somewhere in front of the **Lighting Device**. The default name will be **A** and the default height will be 5' (1,524mm). When prompted choose **Standard 2D**, or make that

choice in the **Tool Preferences**. You can also define that parameter in the OIP with the Focus Point Object selected.

In the OIP, with the Light selected, assign the **Focus** at the very bottom of the window. Turn on **Draw Beam**. This will now illustrate the *Beam and Field* of the instrument graphically in the document. You can also view that same information as a **3D Solid**, or as a **Vertical Beam**, if the light is to be focused on a wall, cyc, or backdrop. That graphic representation will appear in all views. This is useful, but should only be used sparingly and never on a published Light Plot.

In the OIP, a huge number of parameters associated with the Device can be set. Shift-selecting multiple units allows the same parameter to be set for many units. While that's not a good idea for items like Channel, Dimmer, or Circuit, it might be a good idea for color. This information can be displayed adjacent to the unit, used to create Reports, and exported to Lightwright.

While you can change the beam and field in the OIP, that's not a good idea. You can experiment with these parameters. They only affect the one instance, but assuming the information about your lighting device is correct, you would end up with an incorrect display.

Use the software's capabilities to check your work.

Right-click on the **Lighting Device Symbol** and choose **Turn On** from the contextual menu.

Photometer and PhotoGrid Tools

Go to the **Spotlight Tool Set** and choose the **Photometer Tool**, click near the **Focus Point** to insert a **Photometer**, and choose **Show Elevation**, **Show Zero**, and **Calculate using only visible beams** when the Tool Preferences open. The Photometer Object will then display the amount of light at a given point, in Footcandles. Changing the placement of the Object or the elevation will show revised illumination.

The Photometer only assumes or measures white light, even if the lights have been colored.

This is useful for seeing comparisons. Add additional Lighting Units and Focus Point Objects to see the variation. In film and television, this information can be critical. In theatre, you can use these Tools to be sure you have laid out an even wash.

Once you have several units in place, tap the **Photo Grid Tool** and lay out a grid by clicking and dragging to choose the area to measure.

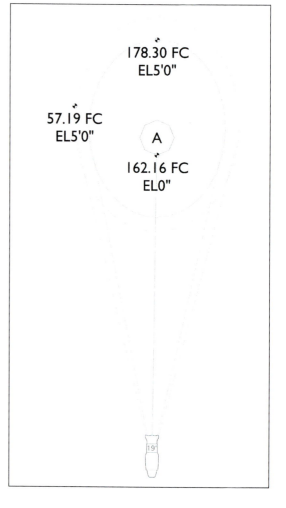

178.30 FC
EL5'0"

57.19 FC
EL5'0"

A

162.16 FC
EL0"

Use the **Edge Placement Mode**, drag a line, **Constrained** with the **shift key** across the window, and encompass the entire area shown by the **Beams**. Click, and then drag down to do the same. Click to terminate the area where the **Photo Grid Object** will take its readings.

For reference, a dark movie theatre would measure about 5 Foot Candles (FC); a normal room, brightly lit would be 30-50FC. A Television News Broadcast or Interview Studio would require about 150FC, and a brightly lit theatrical stage would be 150-300FC.

Use the Photometer Tools to verify your choices.
In Film and Television measuring light is critical.

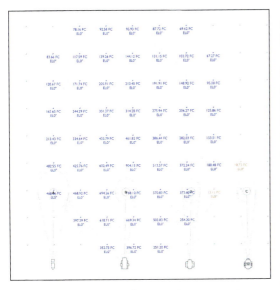

Use these Tools to verify your choices moving forward. Give them their own Class and/or place them on a new Design Layer.

Spotlight Preferences

Whether you are a Lighting Designer, a Set Designer who uses the Spotlight for visualization, a Sound Designer who needs to work in and around the lighting positions/instruments, or a multidisciplinary artist, you really want to add some of these settings to your Stationery file.

Go to **File>Document Setting>Spotlight Preferences**, and tap the **Lighting Device** Tab. Begin by checking the **Enable lighting device auto positioning** box and the **Automatically assign the classes of all lighting devices** box. Set the auto-positioning radius to 18" (457.2mm) and assign the Spotlight Lighting Devices to the **Lighting-Spotlight Lighting Device Class**.

The OIP is an incredible control for manipulating objects, especially Spotlight Lighting Devices. The only drawback is that the amount of information you can control, in a small space, can be daunting, and requires lots of scrolling. There is a solution.

Click the **Lighting Device Parameters** button.

In this dialog, you can select what Data Fields appear in the OIP. Once chosen, sets of Data Fields can be saved. One set of parameters might include functions needed for design, another for focus and rendering, and another for use by the production electrician.

Data Fields can be reordered by dragging the number in the **#** column to suit the individual workflow.

These are **Document Settings**. If you want, or need to keep various sets of data, add them to your stationery file. Factory-specified default parameters cannot be removed, but they can be edited, and hidden in the OIP.

For Design, turn off:
- Circuit Number
- Circuit Name
- The User Fields
- Frame Size
- Beam and Field Angles
- Falloff Distance
- Lamp Rotation (for PAR lamps)
- Shutter Controls (which you might want back for rendering)

Keep Set 3D Orientation, especially if you might want units on the floor to uplight objects.

Save your Set.

Organize and mange your OIP for faster execution of tasks.

The **Additional Default Records Button** allows users to add additional records, and data entry points in the OIP. Any Record can be used in a **Label Legend** to place that information around a **Lighting Device Symbol**. Vectorworks supports unlimited Record Fields, but that is not necessarily a good choice for clear communication. New Record Fields have to be mapped to open fields in Lightwright, if the information they contain will need to be managed in the production paperwork. You can also add parameters for DMX addresses, Mult ID, or Mult circuit.

Rather than the **Spotlight Lighting Device Class**, lights can be classed in a New Class, or in custom Classes determined by values added to **Lighting Device Parameters** in the OIP. Vectorworks will generate the Classes on the fly once the **Prefix** has been set.

It is possible here to color your Lighting Device Symbols; check **Modify lighting device color**, and remember that you can now change the color of the device using the **Attributes Palette**. This might be useful during the design phase for delineating which units are rented from which shop, or to see specials available in the Rep Plot.

> Label Legends are Vectorworks' convention for displaying information around a Lighting Device

Instruments can be colored, either the fill or the pen, by the parameter set in the OIP Color Field. However, light Pen Colors can be hard to read, and dark Fill Colors can make information in the Symbol or the Label Legend difficult to see. It can be pretty.

Label Legend Containers are graphics from the **Default Content** that can house information placed around the Lighting Devices on the plot. A **Label Legend** is Vectorworks' method of organizing this information. This is a graphic convention to help the eye see information. In general, how this is done is the designer's choice, a choice that may vary with the venue and gear.

If you think you may want to keep a number of units with **Draw Beam** turned on, these Preferences allow you to create or assign a Class to the Beams, so they can be quickly activated and deactivated.

The **Universe Tab** allows automatic or manual assignment of Universe IDs.

The **Lightwright Tab** is used when establishing the **Dynamic Link** between Vectorworks and Lightwright.

Click OK to exit the dialog.

> Organize to Design, Organize to Execute.

Focusing Spotlight Lighting Devices

Lighting Device Symbols require Focus Point Objects for Rendering. Additionally, they serve to:
- Allow the designer to verify the instrument throw and beam angle.
- Graphically illustrate where instruments will be focused.

Electricians do not need Focus Points, they have the designer to stand where the light goes, so, they can clutter the plot, sometimes concealing information electricians require.

Designers may want a copy of the Plot that includes the **Focus Point Objects**. So they can remember where to stand.

The **Plot and Model Command** stands vertical lighting positions upright so they can be properly used in rendering, and seen truly in Section Views. Focus Point Objects can interfere with the running of this Command. Class Focus Point Objects, and keep them in their own Design Layer.

Focus Point Objects are for the Designer, not for the Crew.

In 3D views, instruments assigned to **Focus Points** point to the **Focus Point**, allowing designers to see focus issues, clearances, and conflicts. Adjustments can be made in the drawing, before the load in. The 2D portion of the symbol can be angled towards the Focus Point, however that does not make for a clear and legible Light Plot. Once focused, the 3D portion of the symbol will pivot to the Focus Point.

Lighting Devices can be assigned **Focus Points** in the **Focus Data Field** of the **OIP**. Alternately, Spotlight Lighting Devices can be manually focused and Vectorworks will create a Focus Point.

In your blank file, create a slab, and insert a Lighting Device. Go to an isometric view, and with the light selected, go to **Spotlight>Focus Instruments**. You will be given a choice between Focus Point Objects in the document, or **Next Click**. Click on the slab, the light will turn towards the object, and the new Focus Point as specified will be made.

By shift-selecting, multiple units can be focused at one time.

In the Lysistrata-Lighting.vwx file, in the **Lighting Areas Design Layer** insert five **Focus Point Objects** across in zones beneath each **Portal**.

Additionally, **Focus Points** are needed above the Settees, and the Braziers, as well as around the Temple. Heights will all need to be adjusted to compensate for the height of the deck. Those Focus Points that are used for the Temple upper level will have to be further adjusted.

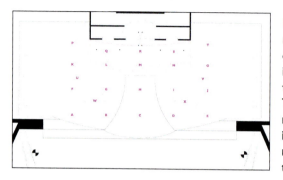

You will need enough lighting areas, as defined by the Focus Point Objects, to isolate different areas of the stage, and light the entire space.

With a **Focus Point Object** selected, options from the **Tool Preferences** can be changed in the **OIP**. There is a standard hybrid symbol, a 2D, a 3D, and a Locus Point. Below the dividing line there are additional choices available from the default content. The Standard 2D shows the graphic, and has a 3D Locus. These disappear in renderings. The options are all editable symbols, including vertical focus objects. Users can add their own content, or modify the defaults once used in an active document. The default content is stored in **Libraries>Defaults>Focus Points** in both the User Folder and the Application Directory.

The Focus Point name can be turned off in the OIP. Names are not restricted to letters. If giving a description in the Focus Point helps, by all means name the Focus Point anything you like.

In the **Application Preferences>Display Tab**, **Display light objects** and **Display 3D loci** should be set to **Only in wireframe**.

Right-clicking on a **Focus Point Object** selects all units focused to that point.

Label Legends

Every **Lighting Device** placed in a document needs some descriptive information to be shown on the Light Plot. The complexity of that information may depend on a number of criteria; the venue, the project, or the crew, for example. The critical point is to provide the information needed where it will be needed. Some information is fine only in the paperwork, some needs to be on the plot. **Label Legends** are the means to display that information.

Once created, Label Legends should be stored in the Lighting Designer's Stationery File.

Label Legends provide critical technical information around and about your lighting units. We are going to require several label legends.

While **Labels Legends** can associate any number of data fields, as established in the Spotlight Preferences, to a lighting unit, it is best to limit that number for clarity. Label Legends only appear in the 2D Top/Plan View.

Label Legends only appear in the Top/Plan View.

It is best to have **Spotlight Lighting Device** Symbols in your file before creating a **Label Legend** so that the Label Legend can be associated with a proper symbol. In the absence of a **Spotlight Lighting Device** Symbol, Vectorworks will insert a generic light in the Layout. You may find that you need different Label Legends for different gear.

Activate a Source 4 Lighting Device Symbol, and go to **Spotlight>Label Legend>Label Legend Manager** and click **Add**. Call the Label Legend **s4**, and click in the left column to select these Fields:
• Unit Number
• Color
• Channel
• Gobo 1
• Focus

The Right Reading column specifies whether the information in the Label Legend will rotate when used on a rotated Instrument Symbol. Leave Non-Rotating unchecked. This keeps the position of the information aligned as designed.

In the right column you can choose to enclose information in a **Container**. Containers are Symbols found in the Default Content. To change a container, you Edit the symbol in the Resource Browser. The container symbols do not appear in your document until you use them.

It is generally suggested that **Channel** number be enclosed in a **Circle**. Click in the Container Column, Channel Row to add the Circle.

Your active Source 4 Instrument should be chosen as the Lighting Instrument Layout Symbol. Tapping the choose Button allows you to change that Symbol.

Click **OK** to return to the **Label Legend Manager** dialog. Check the **s4** Label Legend to make it active, and tap **Edit Layout**, which will open an **Edit Symbol** window. Click and drag the labels from the left column and position them as you like around the instrument Symbol. The SmartCursor and Align Command will assist in aligning the data. Text can be formatted via the Text menu. Click **Exit Symbol** when complete.

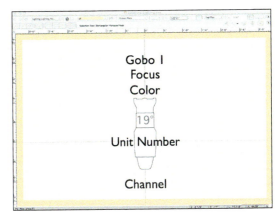

Additional Label Legends may be required to use on other units and/or orientations. This process can simply be repeated, but you may find it easier just to move the legend parts around a unit in the plot.

Select a unit with a Legend assigned, then move the cursor over a data point center mark. Note that the cursor changes shape. With this cursor, move the data around, and snap to arrange.

Once you have the information properly composed, go to **Spotlight>Label Legend>Create Label Legend from Lighting Device,** and you will be prompted to name the new Label Legend. **Edit** after completion if you need to finesse.

Label Legends will automatically size themselves appropriately for the instruments to which they are assigned.

The Label Legend on one or more devices can be changed using the drop-down menu in the OIP.

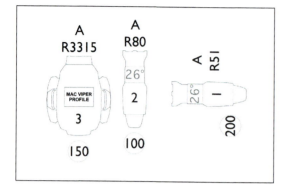

Lighting Positions

In the real-world there are pipes, ladders, and trusses on which lights are hung. In the virtual world, this is virtually the same, except that those items must be **Lighting Position Objects**. When Lighting Devices are attached to Lighting Positions, they automatically find their height, and data can be logically transferred to and from Lightwright.

Lighting Position Objects must be inserted with the Light Position Obj Tool, or converted to Lighting Position Objects.

Lighting Position Objects must be Hybrid Symbols.

Like the real-world, this is another place where sightlines come into play. There will be Front of House (FOH) positions that are visible, but within the framed world of the production, the audience should not be able to see the lights. The trim on the stage electrics must be high enough that when lights are hung on a stage position, they are out of the vertical sightline from the End Seat. Off stage ladders and booms must be located out of the horizontal sightline.

Lighting Position Objects must be **Hybrid Objects**. They can be a round or square Extrude to represent the pipe in 3D, with a 2D Line or Rectangle (designer's choice) showing in the Top/Plan View. The Lighting Position Object must also be placed in Back of the Lighting Device Symbols.

Lighting Devices associated with a **Lighting Position** can be **Auto-Numbered**. With the position selected, tap the Auto-Number Button in the OIP.

Class all of your Lighting Positions as **Lighting-Lighting Positions**.

Truss Objects as Lighting Positions

The Front of House Truss Object exists in this file; it is just not yet a Lighting Position Object.

Select the **Truss Object** and navigate to **Spotlight>Object Conversion>Convert to Light Position**. Name this position **FOH Truss**. In the OIP, set to auto-number, and turn off the position name.

That **Truss Object** now appears in the **Resource Browser** as the **FOH Truss Symbol**. Once converted to a Lighting Position, if you need to Edit the Truss, you must edit the FOH Truss Symbol, to access the Truss configuration in the OIP.

Lighting Position Symbols

For the onstage electrics activate the imported 50' Pipe Symbol. The **Symbol Insertion Tool** will become active as there is nothing special about this symbol. That is, there is nothing to make the Symbol into a Lighting Position. Switch to the **Light Position Obj Tool** from the **Spotlight Tool Set** and insert instances, on the Center Line between the portals and masking. In the OIP, name these positions beginning with the downstage position First Electric, Second Electric, etc.

If you do not select the **Light Position Obj Tool**, Vectorworks will place the Symbols without the Lighting Position attributes. Like the Truss Object, Hybrid Symbols can be converted to Lighting Positions when selected by going to **Spotlight>Object Conversion>Convert to Light Position**.

Elevate the Z Axis of these positions to above the Portal opening in the OIP. Make any **Lighting Instrument Symbol** active, and the **Inst Insertion Tool** from the **Spotlight Tool Set** will become active. Insert an instance of the light at the center of each position. In the OIP these lights should become attached to the positions, and their Z elevation should match the Lighting Position's Z. If they do not, you clicked in the wrong place.

Go to the side view, and draw the sightlines. Move the **Lighting Position Objects** out of view and the **Lighting Instruments** will follow. As they should.

These may not be the finals trims, but they are as low as they can go.

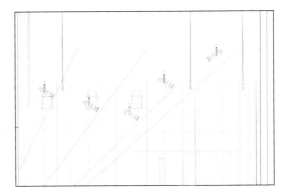

Use the 2D Boom Plan Symbol to locate vertical positions in the wings. Remember, the cast has to be able to get on and off the stage quickly. The booms cannot interfere with the action onstage.

As positions are placed, masking may need to be adjusted, and as you work out lighting angles, positions may need to be moved.

While it is ideal that all of the lighting be concealed, that may not be possible. There will be dance, so there will be shin busters.

At least the traditional black boom bases could be built-into the deck.

The space between the proscenium and the first set of masking, in this case, the first two portals, is referred to as **In-1**. The space or zone between the second portal and the third is called **In-2**. This convention continues logically as you move upstage.

Locate ground placement for booms In-1, In-2 and In-3. Work your sightlines on one side of the stage. **Mirror** and **Duplicate** the Boom Plan Symbols to the opposite side.

Activate the 20' Pipe Symbol with the Light Position Obj Tool and insert three instances, each left and right. Rotate each so they're vertical on the page (running upstage and downstage). Do not be concerned if they are not actually on the page.

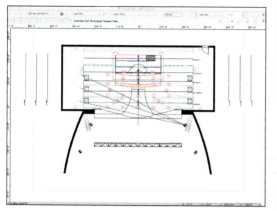

Name these Positions **In-1 Left**, etc. Hide or delete your sightline guides. Delete the lights placed to determine the vertical sightlines.

The Lighting Pipe Tool

Like the **Softgoods Object Tool**, the **Lighting Pipe Tool** uses Polyline drawing, allowing for the creation of standard straight pipes, or anything you can imagine, the shop can build, and the producer will purchase. Similarly, the **Create Objects from Shapes Command** can be used to create Lighting Pipe Objects.

Despite what you might think, the Lighting Pipe Tool does not create **Lighting Position Objects**. The Lighting Pipe PIO is similar to the Truss PIOs, it creates Objects that can be converted to Lighting Positions. There is added functionality.

Draw an **Arc**, using the **Arc by Three Points Mode** that traces the front edge of the balcony. Once drawn, and selected shorten the *Radius* in the OIP so that the pipe sits in front of the edge

of the balcony. There should be enough space so that a large instrument, like the VL-3000 can be mounted and not touch the balcony. Change the **Sweep** in the OIP to 20° and use the **Rotate Tool** to move the center of the **Arc** back to center. Use Command/Control+6 to view the entire Arc Object. Click with the Rotate Tool at the insertion of the Arc (the top) and then at the center of the line (the bottom). Rotate with the **shift key** pressed to constrict the rotation to vertical.

Trace the **Arc** with the **Lighting Pipe Tool** in the **Point on Arc Mode**. Click once at one end, again snapping to center, and double-click on the opposite end. The **Object Properties** dialog and the OIP show the magic in this tool.

Call the **Position Name** *Balcony Rail*, and the **Location** *Balcony*. Raise the **Z** axis so that the Position is in front of the balcony wall. Check **Draw Pipe**, and choose a **Line Type**. Place **End Markers** at **Both** ends. Check **Draw Tick Marks** with the **Origin On Center**; these will help place instruments, even on the curve. The Data Fields that follow set up the graphic attributes of the Object. These can be changed in the OIP after the Object has been created. The Defaults stop and start the Line Type leaving a bit of space before and after the Tick Marks.

Footprint/3D creates a 2D projection of the 3D component in Top/Plan View, if the Lighting Pipe has been offset or rotated. So, a Lighting Pipe Object can be drawn in one location in 3D, and displayed in another location in the 2D Top/Plan View. The Lighting Pipe Object can be rotated in 3D, and still display a proper 2D Top/Plan View on the Light Plot. Rotating on the **J** Axis (perpendicular to the length of the pipe) might cause one instrument to be seen in the Top View over another. While this might be visually dynamic, it would be hard to hang the show without the proper 2D Top/Plan View.

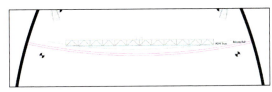

Assign the Lighting-Lighting Positions Class, and tap **Settings** to make that the default for other Lighting Pipe Objects.

The information on this position will interfere with the information associated with the FOH Truss. Eventually, one or the other will need to be moved to a different Design Layer so that the 2D Top/Plan can be displayed in a different location on the plot. The Light Plot will use **Sheet Layers** and **Sheet Layer Viewports**.

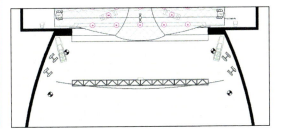

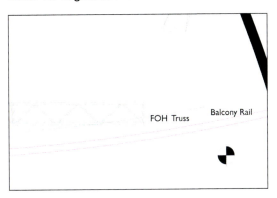

Use **Spotlight>Object Conversion>Convert to Light Position** to create the **Balcony Rail-Sym** and have the **Lighting Position** in your Document. Once created, the Lighting Positions symbols in your Resource Browser can be Moved to the proper folder for organization.

The Balcony Rail position is often used for fill light, adding shadow color that can fill where front light creates shadows, and adding textures or SFX.

The Lighting Pipe Ladder Tool

In a theatre like this there will, or certainly should be, Box Boom positions on the House Right and the House Left. These are wall mounted pipes or ladders. In 2D they would be represented with a variation on the Boom Position Symbol. That variation would simply show the units without the pipe and base. It might include a Rectangle to show the pipe in plan. Create your variation and indicate the plan positions in the Front of House.

It should be clear why the Lighting designer needs to know where the speakers will be going. It should also be clear why the designers need to work together.

Just as the Lighting Pipe Tool could be used to create the onstage electrics, the Lighting Pipe Ladder Tool can also be used for the onstage booms. How you work, and what tools you use is a personal choice, determined by your graphic style and workflow. These are options.

The FOH Box Booms would be named BB-1 Left, for the House Left (not stage left) position nearest the stage. The others would follow logically.

The **Lighting Pipe Ladder Tool** draws in the same manners as the **Photometer Tool**. Choose the **Edge Placement Mode** and open the **Tool Preferences**, which are similar to the **Lighting Pipe Tool**. Include five **Evenly Spaced Rungs**, set the **Location** to **FOH**. For the **Tick Marks**, choose **Split Center** from the drop-down. Class as with the Balcony Rail. Click **OK.**

Click alongside the auditorium space and drag horizontally to begin to define the shape. Tab into the **Floating Data Bar** (FDB) and enter 30" (762mm) for the length; tap and then drag down to start the height. Tab into the FDB and enter 10' (30,480mm) for the specific size. Click to set. In both cases, be sure you're drawing at right angles.

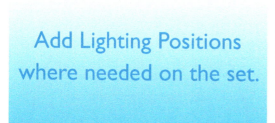

Add Lighting Positions where needed on the set.

Convert to a **Lighting Position** and duplicate as needed. These positions, like the similar positions onstage, will be located in 3D later. The Vertical Positions will require additional Label Legends.

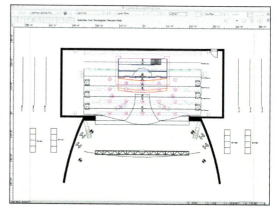

Add additional Lighting Positions as you work. It is probable that additional positions, **Focus Point Objects,** and additional instruments will be needed inside the Temple.

Choosing Correct Instrumentation

If you like, you are welcome to do the math behind this work for yourself, or you can let the application help.

On the FOH Truss, there are instances of different s4's directly in front of the downstage lighting areas. Focus the lights and **Draw Beam**.

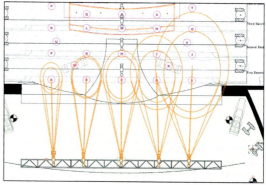

The goal of any system within a lighting design is to produce an even wash. If the design desire is to then break up that even look with gobos, fine, but start with a solid foundation. This experiment does not yield an even wash.

It does yield information required to produce that wash. Use the **PhotoGrid Tool** if that helps.

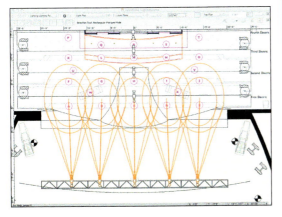

Use this information to create warm and cool front light systems. On the FOH Truss add Vipers for specials between the Warm and Cool for each area. In the center, the speaker is in the way. Place the Viper and check **Set 3D Orientation**. Rotate 180° **X** and elevate that unit so that it is top-mounted on the Truss.

For clarity and ease of reading the plot, front lights should be pointed straight up. Back lights should be pointed straight down. Side lights on an overhead pipe should be pointed towards their side. Specials should align accordingly. Do not angle the Lighting Devices towards their focus on the 2D Top/Plan. That makes for a confusing plot that is difficult to read. That's another rule.

Match the angles within lighting systems for a realistic appearance.

Working through the same process, determine the proper unit to light each area from the front, back, front side (the box booms), and sides. Add Additional Vipers as backlight specials. Add specials for the Settees, and the Braziers. Turn some, not all of the lights on to see how things are looking. Turn those lights off after rendering.

As you add units, it is best practice not to use the **Mirror** and **Duplicate** functions

Matching Angles

As you add additional systems, it is critical to come as close as possible to matching angles. The front light angles should match, the side light angles should match, and the back light angles should match. They do not have to match each other. That's a design choice, or a choice dictated by circumstance.

Adjust placement and trim of the Lighting Positions. Move the Lighting Areas until your focus is just right.

Visualization Palette

Each time you insert a light, it is added to the **Visualization Palette** and assigned a numerical designation. This is true of both **Spotlight Lighting Devices** and **Vectorworks Light Objects**. Instruments can be turned on and off in the Visualization Palette. Lights can also be set to cast shadows or not cast shadows in the Visualization palette. It's a nice trick that we would all love in the real-world.

When a **Purpose** is given to a **Spotlight Lighting Device** in the OIP, the entry in that **Data Field** prefaces the numerical designation. Channel assignments and a list by Channel is also seen in the Visualization Palette.

Adding Color

You can add color from either the OIP or the **Lighting Device Dialog** (double-click on an instrument instance to access). Rosco, Lee, or GAM colors, as well as Hexidecimal, or RGB values, can be entered into the **Color Data Field**. A Rosco color is noted as R36, and a Lee as L36.

Multiple commercial colors can be added as R02+R51 and Vectorworks will calculate the subtrative color mixing and render that color.

Adding Frost

Frost is added and/or specified in the **Color Data Field** of the OIP of the **Lighting Device Dialog**. Frost can stand alone, or be added as R51+R112.

Adding Gobos

Gobos Textures have to be resident in your document. They are added to Lighting Devices by simply entering their number into one of the

Gobo Data Fields in the OIP. They can be rotated, and two gobos can be inserted into any light. Using a steel break-up with a Colorizer or

Prismatic and adding fog takes some time to render, but it is worth the wait.

In the real-world, only certain types of lights can use gobos. That is not true in Vectorworks. So, if you might be using an ellipsoidal zoom fixture, but the symbol does not render the size of the gobo projection accurately, you can add the gobo to a Fresnel or PAR head to get the image right.

In film and television, *Cookies* are often placed in front of high wattage Beam Projectors, or Fresnels. A cookie is a pattern cut into a large sheet of masonite and held in place with grip stands. In Vectorworks, you can assign a Gobo Texture to a 5K or 10K unit to visualize that effect.

Gobos do not render in OpenGL.

> Create and use a logical system for assigning instruments to channels by purpose.

Custom Gobos

Any square graphic image can be imported into Vectorworks as a **Gobo Texture**. Go to **Spotlight>Visualization>Create Gobo Texture** and follow the steps through the creation of the texture. Name the gobo, and accept the defaults. The gobo projection is only the image within a circle enclosed in the square image.

Channeling

Channeling can be done in Vectorworks, or in Lightwright after the dynamic link has been established using Lightwright Data Exchange. In either case develop a numbering system that works logically. Keep systems together numerically.

The Martin Viper requires 26/34 channels. A Source 4, one channel. The VL3000 requires 28 channels. They do not have to be sequential. You might want all of the primary channels for the specials to be sequential. The control channels can be grouped elsewhere.

Use the **Num Channels Data Field** in the OIP to create a notation of the channels required for a specific instrument.

Number your front light something like 1-5 for the warm fronts in the FOH, 6-10 for the cools, 11-15 for the warm front, First Electric, and the like. Keep the numbering together. This makes everyone's life easier during tech.

Aligning Instruments

It is possible to Align and Distribute Lighting Devices with the **Modify>Align Commands**; the Spotlight **Align and Distribute Tool** is designed to be used with Lighting Devices.

Select multiple instruments and then the **Align and Distribute Tool** from the Spotlight Tool Set.

Draw a line to align the insertion points of the instruments. The Length of that Line can be specified In the FDB. After clicking to end the Line, the Tool Dialog opens. Instruments can be simply **Aligned** for graphic clarity, or also **Distributed** along that line at a specified interval.

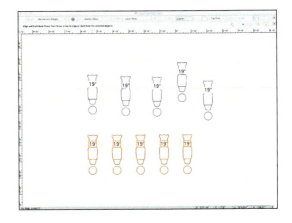

Snapping to the Lighting Position is great, but we all miss from time to time.

Clean and clear graphics are the only way for the design to be executed as intended.

Ganging Tool

If you have assigned Dimmers or Circuits to instruments, you can choose the Ganging tool from the Spotlight tool set and graphically indicate the two-ferring or other ganging.

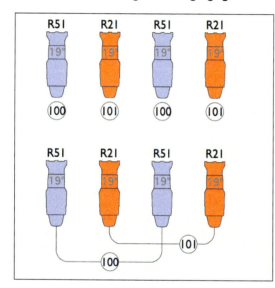

Accessories are either **Accessories**, or **Static Accessories**. A Top Hat is a Static Accessory, something that does not need a Channel or control. This delineation is critical for communicating with Lightwright.

Accessories become attached to the Lighting Device to which they are assigned and move.

Adding **Accessories** will require modified **Label Legends**.

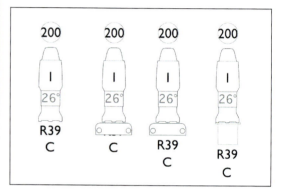

Adding Accessories

Instruments often need accessories like top hats, color scrollers, and barn doors.

Accessories are Hybrid Symbols that have the **Light Info Record** attached, and have had the **Spotlight>Object Conversion>Convert to Accessory Command** run.

Double-clicking or **Activating** an accessory symbol activates the **Accessory Insertion Tool**.

Inserting accessories is a three-click operation. The first click inserts the **Accessory**, the second click sets the rotation, and the cursor changes to a **Bullseye** for the critical third click, on the red highlighted instrument, to associate the accessory with the instrument.

Basic Scripting

The **Magic Wand/Select Similar Tool** is great, but it does not drill down into the specific parameters that can be assigned to a **Spotlight Lighting Device**. Go to **Spotlight>Find and Modify**. Devices can be selected, and then modified, based on specific criteria. If you want to swap out one color in the design for another, set those parameters in the **Find and Modify Dialog**, and that work is then done quickly and efficiently. **Find/Modify** creates a script that selects the units with the specified color, and color can be changed in the **Change Data Field**. There are numerous functions and possibilities beyond changing colors. An electrician or designer circuiting a show can run a script that selects uncircuited instruments. As circuits are assigned, fewer units will be selected.

Don't let the idea of scripting scare you. The **Tools>Custom Selection** and **Tools>Custom Modification** Commands can create simple scripts that can be used immediately, and/or saved for future use. Once a script is saved, there will be a new *Scripts* window, and section of the Resource Browser. To execute the script, double-click on the name. If the window is closed, it can be opened at **Window>Script Palettes>Scripts**.

Complex and frequently used scripts should be saved to the Stationery File.

Custom Lighting Symbols

Vectorworks is one of the few applications that allows the user to create symbols. Vectorworks gives you the flexibility to create symbols, but some rules must be followed for full functionality. Any **Hybrid Symbol** that includes a 3D Locus can be made into a **Lighting Device** by selecting the symbol and going to **Spotlight>Object Conversion>Convert to Instrument**. In this way, you can assign a symbol to represent a lighting device, a practical, or prop lamp, and it will be accounted for in your paperwork.

To have a functioning light, a **Vectorworks Light Object** must be included in the 3D portion of your new symbol, if you do not include one, Vectorworks will add a Light Object when Convert to Instrument is run. When looking to represent a specific lamp type, Vectorworks includes symbols of accurate lamps in the libraries. Illumination Engineering Society (IES) data from manufacturers' specifications, can be imported when making a custom Vectorworks Light Objects.

Whether a table lamp, or the new theatrical fixture you've just invented, be sure that your symbol either uses the **Default Instrument Texture**, or a texture with **Cast Shadows** unchecked for the light to pass out of the geometry. A Back-lit Texture Shader would be the correct choice for a lamp shade.

General Rules for Lighting Instruments

The Geometry of the symbol in both 2D and 3D should be as simple but as accurate as possible. Instruments should be drawn with the front, the end that emits light, oriented towards top. Both the 2D and the 3D need a solid fill so that the objects obscure information below. Lighting Instrument Symbols are not detailed drawings of the accurate device. They need to accurately represent and identify the unit, with minimal detail.

There are three different 3D components: the body, the yoke, and the clamp or base. Each component must be a single **Object** or **Group**. The clamp has been included with each Lighting Device in the libraries. The yoke will rotate around the Z Axis, and the body will rotate at the height of a 3D Locus point that must be placed inside the Object where the unit would pivot.

The 3D portion of the instrument is drawn as if it is hung straight down (along the Z axis) with the yoke oriented along the Y axis. The top of the instrument should be oriented towards the top of the drawing.

Align the 2D and 3D components so that the hanging points align.

The insertion point of the 2D/3D hybrid symbol in Top/Plan View should represent the hanging location of the instrument. The 3D Insertion Point should be the hanging point at the center of the clamp.

Once the symbol has been created, **Import** and **Attach** the **Parts Record** to each of the 3D

components, by Editing the 3D symbol. Select each part and click on the **Data Tab** in the OIP. Attach the **Parts Record** to the part by checking the box next to the name. **Edit** the record by selecting the appropriate record field and changing its value to **True**.

Import and **Attach** the **Light Info Record** to the Lighting Instrument Symbol. The **Light Info M Record** provides metric measurements of the weight and frame size of the instrument object. This Record is required for symbols that could be used in either imperial or metric drawings.

In the **Edit Symbol Window**, click on an empty location to be certain nothing is selected. Click on the **Data Tab** in the OIP. Attach the **Light Info Record** and/or the **Light Info Record M** to the symbol by checking their respective check boxes. **Edit** the **Records** by selecting the **Record Field** and entering the proper values. Not all fields are required.

The **Candlepower**, **Beam Angle**, and **Field Angle Parameters** affect the **PhotoGrid** and **Photometer** object calculations. **Beam Angle** and **Field Angle** parameters affect the **Draw Beam** characteristics. These settings set the defaults for the new symbol, and future instances of the symbol.

Lighting Instrument Symbols should be named with the model name of the lighting instrument.

The Vectorworks Light Object located with a Spotlight Light Device can be Edited after creation. Accurate light information can be specified with the parameters in **Use Emitter**.

The **Light Info Record** can also be attached to the Symbol using the **Spotlight>Reports>Lighting Symbol Maintenance** Command. The symbol can be added by tapping **New**, and the Light Info Record is automatically attached to it. Once in the maintenance list, the Record Data can edited.

Clear graphics, notes, and information speed the reading of the plot.

Auto Plot Tools

The AutoPlot Tools for Vectorworks Spotlight are a shareware set of macro commands that make some functions of Spotlight easier to use. These macros include:

- dimensioning lighting positions
- create Line Set legends from worksheets
- create hybrid pipe symbols
- globally change fixture symbol line weights
- selections based on Lighting Device field values
- macros for facilitating data entry individually and globally
- Label Legend visibility
- Focus Point creation and visibility

The Auto Plot Tools come with their own workspace, and they can be added to existing or custom workspaces.

Invest in add-on products that speed your work.

Instrument Summary Tool

Every Light Plot requires a **Key to Instrumentation** so that the electricians know, at a glance, what actual unit each symbol is representing. Designers cannot assume the crew will know what is in the designer's mind. In fact it is best to assume the crew has no idea what the designer was thinking. The **Instrument Summary Tool** can create both a **Key to Instrumentation**, and **Lighting Position Summaries,** which provide detailed information about the units on a single position.

Go to the Spotlight Tool Set, select the **Instrument Summary Tool,** and open the Tool Preferences. There is a drop-down to choose between:
- Instruments
- Positions

These default sets are saved separately and their use depends on how the Summary is inserted. Investing the time to establish your choices makes it much easier to insert summaries later. Save these settings into your stationery file.

Instruments

Tapping the **Build List Button** opens the two-column Build List Summary Dialog. On the top left there are three Radio Buttons that affect the choices available in the left column. Items from the left column can be moved into the right column to be shown on the document. The Radio Buttons are not exclusive, which is to say that used and unused instruments can be chosen. Delineations and information can also be added from the **Other Elements** options. Items can be moved and reorganized by dragging the numbers in the **#** column.

The **Width** and **Column Offset** are **Page Based Scale**. The **Column Offset** is the overall width of the information. **Compare to Inventory** will deduct the number of instruments used against the inventory created using the **Spotlight>Reports>Lighting Inventory Set-Up Command**.

General text settings for the overall look are set from the **Text Menu** Commands. Certain specific internal headers can be added, and font settings specified in the dialog. Once inserted, the Key to Instrumentation can be adjusted using the OIP.

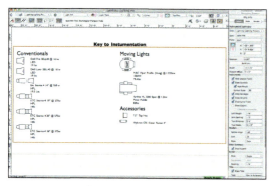

Data for the **Instrument Summary** comes from the **Light Info Record** attached to each Spotlight Lighting Device. That information, like instrument names, can be modified using **Spotlight>Reports>Lighting Symbol Maintenance** Command. **Lighting Symbol Maintenance** has an option to **Update all Lighting Devices,** which will push changed data to any Lighting Devices placed on the Plot.

Lighting Symbol Maintenance also has a **Copy types to Model Name** button, which will copy any data in the **Type Field** to the **Model Name Field**, should those values need to be the same. Those **Fields** do not become linked.

Instrument Summaries can be placed on Design Layers or Sheet Layers. Individual insertions can be **Filtered** to customize the information presented. So, if one Key is required for the Light Plot, a variation or a Position Summary might be more efficient for a Boom Plan Sheet, or a Plot detail.

Positions

The **Positions** settings are very similar to the Instruments settings, but the information is applied differently. Position Summaries are inserted using the OIP, with the Position selected, and by tapping the **Insert Position Summary** button.

Lighting Position Summaries are **Filtered** Instrument Summary information.

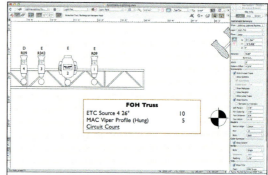

Create Similar Command

Once an object has been inserted into a document, such as a Door, a Window, a Truss, or a Lighting Device, that Object can be used as a template for subsequent Objects. **Create Similar** is available as an option in the Contextual Menu when right-clicking on an Object.

The Tool required to create the object is activated, while the Tool Settings, and any global settings used by the Tool, change to match the source object,

Magic Sheets

Every Designer is going to need a Magic Sheet or Magic Sheets to keep track of units and channels when working with the programmers during tech. Magic sheets are a graphical representation of instruments on the plot, and some associated information. Magic sheets are invaluable for cueing a show.

The **Spotlight>Reports>Generate Paperwork** Command has an option to create **Magic Sheets** from the information on the Plot. Tapping the **Setup** button accesses a number of graphic representations of standard theatre spaces.

It is also possible to use the information in the plot to create your own visual representation of the complex drawing. The gel colors are stored in the **Active Document Color Palette**. Just as Vectorworks can color lights with paint, the application can fill 2D graphic objects with colors similar to the gel colors used for the show.

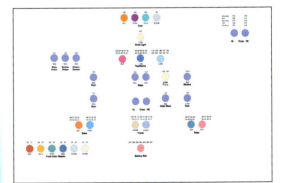

Magic sheets are invaluable when cueing a show.

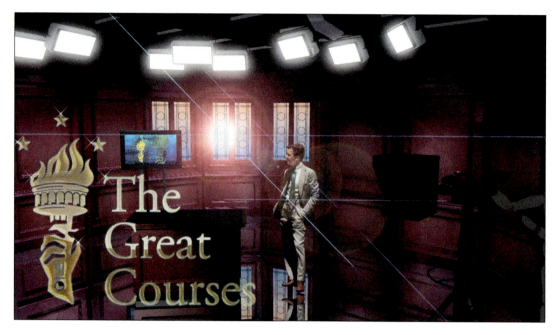

The Teaching Company

The Teaching Company

The Teaching Company Studios

Scenic Designers: Kathleen McDonough & Kevin Lee Allen (KLAD)
Lighting Designer: Shadowstone
Systems Integrator: Human Circuit

17. Visualizations and Animation

Like mathematical proofs, visualizations show results. Visualization is how you prove to directors and clients that you have great ideas. It can be done on site, or it is possible to proof or entirely pre-program the show before a crew has hung 500 or 600 lights. It is possible to pre-program the show in a lounge chair by the pool. Cocktails are best after work.

On a Light Plot, horizontal Lighting Positions and their associated instrumentation have a Z elevation above the deck. The vertical positions are lying on their sides, on that same deck. This is all well and good for publishing a plot, but it does not give you the information needed for a stage section, or to use those instruments in renderings, or animations.

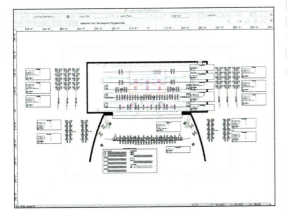

Create Plot and Model View

The **Spotlight>Visualization>Create Plot and Model View** Command is used to stand vertical positions upright, and properly angle them in 3D views. The Command can be run on one position at a time, or all of the positions at once. Running on all at once gangs them together, so it is not possible to properly orient each position.

If you include horizontal positions, or have nothing selected when you run the **Create Plot and Model View** Command, all or none will become vertical.

If you work in a facility with fixed positions, save the Plot and Model views and Definition Layers for the facility in a template file. Even without fixed positions, it is possible to save and reuse specific types of vertical positions.

Turn **Off** the Focus Point Objects Class and Layer.

The **Create Plot and Model View**

Command moves the selected Lighting Position Object and its associated Spotlight Lighting Devices to a new Design Layer and References a Design Layer View Port (DLVP) of the new Design Layer back to your Plot Layer. The DLVP is the 2D representation of the Position to be seen on the plot.

Focus Point Objects cannot be visible when running Create Plot and Model View.

The first, or any time, you run the **Create Plot and Model View** Command, you are given the option of placing the 3D Vertical position on a new or existing Design Layer. The first time, create a Design Layer called *Model*, and thereafter add your vertical positions to this layer.

Select one of the vertical positions, and go to **Spotlight>Visualization>Create Plot and Model View**. The first dialog in the process names the **Definition Layer**. You must run this command for each of the vertical positions. Name the Definition Layers after the position name adding DL as a suffix. Check **Vertical**.

Definition layers are created at the same scale as the original layer. Objects are placed at the same position as they were originally drawn. When viewing the Model or the Plot Layer, turn **Off** the visibility of the **Definition Layers**.

On the **Model Layer**, rotate, elevate and place the positions so that they appear correctly in sections, and elevations. In the Model Layer, Top View, select a vertical position, and rotate such that it aligns with the 2D symbol that indicates placement on the plot. Repeat for each vertical position.

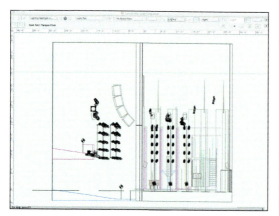

The Design Layers are not used for creating and publishing production documents like a light plot. Different Design Layers and Classes are used to create Sheet Layer Viewports, and Sheet Layers for publication:
- The Definition Layers are used to **Edit** lights, and to modify the plot, and the model.
- Lighting Positions and instruments on different Design Layers can show position placement, and plot details in different Viewports/drawings. Move, or cut and Paste in Place, the DLVPs of the Vertical Positions to a new Design Layer.
- The Model Layer is used when showing stage sections, rendering, and animating.

Vertical Positions-Plan View

The Vertical Position symbols locate the placement of booms and ladders on the light plot. The snappable center is used to dimension the boom location. These symbols must not be placed, or identified as a Spotlight Lighting Device.

Editing Lighting Devices

By default, Spotlight Lighting Devices are not turned on when placed into documents. To turn **On** a Lighting Device, either right-click on the device and choose **Turn On**, or select the Device in the Visualization Palette, and turn it on there.

Inside each Spotlight Lighting Device, there is a Vectorworks Spotlight Object. That Object can be accessed by right-clicking and choosing **Edit Light**. The dialog that follows is similar to the OIP when modifying a Vectorworks Light Object. This is where an intensity level can be set, and where **Lit Fog** may be checked. Who doesn't love fog? Just as, or more so than fog can be controlled on stage, Vectorworks can control the fog in renderings. The more units that use fog, the longer the render time that will be required.

In the Visualization Palette and using Edit Light, shadows can be turned on and off. This is not particularly realistic in theatrical lighting. The soft lights used in film and television cast fewer shadows; turning shadows off for film and television can produce a more realistic rendering.

Double-clicking on an instrument in the plot, or tapping the **Edit** button in the OIP, opens the **Lighting Device Dialog** to reveal four tabs:
• Instrument Properties
• Light Information
• Shutters
• User Data

Instrument Properties, Light Information, and User Data access some of the same information as the OIP, some of which can also be edited in Lightwright. It is a personal decision as to where it is most efficient to work. The answer may vary depending on where you are in developing the project.

The **Shutters Tab** allows the same kind of control over a Lighting Device as can be had in a theatre, or film/television studio. Shutters work as expected on spot units but can also be used on other types of instruments. A Fresnel can be shuttered to simulate barn doors, or flags on a film or television set. In the same way, a gobo can be placed in a film Fresnel to perform as a cookie on set.

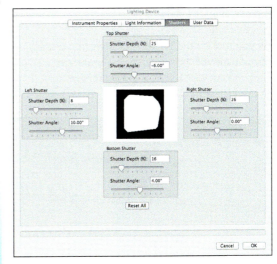

Final Pre-Visualization

Be sure **Ambient Light** is turned **Off**. Check the work progress using either either **Final Quality Renderworks**, or **Custom Renderworks**. Light several moments:
• A Dance Sequence
• A Dramatic Moment
• Day
• Night

Spotlight Lighting Devices do not always work the same way real fixtures work. Use that carefully.

Turn **On** and **Shutter** units to create your desired looks and mood. Adjust intensities. Use the render-as-you-go approach, and modify the design to experiment. Turn on only one **Spotlight Lighting Device**, shutter, and render. See how it looks. Experiment with different gobo textures in different places.

Consider how the lighting and scenic color palettes suit your taste. In a true collaboration this is the final point where the designers can and will make accommodations to one another towards the best design solutions.

Change the scenic textures to things that may better suit your interpretation or tastes. Modify the lighting to suit those changes.

Review different camera views.

As you modify the Lighting Design, be sure any new, or moved instrumentation is associated with the correct **Lighting Positions**.

Animate Scenes

Vectorworks and Renderworks can generate movie files of light cues. After setting one cue of levels, and with that scene rendered in Final Quality Renderworks, go to **Spotlight>Visualization>Manage Scenes** to save that collection of information, and transition timing. **Saved Scenes** can be used to manage and animate transitions, or to render stills of different moments. The same dialog can be used, like a **Saved View**, to return to the specific settings. **Saved Views** do not recall lighting settings.

Once multiple scenes have been saved, a QuickTime movie can be created to preview the transition between cues. These scenes can be of the same view, or different views, if different, Vectorworks will add the sprites to move from one view to another. With multiple scenes saved, select **Spotlight>Visualization>Animate Scenes**, and choose a location to save the file.

Clicking **Save** opens the **Scene Animation** dialog. Choose the two scenes to animate, and enter the time parameters for the **Start** and **End Scenes**. **Edit** the timing for the **Saved Scenes**, if desired. The **Up Time** and **Down Time** used for the animation is taken from the **End Scene**. You must enter a value for the **Hold For** time in seconds for both scenes. Tap the **QuickTime Settings** button to choose a Codec for compression, frame rate, and quality of the animation. Click **OK** to create the animation.

Multiple cues can be edited together, and a musical score can be added using Video editing software, like Final Cut. If a production is using moving, or static projections, and an Object has a chroma key green texture, using the Glow Shader, graphics, or other animations can be mapped onto that Object using a video editor/compositor.

These same Commands can be used to create simple, or complex walkthroughs of film sets, retail environments, installations, or exhibit spaces.

ESP Vision

ESP Vision is a **Cuing Animation and Visualization** software package that works closely with Vectorworks. Use Vectorworks to create the designs and then export the scenic model and the light plot to ESP Vision for offline cuing.

Using Vectorworks and ESP Vision in a professional situation, cueing can be done with your Vectorworks document, consoles, or offline application, programmers, and design staff off-site, which leaves the theatre space available for work calls, or rehearsals. Concert tours can be pre-programmed off-site and set to run at the first venue. Working with Vectorworks and ESP Vision will reduce stress, on-site time, and production costs while inspiring creativity. ESP Vision plug-ins allow designers to customize colors, gobos, lenses, lamps, or any other variable of the fixture. All fixture functions, such as gobo and color wheel rolls, prism effects, beam angles, head speeds, gobo and color wheel rotation speeds and beams can be seen and animated. QuickTime movies can be created for review by and with the director.

It is possible to pre-visualize a production, and spend minimal time, sometimes as short as an hour, tweaking the design in the venue. This is a huge value to the producer, and allows the director to truly see the designer's vision before entering the theatre.

ESP Vision has PIOs and lighting symbols for Vectorworks. Any lighting symbol can be used, so designers are able to maintain their own graphic standards. ESP Vision will convert Spotlight Lighting Devices to its own format during the file transfer. Vision has some simple modeling tools, but most any Vectorworks Object will convert to Vision. Some complex geometry may not convert. Image Props do not transfer.

Vision can create real-time animations from simple looks like cross fading, to complex animations with moving lights in motion, gobos rotating, colors changing, and fog. If the board can program the cue, Vision can render it out.

ESP Vision can be controlled with any commercially available lighting desk, or the offline software.

There are professional and student versions of ESP Vision.

AnimationWorks

AnimationWorks is an add-on set of PIOs for Vectorworks that allow the creation of complex camera, and/or object movements within Vectorworks. These animations can be saved as QuickTime movies and shared, and viewed by anyone.

AnimationWorks does not work with Spotlight Lighting Devices, all lighting must either be Vectorworks Light Objects, or the PIOs own lighting sources. Image Props are, however, supported, so there is that.

Animating scene changes informs the director and the cast, while helping to engineer the physical structure.

AnimationWorks features:
- Creation of camera paths through your model using the Camera Path Tool. Cameras can be static, panned, zoomed, stopped, started, and aimed at either stationary, or moving objects.
- Objects can be made visible or invisible by turning Classes on and off within a movie. This feature can be used to show chasing lights.
- Any object can be animated or moved along a user-defined 3D path; a NURBS Object.
- Lights can be faded up and down within a scene.
- Rotating object animation.
- Sliding object animation.
- Changing Transparency animation, like a scrim through.
- Preview camera animation with look-to point and view extents drawn on screen, zooms, and pans.
- Real-time wireframe or OpenGL previews of either object or camera animations.

Animations can be rendered in segments, so multiple computers can be assigned the rendering task.

Pre-Visualization is key to testing and selling ideas.

It takes time and patience to make a film in real life, and AnimationWorks will require some of both, especially when rendering in Final Quality Renderworks, but the results can be spectacular.

AnimationWorks is a great tool for previewing scene changes, and timing them with the music. This kind of pre-visualization not only informs the Director and other designers of intent, but can also help Technical Directors make hardware, engineering, and mechanical choices.

MA Lighting grandMA Plug-In

MA Lighting, a leading manufacturer of computer lighting consoles, networking components, and digital dimming systems has a PIO that will provide a direct connection between Vectorworks and the grandMA2 console. The grandMA2 has its own built-in visualizer that allows the designer/programmer to program and pre-visualize. With this PIO, Lighting Designers are able to export their lighting data from Vectorworks, and then import that data into grandMA's built-in visualizer to do the pre-programming and visualization.

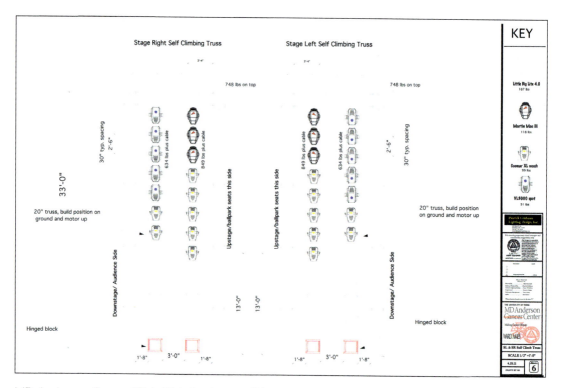

MD Anderson Cancer Clinic 70th Anniversary Dinner

MD Anderson Dinner

MD Anderson Cancer Clinic 70th Anniversary Dinner

MD Anderson Cancer Clinic 70th Anniversary Dinner
Minute Maid Ball Park Field

Scenic Designer: Peter Crawford
Producer: Ward & Ames Events of Houston
Lighting Designer: Herrick Goldman
    Assistant Lighting Designer: Susan Nicholson
Gaffer: Rob Baxter

Dinner for 2,000 was held on the field of Minute Maid Ball Park. Many challenges were imposed by Major League Baseball, as well as tight time and budget. The entire Houston Symphony Orchestra was onstage as well as a performance by The Gatlin Brothers.

18. Working with Lightwright

Transferring data from Vectorworks to, and from, Lightwright 5 is the entertainment industry standard for creating the paperwork required to bring a lighting design to life. Just as the Lighting Designer's Vectorworks file is likely to be shared with other designers, the production electrician, and production staff, the Lightwright file will need to be touched by many. Lightwright can configure data to be used by designers, associates, assistants, and electricians. Each job function will want to organize information differently.

Dynamic Data Transfer with Lightwright

Go to **File>Document Settings>Spotlight Preferences** and then the **Lightwright Tab**. This Preference Tab determines what information about Lighting Devices will be exported to Lightwright to generate paperwork. The dynamic exchange of information between Lightwright and Vectorworks is fully interactive and ongoing, as soon as it is established.

This link can be established at any time in the design process, however it is best practice to have some lights on the plot before linking. Lights can be added to the Vectorworks Light Plot from within Lightwright, however the symbol for any new Lighting Device must pre-exist in the Vectorworks file, or Lightwright/Vectorworks will insert a generic rectangle.

In the **Lightwright Tab** of the **Spotlight Preferences Dialog**, check **Use Automatic Lightwright Data Exchange** and **Perform a complete export on exit**. Save the Lightwright file in the **Same location as the file,** that is, the **Lysistrata Workgroup Folder**.

It is a best practice to save the VWX, XML, and LW5 files in the same folder or directory.

Add **Focus**, **Num Channels**, and other desired data from the **Available Fields** to the **Export Fields**.

> Lightwright is the entertainment industry standard for generating lighting schedules and paperwork.

Save as default establishes choices for future exports; these defaults can always be modified in the future.

Vectorworks will then create an XML file in the Workgroup Folder that can be imported into Lightwright 5. That XML file will be continuously updated as changes are made in either program.

Importing Data into Lightwright

Create a new file in Lightwright 5, and there will be a large button showing the Vectorworks logo. Tap that button to turn **On** and check **Use automatic Vectorworks Data Exchange** and **Reconcile whenever LW receives a full export**. Tap the button to **Choose Vectorworks .xml file**, and navigate to the Workgroup Folder and select the XML file you just created.

Adding Data Fields in Lightwright

The Vectorworks **Focus** and **Num Channels Data Fields** (amongst others) do not automatically transfer to corresponding Data Fields within Lightwright. This is also true of any custom fields you have created in Vectorworks. There can be unlimited Data Fields associated with Spotlight Lighting Devices; if you need to use that additional information within Lightwright, the **Vectorworks Data Fields** need to be mapped to a **Lightwright Worksheet Column**, and the **Data Type** addressed.

These links must be established in Lightwright when creating the connection with the Vectorworks XML file. To make these connections later, the XML file will have to be unlinked and then re-established. Work may be lost.

In the **Focus Row**, click on the **Access Triangle** in the **Lightwright Worksheet Column**, and assign a **User Field**. Repeat this process for any other Data Fields without a corresponding Lightwright Worksheet Column.

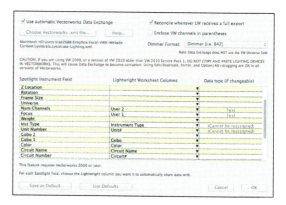

Save the Lightwright 5 file in the same **Workgroup Folder** as your VWX and XML files.

Change the names of the **Lightwright User Fields** used by going to (in Lightwright) **Set-up>Column Names & Definitions**.

Save the VWX, XML, and LW5 files in the same directory.

Once the dynamic link has been established, the Vectorworks Dynamic Data Exchange button at the top of the Lightwright window will appear indicating the link is now made. The data entered in Vectorworks will be available for use, and/or modification in Lightwright.

The **Num Channels** information adds to fixture maintenance in Lightwright 5. The number of channels needed can be *Locked* in Lightwright 5 so that all similar fixtures always have the same number of channels.

Maintaining the Dynamic Link

Once established, the dynamic link to Lightwright will want to be maintained. If the Lysistrata-Lighting.vwx file is Saved As, Vectorworks will create a new XML file (that was established when defining the Lightwright Preferences), but Lightwright will still be linked to the original XML file. The new VWX file and its associated XML file will have to be linked to Lightwright.

Best Practices with Lightwright

Lightwright was developed by Lighting Designer John McKernon and not by Nemetschek Vectorworks. They work together to ensure a smooth workflow, but they are not one product, like Vectorworks Designer. This is a critical point, and it needs emphasis.

Copy files off of the Cloud to work on the file.

Critical Best Practices

Save the Vectorworks XML file in the same location as the VWX file.

The VWX, LW5, and XML files must all be located in the same folder or directory.

If you have a collaborative environment using a service such as Google Drive, or Dropbox, do not work on your files while they are on the server. Move working files to the desktop for modifications. The Cloud servers may be copying parts of the files at any time. When this happens, the file is likely to be locked and cannot be written to by either Vectorworks or Lightwright. Whatever changes are made when the file(s) are locked will not show up in the XML file.

Do not use degree symbols anywhere in your Vectorworks symbols—in the name of the symbol, in the default data/information for the Lighting Device, or in the OIP data. For detailed information on why, search the Lightwright Reference Manual for *degree symbol*.

Use Lightwright 5's Save a Back-up Command to make copies of the LW5 file, but do not Save As. The Save a Back-up Command (similar to the Save a Copy As Command in Vectorworks) automatically turns off Data Exchange in the back-up copy, so it will not interfere with Data Exchange on the original VWX file.

Maintain the dynamic link between Lightwright and Vectorworks.

Do not change the name of the VWX file. To back-up, make a duplicate of the file using a different name, and do not rename the original; this is the same as Saving As. In this way the XML file that Lightwright has been linked to will not change, and you won't have to do a full export on exit and re-link Lightwright to the XML file. Opening the duplicate copy, it will automatically export a new XML file. The new XML will not be linked to Lightwright.

Any lighting devices, static accessories, or accessories added to the plot will be added to the Lightwright file.

Similarly, you can add data to the Lightwright file such as; channel information, color, circuiting, instruments, accessories, and that information will appear in Vectorworks.

Refreshing Instruments

Right-clicking on the document and selecting **Refresh Instruments** (Command/Control+/) from the contextual menu, or going to **Spotlight>Refresh Instruments,** updates light position information and instrument labels to reflect any changes to ensure that all current information is displayed.

Vectorworks can also generate lighting paperwork.

Good, clear paperwork is critical to the design execution.

Perform a Complete Export on Exit

Occasionally, Lightwright will ask you to **Perform a complete export on exit**. In Vectorworks, go to **File>Document Settings>Spotlight Preferences, Lightwright Tab** and check the box to **Perform a complete export on exit**. That box only stays checked for the time you are in the dialog. Check as asked, and Vectorworks will export current data to the XML file when you click **OK.**

Vectorworks Reports and Schedules

Vectorworks can also generate instrument schedules, hook-ups, and other paperwork. Go to **Spotlight>Reports** to choose the desired paperwork. Follow the directions, and make the choices required. **Reports** are **Resources**, and can be edited from the **Resource Browser**.

Lightwright Touch

Why carry a bunch of paper around on stage when in tech, or focusing? Carry an iPad, or an iPhone. Lightwright Touch has been developed by Eric Cornwell of West Side Systems and Pocket Lighting, under license from John McKernon, and is only available for iOS. Lightwright Touch provides mobile viewing and editing of Lightwright 5 lighting paperwork.

In Lightwright 5 the **File>Export Lightwright Touch .lwx** Command will export your show to the Lightwright Touch format. That file is transferrable to the iOS device running Lightwright Touch via iTunes, eMail, or Dropbox. Once transferred the Lightwright data can be accessed, and modified. Changes made in Lightwright Touch, and merged back into Lightwright using the **Lightwright>File>Reconcile with Lightwright Touch .lwx** Command, will update the Lightwright file, and then the Vectorworks Light Plot.

While Lightwright Touch does not do everything that Lightwright can do, it is pretty powerful and valuable:
- Views and Sorts worksheets
- Columns can be added, removed, and rearranged
- Log feature speeds selection of previous displays
- Worksheet data is editable
- Notes can be added to any worksheet row, or to a general notes page
- Lightwright Touch can store and access multiple shows
- View and e-mail notes or changes
- Lightwright Touch supports any device orientation, and multiple font sizes

Of course, you cannot start a new show on Lightwright Touch. Lightwright Touch is an accessory for Lightwright 5, not a replacement, or alternative.

Using Lightwright and Lightwright Touch with Vectorworks, you can read your documents, on stage, in the dark, without a flashlight.

Using Lightwright, and Lightwright Touch with Vectorworks, you can read your documents, on stage, in the dark, without a flashlight.

PLSN Virtual Television Studio

PLSN Virtual Studio

PLSN Virtual Television Studio

PLSN Virtual Television Studio
PLSN Magazine

Editor: Justin Lang
Scenic and Lighting Designer: Kevin Lee Allen

The chroma key green texture, using a Glow Shader, in the Television objects, allows the publication to update the look with each broadcast.

19. Documentation and Publication

Once the design is complete, it is time for the actual drafting. Since the work was developed in 3D, that drafting exists, it just has to be composed so the information is presented in a clear manner. Additionally, once the drafting has been completed, if the designs are modified, much of the drafting will be automatically revised.

Every designer, of every stripe, needs a graphic designer hat. Page Layout is a huge component of creating production documents. Graphic Design and Page Layout are all about communicating ideas. Drafting is about communicating the design ideas to the craftspeople for execution.

Line Weights, use of color, Lines Styles; these things come into play when composing the plates of drafting for the production. There needs to be air on the page around information so the eye can find the information. Do not over-stuff a page.

In each drawing file go to the **Document Preferences** and check **Save Viewport Cache** in the **Display Tab** and set the print and PDF resolutions to 125 in the **Resolution Tab**. A dpi (dots per inch) resolution of 125 is sufficient for plotting with an inkjet plotter.

> Working in 3D facilitates creating and revising the production documents.

The process of creating production documents can be completed by one artist in one document by placing instances of each of the symbols on a **Design Layer** and creating **Viewports** from those **Design Layers** onto **Sheet Layers**. This narrative describes working in a team, or a possible workflow for designers working without assistants. As scary as that might sound.

What is a Title Block?

The Title Block identifies a drawing. What needs to be included? A title block must appear on every drawing that leaves any studio. Whether an early design sketch, or final production documents, the drawing must be identified. The information in the title block may often be different for different functions, but should always include the designer's name, the project, date, title, scale, and sheet number. The sheet number is usually expressed as a number of the total number of sheets in the set. That alerts the user to be sure they have all of the information.

Old school title blocks are very simple, small rectangles in the lower-right-hand corner of a drawing. This approach is often still used by engineers, and for shop drawings in many different types of firms and fields.

Most designers currently opt for a full-height vertical title block up the right-hand side of the plate, or a full-length horizontal along the bottom. In Vectorworks, title blocks are associated with a drawing border on **Sheet Layers** using the **Sheet Border Tool** from the **Dims/Notes Tool Set**. Traditionally, in addition to a title block, each plate of drawings was framed by a box called a border. That tradition does not need to be adhered to, but the **Sheet Border Tool** can provide that graphic. The actual border can be turned off in the **Sheet Border Tool Preferences**, or in the OIP.

The one constant, or rule, here is that the drawing number must be in the lower-right corner, so a print can be folded and that number remains clearly visible. Whatever the orientation of the title block, it pivots from the sheet number.

Vectorworks comes with a selection of title blocks, stored in the default content and accessed when a **Sheet Border Object** is inserted on a **Sheet Layer**. Dissecting a copy of the Default Content is a great way to learn new ways of doing things.

Contents of a Title Block

The contents of a title block can vary widely. Minimally, a title block must contain certain basic information:
- The name of the project
- Drawing Title
- The name of the designer
- The date of the drawing
- Sheet Number, and the number of drawings in the full set
- The scale of the drawing

Additionally, a title block should include:
- The Venue
- Designer's Declaration of Copyright
- Disclaimers
- Designer contact information

Optionally, a title block might include:
- Revision Dates and Notes
- The names of the other designers, TD, crew heads, production manager, director, and producers
- The draftsperson's initials or name
- A Show Graphic
- Client Logo
- Designer's branding or logo
- Some Lighting Designers incorporate the **Key to Instrumentation** in the title block
- Union Stamp
- The Vectorworks file name

Do not underestimate the importance of creating a personal brand.

Personal Branding

Like the work, and the graphic style of the drawings, a designer's personal brand identifies the designer and sets you apart. The typeface you choose for your drawings, and your logo speak volumes. Every designer should have a personal brand and begin to develop that brand early. It will evolve over time.

Craft a logo, a simple graphic element to use on business cards, letterhead, resumes, and your drawings. The logo should work in both black and white, and full-color, should you desire color. Hire or work with a graphic designer if that makes you more comfortable, but everything you produce should seal to who you are.

Spend some time studying graphic design and logos; this will help compose plates, and someday, you might need to design a sign for a production.

Put on your graphic designer hat.

Disclaimers

Disclaimers are included on drawings to assist in absolving designers from legal responsibility should something fail. This disclaimer and variations is widely used:

- These drawings represent visual concepts and construction suggestions only. The designer(s) are not qualified to determine the structural appropriateness of this design. Contractor(s) assume sole responsibility for safe and workmanlike execution conforming to the most stringent applicable federal and local fire and safety codes.

Other disclaimers might appear in the title block or elsewhere on the drawing. These might include:
- Written dimensions on the drawing shall have authority over scaled dimensions.
- Contractors and manufacturers shall verify and be responsible for all dimensions and conditions on the job and shall inform the Designer of any variations from drawings before beginning the work.
- Verify all field measurements.

If a designer expects a shop, carpenter, electrician, prop artist, or others to do something, it needs to be drawn, noted on the drawings, or written in attached specifications.

> If something, anything, needs to be done, it needs to be drawn and specified in the production documents.

Custom Title Blocks

Custom Title Blocks are saved as default content, in the User Folder. Custom Title Blocks are created in their own files, not the file in which the title block will be used. They will be imported.

A Custom Title Block can contain your personal or company branding, project/document information, and Data Fields. Your own title block can then be attached to a **Sheet Border** and inserted onto a **Sheet Layer**. Three steps are required:
- Create a 2D title block graphic at 1:1 scale and save it as a symbol.
- Create a custom Record Format.
- Link the Record Format Data Fields to the title block symbol Text Fields.

Creating a Custom Title Block

This is about process and content; the look of the title block should be the designer's own. To create a custom title block, work in a new file, or a copy of your template file, and work on **The Screen Plane,** and in a **Design Layer** with a scale of 1:1.

Title Block Objects can be **Scaled** in the OIP after they have been attached to a **Sheet Border**. It is nonetheless best practice to make a **Title Block Object** for each size sheet you use. Scaling can be fast and practical, but it does affect the final look of your drawings. You can modify one **Title Block Object** once Completed. **Text Styles** will expedite any modifications. Save each Title Block in its own file in your **User Folder>Libraries>Default Content>Sheet Border-Title Blocks** folder.

Working on a US Arch E page (36" by 48"), allow some empty space between the **Sheet Border Object** and the edge of the page. Typically, there is extra space on the left to allow for the binding of sets of drawings, about 2" (50.8mm), 1/2" (12.7mm) on the right and top, and allow a bit extra on the bottom 3/4" (19.05mm) to add some visual weight. So the **Sheet Border Object** would measure 45 1/2" (1,231.9mm) by 34 3/4" (876.3mm) tall. Those distances are then the limits for full horizontal or full vertical title blocks. The same math works on other size sheets, although the air around the border can decrease as the sheet sizes diminish.

The overall size of the title block should be elegant.

Critical details:
- Draw in the **Screen Plane.**
- Do not use any 3D elements.
- Logos and Graphics are imported as image files.
- Fonts may need to be uploaded to Vectorworks Nomad.

The title block geometry (pen color, line style, and line thickness) and text (font, style, and color) can inherit the **Sheet Border Attributes**, be assigned by **Class**, or retain the attributes used at creation. The **By Class** setting in the **Attributes Palette** indicates that the attributes should be inherited from the sheet border. If an attribute is not set to **By Class**, then its original setting is retained.

Title Blocks take time and patience to set up, but speed all future work.

Title Blocks are part of your Brand!

There have been many illustrations of title blocks throughout the Text. Typically, the title block sits within a boundary box, then specific information is set within additional boxes. These are not rules. The boxes do not have to be rectangles. That said, each type of boundary might want its own **Class** and specific **Attributes**.

Title blocks take some time and patience to establish, but once completed, they expedite the process of compiling sets of drawings.

Text Styles

A **Text Style** is a resource, stored and edited from the **Resource Browser**, that specifies **Text Attributes** such as the font, size, line spacing, font style, text alignment, and text and background colors. Text styles make it easy to apply a consistent look to all text throughout a file. If you change a text style, all objects that use the style are updated. A text style can be applied to objects created with the **Text Tool,** as well as to the text portions of other objects, such as title blocks, dimensions, and callouts.

Text Styles may be familiar to users of word processing applications as **Paragraph Styles**.

To create a text style select the **Text Tool** from the **Basic Tool Set**, and in the **Tool Bar** go to the **Text Style** drop-down menu, and choose **New**. Set the font attributes, name the style and click **OK. Text Styles** can also be created by right-clicking in the **Resource Browser** and selecting **Create New Text Style**, or from existing text, by selecting the **Text Object** with the **Selection Tool**, and switching to the **Text Tool**. Then, go to the drop-down menu in the **Tool Bar**. Select **New**, and the dialog will show the attributes of the selected text. The original text will remain unstyled until the **Text Style** is applied from the OIP.

New **Text Styles** can also be applied to existing text in the OIP.

If using boundary boxes, use the **Smart Cursor** to snap the centers of the text objects to the centers of the rectangles.

Save as Symbol

Once you have composed your title block with placeholder text included, **Select All**, and create a 2D Symbol of the title block. Place the **Insertion Point** at the lower-right corner of the **Title Block Bounding Box**, or the lower-right of the composed area. The symbol inserts in the lower-right corner of the **Sheet Border Object**.

Title Block Record Format

The **Title Block Record Format** will allow data to be associated with objects in a title block, generally **Text Objects**.

In the **Display Tab** of the **Document Preferences**, check **Use Automatic Drawing Coordination** allowing Vectorworks to coordinate sheet names and numbers. This will require specific naming and

Title Block Data Fields require specific naming conventions.

association requirements between the **Title Block Object** and its **Record Format**. When the **Title Block Object** is in a **Sheet Border Object**, double-clicking on the combined object or choosing **Edit** in the OIP allows you to edit the content of the **Title Block Symbol Instance**, as associated with its **Record Format**.

Right-click in the **Resource Browser** to create a **New Record Format**. **Name** the **Record Format** and tap **New** to add **Fields** and **Name** those **Fields** as described below.

Using **Automatic Drawing Coordination** with the **Data Fields, S_Sheet Number_ SN** and **S_ShtTitle Line 1_SD** will enable Vectorworks to generate a Table of Contents (**Spotlight>Reports>Create Sheet List**) for the final drawing package, if all of the sheets are in one file. This is a useful guide for the shops. When the sheets are in multiple files, the **Create Sheet List Command** can get that work started and set up.

A **Record Field** with a **P_** prefix is **Project** related information; so the title of the show, the name of the designer, the number of sheets in the set, and/or the venue can be changed universally. Create **Fields** for the **Project Specific Information** in your title block.

A **Record Field** with the **S_** prefix is **Sheet** specific information; like the drawing name, the sheet number, and/or the scale. When edited, the information in these fields only modifies one sheet at a time. Create **Fields** for the **Sheet Specific Information** in your title block. The **S_Sheet Number_SN** should be a **Text Field**. While it would be logical to assign **Number** to this **Field**, a prefix may want to be added to the sheet number so that the scenic, lighting, and sound sheets have differentiation.

Designs change, to keep track of the changes, add **Revision Fields**. Vectorworks recognizes these specific text blocks to indicate specific information;

- :rNo = Revision number
- :rDate = Revision date
- :rNote = Revision note

Don't forget the colon.

These **Text** fields should have **Left Justification**, and **Word Wrap** on. Set the **Vertical Alignment** to **Top** for the revision text to flow down, and to **Bottom** for the revision text to flow up, creating columns of information.

Attaching the Record Format to the Title Block

To attach the **Record Formats** to the **Title Block**, **Edit** the 2D component of the **Title Block Symbol**. Right-click on the symbol instance in place, and select **Edit 2D**, or right-click on the symbol in the Resource Browser to **Edit>Edit 2D**.

Linking Text to Record Formats

While in the Edit 2D Symbol window, select a placeholder **Text Object** and go to **Tools>Records>Link Text to Record** to link the **Record** to the **Symbol**. One by one, link the placeholder text to the associated **Data Field**.

Save and close the file.

The production drawings should be so complete that if the designer finishes the drawings and gets hit by a bus, the design can be executed.

Creating Production Documents

Open the Portal.vwx file located in your Workgroup Folder. This will be an example; all of the scenic models need to be converted to 2D elevations for construction. The process is also the same for detailing the lighting and audio.

Create a **Viewport** of the Portal in **Top/Plan View** on a **New Sheet Layer**. This is a rare occasion where the same name can be used twice. Name the **Viewport** and the **Drawing Title** both as **Portal Plan**. In the New Sheet Layer Dialog, name the **Sheet Title** as **Portal**, and do not be concerned with the **Sheet Number** as that, like most everything, can be edited later. Click OK to exit the Dialogs. Vectorworks will shift the view to the new Sheet Layer

If required, go to **File>Page Set-up** and change the page to US Arch E.

Adding the Sheet Border Object

Go to the **Dims/Notes Tool Set**, select the **Sheet Border Tool**, and click on the sheet. With **Lock to Page Center** checked, the **Sheet Border Object** will always find the center of the page.

Add your **Title Block Object** from the **Default Content**.

With the **Sheet Border Object** selected, go to the OIP and un-check **Show Grids**. Tap the **Border Settings** Button to change the margin settings to fit the **Title Block Object**.

Sheet Border Settings	
Drawing Size (in)	
Horizontal Dimension:	48
Vertical Dimension:	36
Dimensions Shown Are:	Outside Dimensions ⇕
Margins (in)	
Left:	2
Right:	0.5
Top:	0.5
Bottom:	0.75
Zones/Grids	
Vertical Zones:	7
Grid Text Order:	Top to Bottom ⇕
Horizontal Zones:	9
Grid Number Order:	Left to Right ⇕
Grid Label Size:	18 ⇕
	Reset to Default Values
	Cancel OK

The **Title Block** is aligned to the **Sheet Border** and the **Sheet Title** has retrieved information from the **Sheet Layer** settings.

The choice of Title Block, and **Lock to Page Center** can be set in the Sheet Border Tool Preferences. To speed work in other files, the Sheet Border Object, and Title Block can be copied and pasted.

Double-click the Sheet Border, the Title Block, or, with the Sheet Border selected, click the **Edit Title Block** button in the OIP to edit the information connected to the Data Fields in the Title Block Record Format.

Working with Viewports

A 1/2" or 1:25 scale **Viewport** of the **Top/Plan View** has been placed on the **Sheet Layer**. Alt/Option select, and drag the viewport up to add a copy, press the shift key while dragging to keep the copy aligned with the original. In the OIP, change the new Viewport to the **Front View**. Repeat to have copies to use as a 1:2 scale detail, and a 1/4" or 1:50 scale isometric view.

The OIP offers tremendous control over the Viewport. Some of these choices can be made when creating a Viewport. First off, users can control the visible Classes and Layers seen in the Viewport, the standard view, background and foreground render, Renderworks background, and lighting.

The Foreground and Background rendering options can be used to add a compositing effect to a view. The **Background** render is the primary rendering mode. **Foreground Rendering** allows the addition of a **Hidden Line** or **Dashed Hidden Line** render over. So an object can be rendered in color, with some technical information composited over the color.

Control the appearance of Viewports using the OIP.

When a Viewport becomes out of date, the **Update** button will turn red and become active. Wireframe views update automatically, but other Rendering modes have to be updated when changes are made, typically back on the Design Layer, or when the rendering mode is changed in the OIP. In the **Document Preferences**, **Save viewport cache** and **Display viewport out-of-date border** should be checked. The **Border** adds a visual alert that a Viewport needs to be updated. The **Cache** saves Viewport renderings.

Viewports can also be updated on **Export** and using the **View>Update All Viewports** and the **View>Update Selected Viewports** Commands.

Change the **Background** render on the Front Elevation to **Hidden Line**, and the isometric to **Final Quality Renderworks**. **Update** both Viewports.

Detailing a Drawing

Right-click on the Front Viewport. The cursor must be positioned over a line in the Viewport to reveal the editing options:
• Edit
• Edit Annotations
• Edit Crop
• Edit Design Layer
• Edit Camera
• Update

Open the **Figures.vwx** file and **Import** or **Reference** a figure or figures to use in annotating the elevation. Elevations and sections should always have a figure included to quickly show the viewer the scale of the objects in reference to the human body.

Right-click on the Viewport of the Front Elevation, and select **Edit Annotations** to enter the **Annotation Space** of the Viewport.

Design Layers can have only one scale. Sheet Layers are always Full Scale, 1:1, or actual, those terms all mean the same thing. Viewports can each have a scale, but Viewports of different scales can exist on the same sheet.

Within the Annotation Space of the Front Elevation Viewport, place a figure instance at the bottom center of the portal opening. If you try to place the instance outside of the Annotation Space, on the Sheet Layer, the figure will be Actual Size, much bigger than the page.

Use the **Constrained Linear Dimension Tool**, located in the **Basic Tool Set** and the **Dims/Notes Tool Set**, using both the **Constrained Linear Mode** and the **Constrained Chain Mode** to add some basic overall dimensions.

Wherever possible, notes and dimensions should not appear over the drawing object. That view should be as unfettered as possible. That said, designers should indicate where they would like the scenery broken for shipment from the shop to the theatre. Those break lines must often appear on the object, but notes describing breaks, or other indicators appear outside of the boundaries of the object.

The **Callout Tool** in the **Basic Tool Set** has a number of options available in the **Tool Preferences** for formatting the look of an **Identifier**. The Preferences also allow access to a **Database** of frequently used **Notes**. Using the **Towards Text Mode**, click to insert an arrow, and then drag to place the note. Pressing the **shift key** while dragging constrains the angle of the line that attaches the note to the object to which the note refers.

When specifying a commercial product it is important to include the product specifications, or MDS (Material Data Safety information). Image files, and PDFs can be imported and placed into Vectorworks documents, saving hours of data entry. Another way to attach information is using a **Hyperlink Object**, which can also open other applications, or Saved Views and Sheet Layers within Vectorworks.

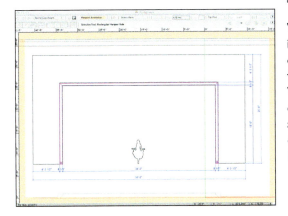

A **Hyperlink Object** requires a Symbol for placement, that can be either text and/or geometry, and can be created from a custom symbol. Hyperlinks are easy to customize and can be batch edited from a worksheet. Hyperlinks to websites can be exported when drawings are exported to PDF; hyperlinks from a batch PDF export can navigate to sheet layers in the drawing.

Select the **Hyperlink Tool** from the **Dims/Notes Tool Set**. Click the **Tool Preferences** from the **Tool Bar**, or double-click the **Tool** to specify the parameters. Once inserted, that link can be inserted again by selecting the Tool, and tapping in the document. Subsequent insertions can be Edited in the OIP without affecting the original instance.

When the **Hyperlink Settings Dialog** opens, choose specifications, and a link for the proper results. For the first time flying this Tool, choose the **Text Link Symbol**. Once the Link has been placed, and is selected, go to the OIP, click **Edit**, and then **Edit Symbol** to format the text to match your graphic standards.

Every drawing needs a label. This will be a sheet with five different views. Choose the **Drawing Label Tool** from the **Dims/Notes Tool Set** and in the **Tool Preferences**, set the **Number Style** to **Drawing and Sheet**, and the **Line Length Mode** to **Control Point**. Insert the Drawing Label Object at the left side of the Portal, and grab the **Control Point** and drag to continue the Line to the right side of the dimensions. In the OIP, the **Drawing Title** will have picked up the name of the Viewport. Since this is a copy, and different view, that needs to be corrected. The OIP will begin to automatically number the drawings. Call this **B** and the sheet number will be automatically completed.

There is a class, **D-Drawing Labels**, for these objects.

In the OIP, adjust the text and overall presentation of the Object to suit your graphic style. Change those same parameters in the **Drawing Label Tool Preferences**, and save those **Preferences** in your **Stationery File**.

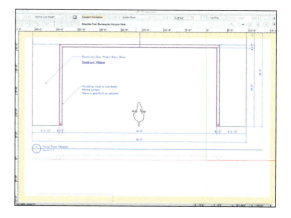

Exit the **Viewport Annotation Space**.

Enter the **Viewport Annotation Space** of the **Plan View Viewport**. Add a **Drawing Label Object**, and call this view **A**. Zoom in to the Stage Left edge of the portal opening. Draw an Oval with no fill around the moulding detail. From the **Dims/Notes Tool Set**, select the **Reference Marker Tool** and set the **Arrow Angle** to **90°** with the **Drawing Number** set to **D**. Specify the Sheet Number. Click OK and insert the object pointing at the bottom of the oval. Adjust the **Object Parameters** in the OIP, and save them in your stationery file.

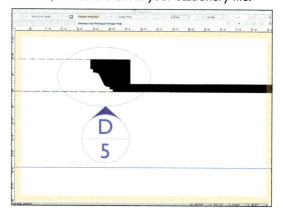

Crop Visible should be unchecked in the OIP, that can be changed if you want to see the crop shape. Having a visible crop is sometimes useful as a graphic element to draw attention to a detail.

Viewport Crops are essential for clarity on the **Light Plot**. **Vertical Positions** can be *Cropped* out of the **Plot** and placed on their own sheet. **Crops** showing single **Positions** can be used to create a sheet of **Hanging Cards**.

Class Overrides

This **Reference Marker** will refer the viewer to a detail on this sheet. On the Scenic Design Plan of the overall set, there should be a **Reference Marker** pointing to each portal, referring the viewer to view **A** on this sheet of details. This is true of each scenic element. The same might be true of a chandelier detailed by the Lighting Designer, or an audio reference.

Exit and Label the Isometric View.

Select the other Plan View Viewport and change the scale to 1:2 in the OIP.

Cropping a Viewport

Move the Viewport such that the Stage Left moulding area sits on the page. Right-click and select **Edit Crop**. Draw an **Oval** that encompasses an area similar to the area enclosed by the Oval in Drawing A. The area inside the 2D shape will remain visible. Any 2D shape can be used. Crops are not restricted to shapes made by Tools. Any 2D shape or combination of shapes that have been Added, Clipped, or Reshaped can be used as Crop Objects. However, you must end up with only one shape. Only one **Crop Object** can exist in a single Viewport. Exit the **Crop**.

Select the **Viewport** and go to the OIP. Tap the **Classes** Button. Highlight the **Portal-2D** Class, check **Class overrides**, and click **Edit** to change the graphic attributes of the Class in this Viewport. Multiple Classes can be selected using the standard Shift + Select to select adjacent classes, Command/Ctrl + Select to select non-adjacent classes, and edited at one time.

Since this is, essentially, a Section View, the Viewport should look like a Section. Makes those changes to the **Attributes** and Exit the Dialog.

Class overrides only change the **Object Attributes** within the specific **Viewport**. Modifications made in one Viewport can be imported to other Viewports.

When modeling, it has been useful to use different Pen colors to differentiate elements and Attributes. For the final drafting some or all of those pen colors should be changed to Black.

Attributes of **Lighting Devices** changed in the **Spotlight Preferences, Lighting Device Tab** can be **Overridden** for printed documents. Similarly, the Lighting Designer and the Sound Designer may not want to see the **Hatch** used in the Set Designer's plan of the show deck. A **Class Override** can eliminate that **Hatch**, just as it can gray out the theatre architecture fill, or the scenic architecture fills. **Graying** those **Design Layers** in the **Viewport** will help, but may not always be enough to focus attention on the **Lighting Devices**, or **Speaker Objects**.

Annotate the **Viewport** with dimensions and labeling. If a stock moulding piece had been used here, this would be the place to identify that moulding, and the supplier.

On the Sheet Layer, outside of the Viewports, draw a Rectangle. Right-click in the Resource Browser to create a **New Image**. Choose **Reuse an Image from Another Resource** and then **Gold-Rough Color** from the drop-down menu. Select the Rectangle, go to the **Attributes Palette** and choose **Image** from the **Fill** drop-down menu. The texture image should fill the Rectangle. Click the button in the **Attributes Palette,** next to the **Fill** preview to **Edit**.

Label this element as *Paint Sample,* drawing *E,* and Save. You have been Saving, right?

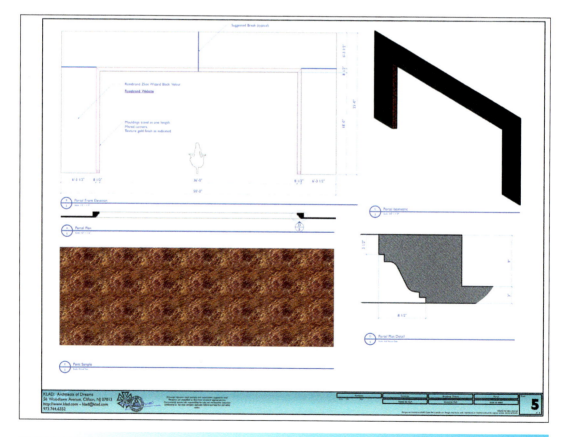

The Line Set Schedule

Every full stage Plan, Plot, or Section must include a hanging schedule. This is one more place to create a shared resource. Open the Lysistrata-Lighting.vwx file and create a new Design Layer above the Light Plot Design Layer.

On the **Line Set Schedule**, items downstage of the Plaster Line are negative numbers, upstage of the Plaster Line measurements are positive. Work in the **Gray-Snap Others** mode set in the **Design Layer Tab** of the **Navigation Palette**. Once drawn, when finessing, **Active Only** is probably better.

Draw a short horizontal Line (6-12" or 15-30mm) snapping first to the Datum that locates the center of the Fire Curtain. Repeat for the onstage electrics, portals, soft goods, and the LED Screen. Use **Absolute Positioning** in the OIP to place these at 0 on the X Axis, and their proper Y position.

With nothing selected go to **Text>Alignment>Left** and **Center**. With the **Text Tool**, **Snap** to a **Line** and enter the distance from the **Plaster Line** and identify what will be hanging in that place. Move the text so there is a bit of air between the line and the text.

Often Electrics are identified by a red **Pen** color. The entire Schedule can be enclosed in a box.

Once drawn, select all of the elements, and create a Symbol. Place the **Insertion Point** of the Symbol at 0-0, and add a **Locus Point Object** if required.

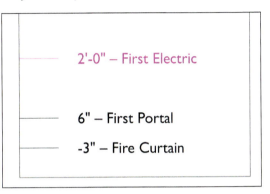

2'-0" – First Electric

6" – First Portal

-3" – Fire Curtain

Stage Plans and Sections

This process is similar for Scenic Lighting, and Sound. Work in the Lysistrata-Sound.vwx file. Also open the Lysistrata-Lighting.vwx and Portal. vwx files.

Create two new Sheet Layers:
- A1-Sound Plot
- A2- Sound Section

Since the environment is symmetrical, only one stage section is needed. If the set and therefore everything else were asymmetrical, a Stage Right and a Stage Left Section would be required.

Copy the **Sheet Border Object** and **Title Block Object** from the Portal.vwx file onto each Sheet Layer. The **Sheet Names** and **Sheet Numbers** will be entered as appropriate. There will be only these two drawings in the set.

Reference or Import a figure symbol from the Portal.vwx file, and close. Reference the Line Set

Schedule Symbol from the Lysistrata-Lighting.vwx file and close that as well. Go to the Sound Plot Layer, with the scenery, theatre, and masking visible.

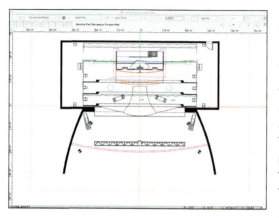

From the **Top/Plan View**, go to **View>Create Viewport** and create the **Sound Plot Viewport** with the same **Drawing Title**. Click **OK.**

Working in their respective classes, add the **Centerline** and **Plaster Line**, snapping to the **Datum** at 0-0. Use the **Center Line Marker Tool** from the **Dims/Notes Tool Set** to indicate the bottom of the **Centerline**. Insert an **Instance** of the **Line Set Schedule Symbol**, snapping to the same **Datum**. Move it out of the theatre, pressing the shift key (once you start moving) to constrain the position. Alternately, use the **Move** Command.

Since this is the only drawing on the sheet, the **Drawing Label Object** is optional.

Adding Scale Bars

Working in the **D-GraphicScale** Class, select the **Scale Bar Tool** from the **Dims/Notes Tool Set**. Set the Preferences to a Printed Height of 1/2" (12.7mm) with the **Minor Length** at one foot and **Major Length** at

four feet with eight **Major Divisions**. Set the style to **Flip** and place at the center line.

Mirror the Object to the other side of the **Centerline**. Run **Vertical Scale Bars** from the **Plaster Line**. It is quick to **Rotate** the horizontals in the **Rotate** and **Duplicate Mode**. Adjust the number of **Major Lengths** as needed.

The **Scale Bar Objects** are reference points useful to stage managers in rehearsal, and to crew onstage looking for a rough starting point. They also help check printed dimensions; printers are not always accurate, and despite any warnings added, people will put a scale ruler on the prints.

Annotating the Plan

Right now, the set design is very dominant. Simply selecting the **Viewport Object** and tapping **Layers** in the OIP and setting the architecture and scenic layers visibility to **Gray** may suffice. It is more likely that Viewport Class Overrides will be required.

Once the Sound Design is the dominant feature of the drawing, it is possible to add some dimensions indicating proper placement of the Audio Objects. Dimensions on plans are from the 0-0 Datum.

> The subject of the sheet must dominate other information included as reference.

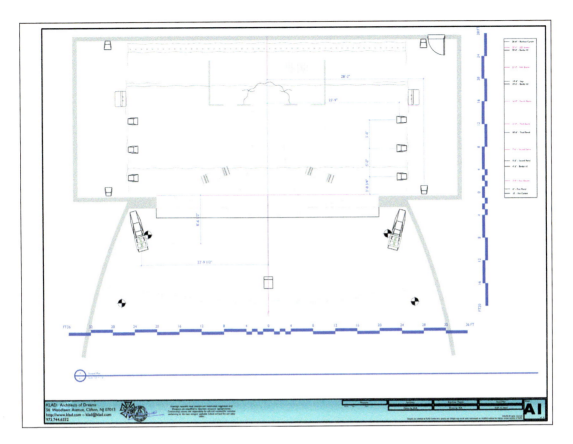

Creating the Stage Section

Return to the **Sound Plot Design Layer** and create a **Stage Left Section Viewport** by going to **View>Create Section Viewport** and cutting down the **Centerline**. Place the Stage Right Section on Sheet Layer 02, and name appropriately.

Early on you should have edited the **Section Style Class** definition and saved to your Stationery Document. That Class is automatically created the first time a Section Viewport is created in a document. It is ugly and non-standard. The Pen Line should be .5-.75 thickness, and the Fill should be a diagonal line Hatch or Pattern. Edit the Class definition, if required.

If the Section Viewport does not adopt the characteristics of the Section Style Class, select the Section Viewport on the Sheet Layer and tap **Advanced Properties** in the OIP. Change the **Attribute Class** to Section Style using the drop-down menu.

Annotate as the Plan View, adding figures.

Create Sheet List

The **Create Sheet List** Command comes with the Architect or Designer package. Go to **Tools>Workspaces>Architect** to activate the **Architect Workspace**. Select **Tools>Reports>Create Sheet List**.

Vectorworks will create a **Worksheet** called **Sheet List**, which is then stored in the **Resource Browser**. The **Sheet List** is also

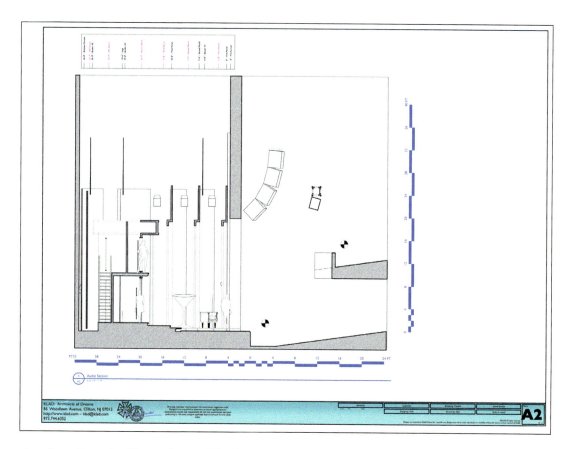

placed on the active **Sheet Layer**. The Sheet List is a **Table of Contents** for the set of drawings. This is a useful reference for everyone involved in the execution of the design.

When inserted, the Sheet List will likely not fit your graphic style. Right-click on the **Sheet List** in the **Resource Browser**, and select **Open** from the **Contextual Menu**.

Worksheets have a standard spreadsheet interface. Select all of the cells and click the access arrow in the upper-left to change the font. Select the Sheet Titles column, and then click the access arrow to change the width so that the column fits the text. Delete any excess rows and lose the **Sheet List Edit Window**. The list inserted on the sheet will then be updated.

Return to your own or the Spotlight Workspace, and add the Command to your Workspace. Go to **Tools>Workspaces>Edit Workspace**. Edit a copy of the Spotlight workspace, or your own Workspace. Locate the **Create Sheet List** Command in the left column and drag it over to a menu that works for your workflow on the right.

The Table of Contents should be immediately visible on the first sheet of your set of drawings. If compiling that set from multiple files, the Create Sheet List Command can get the process started, but the sheets not in the file where the Worksheet was created will have to be entered manually.

Create a cover sheet as bold as your design.

Creating a Camera Viewport

Lighting and Scenic Designers might want to create a cover sheet for their sets of drawings that includes a rendering, especially if you have a great plotter. The cover sheet might also include General Notes and the Sheet List. This sheet will be the first thing anyone sees when they open a PDF, or print set. Make it good, make it bold.

Choose an exiting **Renderworks Camera Object**, or create a new Camera View. With the **Renderworks Camera Object** selected, in the **Top/Plan view**, go to **View>Create Viewport**. Allow the Viewport to be associated with the camera. Name and place the Viewport. Vectorworks will shift to the Sheet Layer. The original camera object will no longer be available in the Design Layer. If you wish to preserve the camera object, copy it, then return to the Design Layer and Paste in Place.

The Camera View can be Edited on the Sheet Layer by right-clicking and selecting **Edit Camera** from the Contextual Menu.

Adjust the size of the Viewport on the sheet, and select **Final Quality Renderworks** in the OIP. The **Foreground** and **Background Rendering** options can be used for great effect with a **Camera Viewport**. For example, a **Sketch Style** (line variations) can be drawn over an **Artistic Renderworks Style** (color variations).

Camera Viewports can render while Vectorworks is working. Once the geometry has generated, the rendering work shifts to the external **Cinema 4D Rendering Engine**. As soon as that App is rendering, Vectorworks can perform other tasks, except modifying the model being rendered.

The teapot icon over the rendering indicates when Vectorworks is free.

The Publish Command

Once all of the detailing is complete, line weights have been checked, each page reviewed for readability and communication, it is time to assemble the pieces, whether from one master file, or many. The **Publish Command** can export any number of **Sheet Layers**, and/or **Saved Views** from the current file, and files from a specified folder to DXF/DWG, DWF, and/or PDF file formats. It is best practice to print Vectorworks files from PDF rather than from the native format, especially when sending to a service bureau. PDF is a universal format.

Go to **File>Publish**, Saved Views and Sheet Layers from the current file will be displayed as

Save and Publish different sets of drawings for different users.

options in the left column. Tap the **Select Folder** Button and choose your **Workgroup**, or a project folder. The left column of the dialog will then display every **Sheet Layer** and **Saved View** in every file in that folder.

Highlight to select the sheets desired in the left column, and tap the **>** Button: all of the sheets can be added by clicking the **>>** Button, whether anything is selected or not. Publish defaults to exporting PDF.

Once sheets have been moved into the right column, they can be re-ordered by clicking and dragging in the **#** column. Scenic files can be added to Audio or Lighting sets, to provide detail information when speakers, microphones, or Lighting Devices need to be built-into the scenery.

The scenery shop might not be interested in the audio documents while the Producer, Production Manager, Technical Director, or others might want full and complete drawings from every department together, either in hard copy or on a portable device. From a PDF it is easy to print documents at 50% or 25% actual size so that the management does not have to wrestle with large sheet sizes. Sheet layers do not have to all be the same sheet size; stage management is not likely to love the large sheets, and is really likely to need plans in a letter or A4 size. Separate sets can be created and saved for specific sheet sizes.

Sets of drawings can be saved for re-publication after revisions. Sets can include more than one file format. When files are selected from the left and moved to the right, they are also removed from the list in the left column. Checking **Show All Items** either keeps those files in place, or returns them to the **Available** column. It is possible then to have the same sheet, represented multiple times, in the **Publish** column.

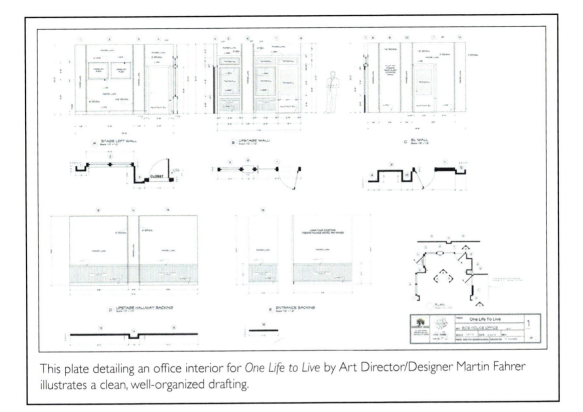

This plate detailing an office interior for *One Life to Live* by Art Director/Designer Martin Fahrer illustrates a clean, well-organized drafting.

I Love You, You're Perfect, Now Change
Paint Elevation by the author

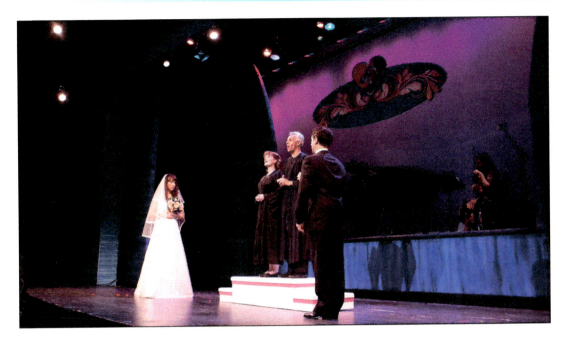

I Love You, You're Perfect, Now Change
Lyn Philistine, Leslie Henstock, Neal Mayer, Christopher Sutton

I Love You, You're Perfect, Now Change
The Surflight Theatre

Artistic Director: Roy Miller
Executive Producer: Timothy Laczynski
Director: Christopher Sutton
Scenic Designers: Kathleen McDonough & Kevin Lee Allen
Costume Designer: Rachel Guilfoyle
Lighting Designer: Sam Gordon

This design began as NapkinCAD, well, actually PlacematCAD, and worked its way into Vectorworks by way of Adobe Photoshop and Adobe Illustrator. The image at left shows the original incarnation of the hanging element in the photo on the right. This piece was designed in Adobe Illustrator, with paint detail, scanned and modified in Adobe Photoshop, added. That element was modeled and rendered in Vectorworks for presentations and construction.

20. Working in the Cloud

We can't always work from the comfort of our design studios; sometimes we must work by the hotel pool.

Theatrical production typically requires all kinds of paper. Different size paper. Cumbersome paper. There are ways to deal with this issue.

Services like Dropbox, iCloud, and Google Drive facilitate communication, can establish a wide area network, and add a level of back up. They are not Vectorworks specific and have no functionality beyond storage and sharing.

Vectorworks Service Select

The Vectorworks Service Select subscription program offers free software updates, training resources, videos, and additional content files. Only members of Vectorworks Service Select have access to Nemetschek Vectorworks web and mobile solutions; Vectorworks Cloud Services and the Vectorworks Nomad app, available for iOS, Android, and Kindle Fire.

Use the Cloud to speed work and facilitate collaboration.

Vectorworks Cloud Services

Vectorworks Cloud Services assists with file sharing and making design decisions from any location. Changes to desktop (or laptop) Vectorworks files that include Sheet Layers are automatically synchronized to 5GB of private Cloud-based storage as PDF files. Those PDF files can be accessed, annotated, and marked up using the Vectorworks Nomad App. Changes are synchronized back to the Cloud.

Vectorworks Cloud Services provides a Cloud-based workflow for creating presentations, shifting calculations needed to generate sections, elevations, and renderings from the desktop to the Cloud. Vectorworks Cloud Services can be used to shift rendering from the computer to the Cloud. There can be additional charges for this feature based on the complexity of the model.

Drawings stored using Vectorworks Cloud Services can be shared with colleagues and collaborators as needed. Subscribers can send or share files with non-subscribers allowing a two-week window of access.

Vectorworks Nomad

The Vectorworks Nomad application is available for Mac OS, Windows, iOS, Android, and Kindle Fire. Nomad can store your Vectorworks documents in the Cloud for access anywhere.

Vectorworks Nomad automatically creates PDF files from Sheet Layers in documents saved on the Vectorworks Cloud, or Dropbox. Those PDF files can be used for presentation, shop visits, Focus Calls, or to mark up changes to be made later, back in the design studio.

The Nomad Application creates a folder on the desktop. Files stored there are synchronized to the Cloud. Nomad on the desktop can be linked with your Dropbox account and set to process some or all of the Vectorworks files stored on Dropbox.

On a Mac, File Aliases can be used with Nomad.

Fonts and Vectorworks Nomad

Nomad has an extensive but nonetheless limited selection of fonts available for processing your Vectorworks files into PDFs. That list changes, and is added to frequently. The list is available on the Vectorworks Cloud Services website.

If your graphic standards require a font or fonts that Nomad does not include, the font file(s) can simply be copied to your Vectorworks Nomad folder. Many designers use specific fonts, and many others will use a specialty font for the title of the show.

Specific font mappings or changes of one font to another can be set in the **Vectorworks Preferences**, **Display Tab**.

Vectorworks Nomad will send a very nice e-mail if it cannot find the fonts used in your documents.

Fonts are system resources for Nomad, just like the fonts on your system.

Use the Cloud.

Work anywhere.

Chase Bank Flagship Signage at 3 Times Square
Rendering and animation by the author.

Chase Bank Flagship Signage at 3 Times Square
Photo by Tom Morra.

Chase Bank Flagship Signage
New York City

Artist/Animator: Kevin Lee Allen
   Design Assistant: Matthew William Anastasio
Fabricator: Spectrum Signs

Index